ID0960904

More Praise for *Ice Cream Social*

"The pioneering experience of Ben & Jerry's shows that corporate social responsibility can, thankfully, be contagious. Brad Edmondson takes us behind the scenes to tell this riveting and timely story."
—United States Senator Patrick Leahy

"This book reveals the true ingredients that go into every pint of Ben & Jerry's: GMO-free cream, fair-trade cane sugar, and a lot of blood, sweat, and tears."
—Eric Utne, founder, *Utne Reader*

"What once was radical is becoming mainstream. By earning B Corp certification, Ben & Jerry's has proven that you can sell without selling out and scale with integrity. Much of the global movement to redefine success in business stands on its shoulders, and much of what we know about better practices and better governance can be traced to lessons the company learned the hard way. Finally, this important story has been well and completely told."
—Jay Coen Gilbert, cofounder, B Lab

"Brad Edmondson vividly conveys the passion, conflicts, and raw humanity behind an iconic brand. He gives us an uncensored look at how smart, caring people poured their hearts and souls into making Ben & Jerry's the standard-bearer for 'caring capitalism.' The story leaves the reader in awe of all they achieved, and it also imparts invaluable lessons by talking frankly about their failures. It puts on full display the contradictions and painful choices that eventually confront all successful mission-driven businesses. It's a journey into uncharted territory."
—Rink Dickinson, cofounder and copresident, and Rob Everts, copresident, Equal Exchange

"The founders of Ben & Jerry's put up a long and determined fight to keep their dream of a socially responsible company intact. Cutthroat capitalism doesn't make it easy for entrepreneurs who want living wages for their employees, environmentally sustainable ingredients, and socially beneficial business practices. Brad Edmondson gives us a fascinating look behind the scenes of a company as beloved as the ice cream it makes."
—Barbara Ehrenreich, *New York Times* bestselling author and Founding Editor, Economic Hardship Reporting Project

Ice Cream Social

ICE CREAM SOCIAL

The Struggle for the Soul of Ben & Jerry's

Brad Edmondson

Foreword by Annie Leonard
Epilogue by Jeff Furman, Chairman,
Ben & Jerry's Board of Directors

BK

Berrett–Koehler Publishers, Inc.
San Francisco
a BK Business book

Berrett-Koehler Publishers, Inc.
235 Montgomery Street, Suite 650 • San Francisco, CA 94104-2916
Tel: (415) 288-0260   Fax: (415) 362-2512 • www.bkconnection.com

ORDERING INFORMATION
Quantity sales. Special discounts are available on quantity purchases by corporations,
associations, and others. For details, contact the "Special Sales Department" at the Berrett-
Koehler address above.

Individual sales. Berrett-Koehler publications are available through most bookstores. They
can also be ordered directly from Berrett-Koehler: Tel: (800) 929-2929; Fax: (802) 864-7626;
www.bkconnection.com

Orders for college textbook/course adoption use. Please contact Berrett-Koehler: Tel: (800) 929-
2929; Fax: (802) 864-7626.

Orders by U.S. trade bookstores and wholesalers. Please contact Ingram Publisher Services,
Tel: (800) 509-4887; Fax: (800) 838-1149; E-mail: customer.service@ingrampublisher-
services.com; or visit www.ingrampublisherservices.com/Ordering for details about elec-
tronic ordering.

Berrett-Koehler and the BK logo are registered trademarks of Berrett-Koehler Publishers, Inc.

Printed in the United States of America

Berrett-Koehler books are printed on long-lasting acid-free paper. When it is available, we
choose paper that has been manufactured by environmentally responsible processes. These
may include using trees grown in sustainable forests, incorporating recycled paper, mini-
mizing chlorine in bleaching, or recycling the energy produced at the paper mill.

LIBRARY OF CONGRESS CATALOGING-IN-PUBLICATION DATA
Edmondson, Brad.
Ice cream social: the struggle for the soul of Ben & Jerry's / Brad Edmondson;
foreword by Annie Leonard; epilogue by Jeff Furman.—First edition.
    pages   cm
Includes bibliographical references and index.
ISBN 978-1-60994-813-9 (pbk.)
1. Ben & Jerry's (Firm) 2. Ice cream industry—United States. 3. Social responsibility of
business. I. Title.
HD9281.U54B4636 2013
338.7'63740973—dc23
                                                                      2013036477

First Edition

18 17 16 15 14   10 9 8 7 6 5 4 3 2 1

Cover design by Irene Morris Design. Project management and interior design by
VJB/Scribe. Copyeditor: John Pierce. Proofreader: Don Roberts. Indexer: George Draffan.

Contents

Foreword by Annie Leonard ix
Prologue xi
Main Characters xv

- One

"We're Completely Insane, and We Need Your Help!" 1

1978

Ben Cohen and Jerry Greenfield never planned to become business icons when they opened an ice cream shop in Burlington, Vermont, in 1978. Neither did their friend Jeff Furman, who was a key player from the beginning. Twenty-two years later, Ben and Jerry resigned from the board of directors when the company was sold to Unilever for $326 million. But Jeff stayed to fight for a new vision of business that links the owners' prosperity to employees, communities, and the environment.

- Two

A New Kind of Start-up 14

1981

The growth train started rolling when Ben & Jerry's sold its first pints in 1981. As growth accelerated, Ben and Jeff seized the opportunity to build a different kind of business. The board of directors used trial and error to invent a mission that gave equal emphasis to three goals—great ice cream, social purpose, and profit. When it worked, the world started to notice.

- Three

Progressive Sweatshop 34

1988

Between 1988 and 1990, an admiring media profiled Ben & Jerry's as a "socially responsible business." But integrating the social mission into daily operations proved a complicated struggle. The company's pioneering attempts to pursue a three-part mission made history, but the ride was anything but smooth.

Four
Staffing the Social Mission   52

1990   Between 1990 and 1992, skilled managers started imple-
menting the three-part mission in strategic ways. The
company's most important contributions during this
period were the annual reports that introduced social
auditing to American businesses.

Five
Money Starts Talking   69

1993   1993 was the year it all went wrong. A decade of rapid
growth ended six months after Ben & Jerry's broke
ground on an expensive new ice cream plant. As a management crisis deepened, the board abandoned the company's celebrated salary ratio in 1994 and decided to look
for a CEO with mainstream corporate experience.

Six
Yo, I'm Not Your CEO   96

1994   Between 1994 and 1996, the social mission became more
integrated into operations as social audits sharpened
the company's focus on measurable results. But the first
attempt to find a "professional" CEO failed, and in des-
peration, the board made a quick decision that proved
disastrous.

Seven
The Gulf Was So Wide   115

1997   In January 1997, a new CEO started focusing on maximizing value for the shareholders of Ben & Jerry's, which
made the company an attractive target for a takeover. As
the CEO groomed the company for a sale, the board did
not face the growing risk.

• Eight
• **Leading with Progressive Values   126**

Late
1990s

In the late 1990s, Ben & Jerry's made several important
social mission advances, including an effective campaign
against bovine growth hormone, a statement of Leading by Progressive Values, improved rules for values-led
sourcing, and taking the three-part mission overseas.

• Nine
• **Unacceptable Choices   138**

By the late 1990s, consolidation in the ice cream industry
made it difficult for Ben & Jerry's to continue as an independent company, even though most board members
did not want to sell. Ben became estranged, board meetings resembled legal depositions, and it often seemed that
investment bankers were calling the shots.

• Ten
• **The Sale Agreements   157**

2000

Unilever wanted Ben & Jerry's badly, and its top executives were willing to keep the social mission if that would
clinch the deal. In 2000, after a long struggle, Ben & Jerry's sold, but only after Unilever signed sale agreements
that created an independent board with legal authority to protect the social mission and product quality in
perpetuity.

• Eleven
• **A Thousand Cuts   181**

The three-part mission went on a long detour after Ben &
Jerry's was sold in 2000. Unilever assigned the company
to a manager who cut costs aggressively and violated the
sale agreements in increasingly blatant ways, and it took
seven years for the board to mount a counterattack.

Twelve

Counterattack   207

2008   In 2008, the activist spirit of Ben & Jerry's reignited as the
board pushed Unilever to take the sale agreements seriously. While they negotiated, they also prepared a lawsuit and a public relations campaign. They almost went
through with it, too.

Thirteen

Pursuing Linked Prosperity   233

2010   In 2010, Ben & Jerry's made peace with Unilever, and the
three-part mission roared back to life. A talented CEO
and profits from international expansion made it easy to
set audacious goals. While things are far from perfect, the
company has recommitted to its struggle to change the
world while also making great ice cream profitably.

Epilogue by Jeff Furman   253

What does it all mean? In this epilogue, the man known
as "the ampersand in Ben & Jerry's" reflects on four
decades of trying to advance the three-part mission and
linked prosperity, and on the eternal struggle to remember people's names.

Reflection by Anuradha Mittal   263

Why the most important question for moving forward on
linked prosperity is "How can we be more unreasonable?"

   Notes   265
   Sources and Further Reading   268
   Photo Credits   270
   Index   271
   About the Author   277

Foreword

When I heard the title of Brad Edmondson's book, my first thought was, "the *soul* of Ben & Jerry's?" Ben & Jerry's is a corporation. It doesn't have a soul. The US Supreme Court may not be able to fully distinguish between corporations and people, but I can. Corporations aren't people, and they don't have souls.

Then I read the book. And it became clear that the *people* in the Ben & Jerry's story definitely have souls. The founders, workers, board of directors, and ice cream lovers everywhere pour their souls into this company.

Some businesses require their owners and workers to check their souls, their consciences, and their values at the door. The story of Ben & Jerry's is a story of what happens if people are allowed, even encouraged, to bring their consciences to work with them. In today's soulless corporate culture, how can such a business exist? What would it even look like? How could it remain true to its values? And if an ice cream company can do it, why not every company?

Ben & Jerry's, like a few other remarkable American companies, shows that another way of doing business is possible. The company has consistently walked the talk on environmental and social issues. It stands for something important, delivers on its promises, and provides a good product, creating a win-win-win. This book tells the story of a beloved company moving forward on principles that respect people and the planet—and in doing so, gives us a taste of how business could be.

Brad Edmondson takes us inside the beginnings of Ben & Jerry's, charting the origins of its social mission and its rise to become an American icon beloved by hippies, yuppies, kids, and CEOs alike. But then the plot thickens, as this small Vermont outfit with roots in the counterculture gets bigger and struggles to keep its identity—its soul—in the world of multinational brands.

Although there has been extensive media coverage of the sale of Ben & Jerry's to Unilever, this book is the first to tell the whole story: how the company fought to keep its three-part mission intact after the sale, how those principles were compromised in the decade following the sale, and how the two parties have ultimately learned to work together to preserve the brand's vitality and integrity.

Just as Ben & Jerry's is no ordinary business, this is no ordinary business book. It's fast-paced, it has compelling, fully realized characters, and the narrative is gripping. The chapters about the Unilever takeover were my favorites. I knew the ending, and I still couldn't put the book down. That made it difficult to eat my Cherry Garcia at the same time.

Annie Leonard
Berkeley, California, June 2013

Annie Leonard is founder of the Story of Stuff Project
(*www.storyofstuff.org*), which makes videos and other
educational material on the effects of corporate globalization,
waste, and consumerism.

Prologue

I met Jeff Furman in 1998, when he offered to rent me a corner of the large room he said was his office. I knew that Jeff had degrees in accounting and law and that he also had something to do with Ben & Jerry's, but I didn't know exactly what that was. Perhaps Jeff worked for a local not-for-profit group that hires teenagers, which operated the ice cream shop directly below the office and had its papers and junk taking up most of the room. Or maybe he worked for the Ithaca Skate Park—one afternoon I had to pick my way past a group of teenagers who were politely holding a meeting, some of them balancing on skateboards while they talked. It was a chaotic but friendly place, and everyone around Jeff was doing something interesting.

Jeff used the office mostly to change clothes before he went for his daily run. He had a small desk in one corner, mounded over with dusty papers, and balanced on top of the mound was a spectacularly grimy, sticky telephone. The phone looked like it belonged in a dairy barn. A lot of people used it, and many of them worked downstairs, where they handled ice cream. Every so often Jeff would come in and talk on that phone for a while, and then he'd leave.

I was alone in that room one day, wandering around the way writers do, when I noticed that Jeff had taped, right above his telephone, a quote from Dostoevsky's *Notes from Underground*: "I admit that twice two makes four is an excellent thing, but if we are to give everything its due, twice two makes five is sometimes a very charming thing too." After that, I couldn't stand it anymore, so I asked Jeff what kind of accountant he was. He smiled and said that he was training to be an *alter kocker*, which is a Yiddish term for a

foul-tempered, forgetful old troublemaker. We started hanging out in coffee shops, and over the next fifteen years, he
gradually answered my question.

Jeff is an interesting guy, but I learned that he was protecting something even more interesting. He is the co-creator
and guardian of the social mission of Ben & Jerry's, and a
stubborn advocate for a vision of business the company calls
"linked prosperity." This is the simple but radical idea that
when the company benefits, everything it touches should
also benefit, including employees, suppliers, customers, communities, and the environment. One day, Jeff suggested that
I write a magazine article about linked prosperity at Ben &
Jerry's. This book is the result.

The journey of linked prosperity spans four decades, has
a cast of thousands, and contains as much human drama
and unexpected plot twists as anything by Dostoevsky. I
spent a solid year learning about it, interviewing more than
three dozen people and digesting several hundred pounds
of company reports and internal documents. (If a source is
not attributed in this book, it comes either from these personal interviews or company documents.) It was all I could
do just to tell the story, dear reader, so please do not expect a
typical business book with a lot of easily summarized "take-
aways." This is a story about inspiring, fallible people and
their shared quest to attain a goal they know they will never
reach. They fail and struggle, and sometimes they think they
have failed even when they have succeeded. They are also
extremely funny, and they make a product few can resist.

If we are to give everything its due, the story of linked
prosperity is a very charming thing. But it is also a very complicated and provocative thing. It raises so many big, fascinating ideas that beg for discussion: What is fair compensation?
When publicly traded businesses invest in social change,
how do you define success? If you liberate a hen from her
cage, is she happier, and what is that worth? And so on. To

encourage those discussions in informal groups, I have prepared a study guide with free documents and links at www
.bradedmondson.com.

I was welcomed by almost everyone I approached while writing this book, with the notable exceptions of Ben Cohen and Jerry Greenfield, who said they didn't want to relive the past (see "human drama," above). That was okay, because this book isn't really about them, or Jeff, or any other person. It is about the extraordinary organization a small group of committed people helped create and how they managed, almost despite themselves, to preserve their vision for future generations.

Jeff was patient, honest, and unfailingly helpful during the long process of writing and revising this book. I am equally indebted to his spouse, Sara Hess (favorite flavor: Liz Lemon Frozen Yogurt), who read and commented on each chapter with the wisdom of someone who was paying attention as she watched the whole thing happen. Twenty percent of the book's royalties are going to a not-for-profit organization Jeff and Sara maintain to support community organizations, and that doesn't begin to repay the debt of gratitude I feel toward them.

This book is an entirely independent effort. It is not endorsed and was not financially supported by either Ben & Jerry's or Unilever. So I am especially grateful to the people of Ben & Jerry's who remained engaged through months of writing and fact-checking, especially Chuck Lacy, Liz Bankowski, Howard Fuguet, Lisa Wernhoff, Michael Graning, Debra Heintz, Rob Michalak, and Jostein Solheim. Everyone I spoke with was cooperative and generous with their time and attention. As I kept pushing and probing, their genuineness convinced me that their commitment to linked prosperity is also genuine.

I am fortunate to have large groups of friends who supported, encouraged, and challenged me in ways too numerous to mention. I would particularly like to thank Jon Crispin for the author photo; the staff of the Finger Lakes Land Trust for being nice to the writer who works upstairs; Nancy Wells, Henry Tepper, Fred Connor, and Stephanie Sechler, for their friendship and encouragement; my children, Will and Emma, whose intelligence and work ethic give me something to aspire to; and my wife, Tania Werbizky, for always believing in me and never giving up.

I could not have written this book without Tania, or without Jack Greer, David and Sharon Schuman, James McConkey, John Marcham, S.K. List, Cheryl Russell, Robert Wilson, and many other editors and teachers who insisted that I go back, again and again, until I got the story. This book is dedicated to all of them.

Brad Edmondson
Ithaca, New York
July 2013

Main Characters

In alphabetical order, with jobs and (favorite Ben & Jerry's flavor):

Andrea Asch, manager of natural resources use since 1992 (From Russia with Buzz)

Liz Bankowski, board, 1990–99, director of social mission, 1991–2001, Ben & Jerry's Foundation board since 1994 (Cherry Garcia)

Bruce Bowman, chief operations officer, 1985–2000

Jane Bowman, human resources director since 2005 (Vanilla Heath Bar Crunch)

Merritt Chandler, board 1987–96 (Peace Pops)

Ben Cohen, cofounder, board 1977–2000, chair 1977–98, vice chair 1998–2000 (Cherry Garcia)

Yves Couette, CEO, board, 2001–4

Daryn Dodson, board since 2012 (Phish Food)

Tom D'Urso, treasurer, 1994–2000 (Pistachio Pistachio)

Jon Entine, investigative journalist (doesn't eat Ben & Jerry's)

Pierre Ferrari, board since 1997, chair, 2007–10 (Cherry Garcia)

Walt Freese, chief marketing officer, 2001–4, CEO, 2005–10, board 2005–10

Howard "Howie" Fuguet, legal counsel 1984–2000 and 2009–11 (Coffee Coffee Buzz Buzz Buzz)

Jeff Furman, board since 1982, board chair since 2010, and board of Ben & Jerry's Foundation since 1985 (Cherry Garcia Frozen Yogurt, for health reasons)

Richard Goldstein, head of Unilever North America until 2000 (Mint Chocolate Cookie)

Jerry Greenfield, cofounder, board 1990–2000, vice chair 1990–98, chair 1998–2000, Ben & Jerry's Foundation board since 1985 (Coconut Almond Fudge Chip)

Sean Greenwood, scooper, truck driver, and public relations, 1988–2003, and director of public relations since 2005 (Cherry Garcia, "fresh off the line")

Debra Heintz, various jobs since 1994 including materials and distribution manager, and director of retail operations (Wavy Gravy)

Jennifer Henderson, board of directors since 1996, board chair 2000–2007 (New York Super Fudge Chunk)

Robert Holland, CEO, board, 1995–96 (Sweet Potato Pie)

Helen Jones, director of brand development for the UK and Europe (1995–2009), board since 2010 (Phish Food)

Charles M. "Chuck" Lacy, general manager and president, 1988–94, board 1990–95 (Coffee Heath Bar Crunch)

Fred "Chico" Lager, general manager, president, and CEO, 1981–90; board, 1981–97 (Heath Bar Crunch)

John Le Boutillier, head of Unilever's North American Ice Cream division, 2008–12, president of Unilever Canada since 2012 (Chocolate Fudge Brownie)

Rob Michalak, public relations czar, 1989–98, global director of social mission since 2006 (Vanilla Caramel Fudge)

Fred Miller, board 1992–2000 (New York Super Fudge Chunk)

Anuradha Mittal, board since 2007 (Americone Dream)

Terry Mollner, board since 2000 (Chocolate Fudge Brownie)

Henry Morgan, board 1987–2000

Perry Odak, CEO, board, 1997–2000

Carol O'Neill, franchise site selection manager, senior contract administrator, since 1985 (New York Super Fudge Chunk)

Paul Polman, CEO of Unilever since 2009

Fran Rathke, chief financial officer, 1990–2000

Ronald Soiefer, chief counsel, Unilever USA until 2012, board ex-officio 2000–2012 (Soiefer's Sweet Soiree—see chapter 12)

Jostein Solheim, CEO of Ben & Jerry's and board since 2010 (Chunky Monkey)

Dave Stever, several jobs, including chief marketing officer, since 1987 (Chocolate Chip Cookie Dough)

Naomi Tannen, Ben & Jerry's Foundation board, 1985–94 (Liz Lemon Frozen Yogurt)

Kees van der Graaf, global ice cream strategy and other senior executive positions for Unilever until 2009, Ben & Jerry's board since 2009 (Chocolate Chip Cookie Dough)

Eric Walsh, head of Unilever's North American Ice Cream division until 2008 (Americone Dream)

Lisa Wernhoff, designer and archivist since 1986 (Chocolate Cointreau Orange Fudge)

Judy Wicks, founder, White Dog Café, Philadelphia, Pennsylvania; former board chair, Social Venture Network; cofounder and board member, Business Alliance for Living Local Economies (Coconut Almond Fudge Chip)

ONE

"We're Completely Insane, and We Need Your Help!"

Jennifer Henderson can't forget the day in 1988 that she met Ben Cohen, Jerry Greenfield, and Jeff Furman. "Ben and Jerry were famous, and I was a young community organizer, so I was excited," she said. "They were starting a new organization, and they wanted a bunch of people to get on board.

"We met in a big room that had a thin wooden divider down the middle. They started talking, and pretty soon Ben got all excited. He was waving his arms and saying all kinds of things, like how he was going to prevent war by printing up a million bumper stickers. He was shouting and getting red in the face and I was thinking, this guy needs professional help. They all had long hair, Ben and Jeff had big wild beards, and they were wearing old T-shirts. Jerry was just sitting there beaming. Jeff was very calm, like he knew some secret reason why this was actually going to work. It was not at all what I expected.

"We took a break, and I went to the other side of the divider and called a girlfriend and told her that I had met these crazy people, and she just wouldn't believe what they were like. I forgot that the divider was really thin, so everybody could hear me. When I came back in, Ben rushed up to me and said, 'Yes! You're right! We're completely insane, and we need your help!' Then they took us down the street

1

to where they had a store, and Ben scooped us all ice cream cones. He didn't introduce himself to the people there or anything. He just walked behind the counter and started in, with everybody staring at him.

"I thought about them all the way home. Jerry was really sweet. Jeff was smart and funny. Ben scared me, but he was also funny, and he said something I couldn't get out of my mind. He said that businesses are the most powerful institutions in the world, and they could become the world's most powerful forces for social change. It seemed to me that they were on to something, so I signed up."

Jennifer started consulting with Ben & Jerry's just as they committed to a radical vision of business. She stayed with the company through an epic struggle, including a change of ownership, as it kept trying to live up to that vision. Although Ben & Jerry's has been a wholly owned subsidiary of the world's second-largest food company since 2000, it is still committed to a different way of doing business. This book is about that difference.

Jennifer has been on the board of directors of Ben & Jerry's for eighteen years. The company's annual sales were $167 million when she showed up; now they are somewhere around $500 million, and the company has devoted customers on every continent except Antarctica. It is the kind of company that might consider setting up a shop there, too.

A few years before Ben Cohen met Jennifer, he decided that scooping ice cream wasn't enough. Ben and Jeff Furman led the company through several years of experimenting, sometimes painfully, with the idea that business could be a force for progressive social change as well as a machine for making money. Ben & Jerry's became a leader in the movement to make businesses more socially responsible, and the company pursued what it called a "double bottom line" while operating as a publicly traded company from 1984 until 2000. They were among the first companies to adopt

Top: The first Ben & Jerry's store in Burlington, Vermont, shortly after it opened on May 5, 1978. Bottom: The first Free Cone Day, May 1979.

policies that are now widely known, such as paying a living wage, publishing audited reviews of social and environmental performance, and teaming up with not-for-profit organizations, to name a few.

Ben & Jerry's took radical, crazy-sounding ideas and proved they could work. It made it easier for other companies to try these ideas. And behind all its efforts was one big idea the company called "linked prosperity." As the company prospered, it said, all of the employees, suppliers, customers, and other living things that had contributed to its success should prosper as well.

The company's mission had three parts that were equal and interrelated. It wanted to make the world's best ice cream, to pursue progressive social change, and to provide fair compensation to employees and shareholders alike. Ben & Jerry's stuck to these principles as it became an international brand with passionately dedicated customers. But the company eventually grew beyond the managerial abilities of its board, and after years of struggling, the board was forced to sell the company to Unilever. Ben walked away from the deal with $41 million. Jerry got $9.5 million. Jeff got about $1 million. Yet Ben and Jerry have also said that losing control of their company was one of the worst experiences of their lives, and they still don't want to talk about it. It's a hard subject for Jeff, too.

The social mission did survive the sale, however. The founders and the board accepted Unilever's offer only after negotiating a detailed agreement that guaranteed them a continuing role in the company and gave them legally enforceable powers. Under the agreement, Unilever is the sole shareholder of Ben & Jerry's, and it controls the company's economic and operational decisions. But Ben & Jerry's also has a separate board of directors that is not controlled by Unilever. This board elects its own members, and it exists in perpetuity. It acts as a watchdog and has the legal authority to block proposals that lessen product quality or the social mission. As sales increase, investment in the social mission must also increase.

The story of the company's endless pursuit of linked prosperity offers answers to the questions Ben put in Jennifer's mind: What would the world look like if businesses got serious about pursuing social and environmental justice? What if a business was directed toward several equally important goals, with profit being only one of them? And what would happen if social justice activists controlled the board of directors of a large, global enterprise? Could that work?

There's a second, related question. It's the question of legacy. Thousands of business owners do value their employees, the natural environment, and the community at least as highly as their own bank accounts. But investing in these areas rarely produces an immediate financial return, and many investors see social investments as unnecessary costs. So how can socially responsible businesses retain their progressive values after the founding generations retire? Or, to put it another way, how can someone give up control of a successful enterprise without throwing away its purpose?

The Ampersand

In this story, the good guys and the bad guys are not always where you might expect them to be. For example, Ben Cohen and Jerry Greenfield are widely known as pioneers of socially responsible business. But the people who wrote the sale agreements that preserved Ben & Jerry's as a socially responsible business were elite corporate lawyers, about as far from Vermont hippies as you can get. Several Unilever executives have become so enthusiastic about the drive for linked prosperity that they have said and done risky things to promote it. And the social mission's most steadfast champion—the only person who consistently fought for it at every stage of the story—describes himself as an activist first, and adds that he has little interest in being a business executive.

Jeff Furman's coworkers often describe him as "the ampersand in Ben & Jerry's." He became friends with Ben and Jerry years before they scooped their first cone. He helped them write the company's first business plan in 1977 by borrowing a similar plan from a pizza joint and substituting the word "cone" whenever that plan used the word "slice." He did a lot of different tasks for the company as it struggled to get going; he joined the company's board in 1982, and he was a key contributor during its decade of rapid growth. He is still on the board in 2014, and since 2010 he has been its chair.

Jeff really is a lawyer and an accountant, but not in an ordinary sense. One Unilever executive refers to him as "a lawyer in disguise." He is a balding guy with a fringe of long hair that he tucks behind his ears. He smiles a lot, trims his beard only occasionally, wears a T-shirt every day—no matter how cold it is—and spends his time working with not-for-profit groups and businesses that have progressive values. And he didn't even meet Ben or Jerry until he was thirty.

Jeff got a degree in accounting in 1965 and a degree in law in 1969, but as the 1970s began, he was not exactly on a career track. In fact, he couldn't keep a job. He was a parole officer until he was given a gun and told to prevent a suspect from fleeing out the back door. He couldn't even bring himself to load the thing. Boston University fired him for spreading the word about an antiwar protest. What he did like was working for the Workers Defense League, representing blue-collar folks and conscientious objectors. That experience gave him strong feelings of compassion for people who hold entry-level jobs. It was a big reason why he later suggested that Ben & Jerry's adopt the policy of paying the company's top employees no more than five times its starting salary, and it is why the company continues to pay a living wage to its employees today.

Jeff met Ben Cohen at Highland Community, an innovative school for twenty-five emotionally troubled teenagers near the isolated mountain town of Paradox, New York. Jeff did administrative work, and Ben taught pottery. Naomi Tannen, the school's founder and director, was a powerful influence on both of them. Jeff says that they were Naomi's employees, not her students, but it could have gone either way. "She had a dream, and she pursued it relentlessly," said Jeff. "She was also tolerant of eccentric people, as long as they were pointed in the right direction. I think Ben and I both learned a lot from her example."

Jeff was raised in a Jewish family, and so was Ben; Jeff grew up in Queens, and Ben grew up on Long Island, less than twenty miles away; they both had been cab drivers; they both liked to laugh and do silly things; et cetera, et cetera. Hilarity ensued. Ben soon introduced Jeff to Jerry Greenfield, who had been Ben's best friend since they struggled through the seventh grade together. Jerry was cut from the same cloth. The three men shared ideals that were formed in the 1960s and tempered by Vietnam and Watergate. They were smart and creative but ambivalent toward government, suspicious of big business, painfully aware of injustice, and looking for better ways to live.

The business Ben, Jerry, and Jeff built sprang from these values. Selling ice cream wasn't their real purpose. If it didn't come from the heart, they weren't interested. As the years went by and the business got bigger, they kept pushing for ways to make things more interesting, more political, and more fun. They went farther than they ever thought they would. Calvin Trillin wrote that Ben represented "one of the people who carried the style of the sixties into consumer businesses aimed at their contemporaries, and whose response to success is to express not gratitude for living in a land of opportunity but astonishment at a world so weird that people like themselves are considered respectable businessmen."[1]

For the first five years of their ice cream business, Ben
and Jerry found themselves working a lot of eighty-hour
weeks, a lifestyle neither of them enjoyed. The money was
not that great, either. They briefly decided to sell the business in 1982, when it might have been worth $500,000, and
they asked Jeff to help with the legal and financial questions.
Jerry moved away from Vermont then, but Ben changed his
mind and decided not to sell. (Jeff persuaded Jerry to hold on
to 10 percent of the company's stock and stay on as a consultant; Jerry returned to the board of directors in 1990 and
stayed until the company was sold in 2000). And then the
broker that Ben & Jerry's had hired to sell the business sued
for breach of contract and won $100,000.

The moment the judgment was announced, Jeff ran down
the street from the courtroom to Merchants Bank in Burlington, Vermont. Ben and Jerry followed close behind, with the
county sheriff literally on their heels. The guys persuaded
the banker, a friend of theirs, to let them withdraw the entire
contents of the company's accounts and give it to them in
cash. Then Jeff flew home to New York, where the court
couldn't get at the money, with $90,000 on his lap in a paper
bag. When he got home, he dumped the money on the bed,
turned to his girlfriend, Sara, and said, "Look what I found!"
(Maybe he was trying to impress her; in any event, she later
married him.) Jeff kept the money in a safe-deposit box until
the lawsuit was settled, and then sent it back to Vermont.
Ben and Jerry never doubted that he would.

Stories about the early years of Ben & Jerry's are often
funny because these guys did not do things the way normal
businesspeople do. For example, Jeff shared his Ithaca office
with several others, including me and the not-for-profit group
that owned the ice cream shop downstairs. Jeff called it a
"PartnerShop." He came up with that idea when the board of
Ben & Jerry's asked him to manage the franchising of stores.
Some of the stores were just normal franchises, where the

company licenses its logo, formulas, and other valuable property to someone who uses them to make a profit. But Jeff also thought it would be cool to franchise some stores to not-for-profit organizations that give young people job experience. As a side benefit, Jeff's Ithaca office occasionally filled up with teenagers who were trying to organize a skate park. It wasn't part of a grand design. It was just Jeff's way of using a creative twist to combine two of his interests.

Another World Is Possible

One summer day in 1999, Jeff came into the office above the Ithaca store and made a call on his grimy telephone. I didn't listen to his side of the conversation at first, but then I noticed that he seemed to be getting more serious, and he was using lawyerly words like "share price," "suit," "counter-suit," and "fly to Amsterdam." He also stared at the ceiling after he hung up the phone, the way people do when they've heard upsetting news. He told me that things were not going well at Ben & Jerry's, and that he couldn't go into the details. Then he left.

Ben, Jerry, and Jeff did not want to sell their company. Although they still regarded a lot of their duties as chores, they also enjoyed their success. They were responsible for the jobs of about eight hundred people, many of whom they counted as friends. The business had come from their hearts. They struggled for a year and a half to find some viable alternative to giving up control, but they failed. They settled for Unilever.

In 1999, Ben & Jerry's was rooted in the idea of linked prosperity. It was making progress in a campaign to reduce the environmental impact and increase the sustainability of its business at every stage of its operations, from reducing the nitrogen and phosphorus output at its dairy farms to eliminating bleached paperboard in its containers. It was doing all kinds of things to improve conditions in its factories and its suppliers' farms, and it paid employees a carefully calibrated "living wage" that was well above the market rate. It was trying to "lead with progressive values" in all phases of its business, according to a statement the board adopted in 1997. Jeff feared that all of this might be lost, and the thought was agonizing.

Ben ended up having quadruple bypass heart surgery a few months after the sale went through; the stress of losing his company might have had as much to do with his heart problem as had decades of taste-testing ice cream. Unilever offered Ben and Jerry seats on the post-sale board of directors, but they never took them. Both men are technically employees of Unilever today, but they do not have job descriptions. And Ben can be sharply critical of Unilever—although, as the founders and brand icons, he and Jerry still have some influence on the company that bears their names.

Jeff, on the other hand, stayed on the board. He wanted to try to keep the company's social mission alive. He had invested a great deal of time and effort in the social mission, and he felt responsible for the welfare of employees. In fact, the sale agreements had given him the power to sue Unilever if it didn't live up to its promise to pay a living wage. The agreements also empowered the board to block any changes in the product formula and to ensure that the company would continue to invest in social initiatives. Jeff couldn't just walk away.

In the years that followed the Summer of the Grimy Telephone, Jeff and the other board members of Ben & Jerry's struggled to find effective ways to pursue linked prosperity within the strictures of a huge multinational corporation. They traveled a dangerous, twisting road. They didn't always live up to their responsibilities, and the whole thing almost ended up in court. But after a decade of struggle, Ben & Jerry's and Unilever found ways of working together.

Once again, the company is making an honest effort to walk the talk on the social mission. It is still taking risks few other companies would consider, and it still sets an example for other companies to emulate.

When Jeff became chair of the board of Ben & Jerry's in 2010, he was also involved in supporting the US Social Forum, a national gathering of progressive groups held in Detroit in July that year. He decided it would be fun to persuade hundreds of people from all over the country to ride their bicycles to Detroit—the Motor City, after all—as a way of spreading the Social Forum's message, "Another World Is Possible." Jeff was a fit sixty-six-year-old then, still a runner, and although he did not have a lot of experience with bicycles, he resolved to organize a delegation of riders to go from Ithaca to Detroit on a winding route of nearly five hundred miles. I offered to help him train and to ride with him part of the way.

After the first day's ride, we found ourselves in Seneca Falls, New York, population 6,700. We were two middle-aged guys on the loose, but we were also quite tired and sore. Most of the other riders were several decades younger than us. They were at a nearby campground, eating food cooked on a camp stove, singing around a campfire, and sleeping in tents; we were at a comfy motel in the village, looking forward to a hot shower, a decent restaurant, and an early night. After we finished dinner and called our wives, we had just enough energy left to stroll down Main Street, where we found the Women's Rights National Historical Park.

The park commemorates a meeting that took place in 1848. More than two hundred women and several men gathered in Seneca Falls to draft a Declaration of Sentiments. The document states that "all men and women are created equal" and calls for women to be given the right to vote, hold decent jobs, and own property. When women finally did get the right to vote, seventy-two years later, only one of the people who signed the 1848 document was still alive and eligible to cast a ballot. Charlotte Woodward had been just eighteen when she went to Seneca Falls. But when the Nineteenth Amendment passed and she became eligible to register, she was ninety years old and too sick to leave the house. So none of the 1848 attendees ever actually voted.

We sat on a bench in the evening light after reading the historical markers, enjoying the calm that comes after a hard workout. "Riding to the US Social Forum on a bicycle is sort of like running Ben & Jerry's," Jeff said. "It's about looking for alternative ways to make the job more interesting, more political, and more fun. The company ran on that same kind of energy."

There was a long pause. "That's smart," I said. "Change happens so slowly that you'd better figure out how to enjoy yourself while you're fighting for it." I was paraphrasing the columnist Molly Ivins, who wrote, "We have to have fun while trying to stave off the forces of darkness because we hardly ever win, so it's the only fun we get to have. We find beer and imagination helpful."[2]

Charlotte Woodward spent her whole life struggling for the right to vote, and when the day finally came, she couldn't do it. But perhaps she was not all that bothered about missing her chance. After all, she wasn't fighting for herself. She had been struggling for the rights of women all her life. Perhaps she knew in 1910 what Dr. Martin Luther King said the night before he was killed in 1968: that it might take more than one lifetime for us to get to the mountaintop.

Ben, Jerry, Jeff, and their colleagues made mistakes as they built their business, but they never gave up on their belief that another world is possible. They found that maintaining a three-part mission takes constant effort when you are surrounded by businesses that focus on profits above everything else. To succeed, you must persuade everyone in the organization to buy in and participate in the struggle. Because your expectations are higher, what looks like success to an outsider might feel like failure. There will always be a temptation to take the easy way. You can always get credit, pocket the money, and let things slide. That happened at Ben & Jerry's more than once, and there's no guarantee that it won't happen again.

What is certain is that the struggle to reconcile profits with social justice will never end. The Ben & Jerry's story shows that the struggle can also be fun, when you're doing it right.

TWO

A New Kind of Start-up

Before you can understand how Ben, Jerry, Jeff, and their friends devised a new way of doing business, you must understand the times that produced them. They stumbled into their success by entering a new market niche at exactly the right moment. They called their ice cream "homemade," but the industry named it "super-premium." This kind of ice cream is usually sold in pints and has a high fat content. Premium ice cream is somewhat less rich and dense and is usually sold in larger containers. There are regular and economy versions of ice cream, too, but Ben and his customers didn't see the point of them.

Ben & Jerry's ice cream is about 16 percent butterfat, and the company does not allow much air into the mix. This makes the product dense. When properly frozen, it is as hard as a rock, which means that it is best enjoyed when partially thawed. It is more trouble to handle, more fattening, and more expensive than regular ice cream, but none of that mattered to Ben and Jerry in 1977. Only the taste mattered.

If the founders had been advancing a social mission back then, they might have hesitated to sell a product that is so high in saturated fat. But they didn't give it a second thought. They were both twenty-six. They loved selling ice cream because it made people happy. If you gave it away, you could have a party anywhere, anytime you wanted, with almost anyone.

Those were the days when hippies were turning into

capitalists. Old-fashioned ice cream parlors, bicycle stores, and head shops were opening all over the place. Many of them were in college towns like Burlington, where you could wear your hair long and smoke a joint on your lunch break. It might be hard to believe now, but most of the founders of these businesses, including Ben and Jerry, did not have a well-crafted "social mission." In fact, many of them were ambivalent about politics because the mechanisms of electoral politics did not reflect their values. Ben and Jerry belonged to a diaspora of baby boomers who converged on Burlington in search of euphoria. They scooped ice cream for a decade before they started trying to change the world.

In the fall of 1977, a young man threw a dart at a map. The dart hit Vermont, so he and a friend got in their old car and drove there. People really did that back then. The young man made it to Vermont, but the car died soon afterward, so he hitchhiked into town a lot. One day, a beat-up old Volvo stopped and the driver gave him a ride all the way home, which was really nice of him. The driver was Jerry. He told the hitchhiker that he and his buddy, Ben, had just leased a gas station in Burlington. They were going to renovate it and sell food.

Ice Cream for the People

Ben and Jerry froze their butts off in that gas station all winter, demolishing, framing, and finishing. At night, they huddled around a wood stove in a poorly insulated house, living on crackers, sardines, and test batches of ice cream they cranked themselves. Their big idea was throwing candy, nuts, and other tasty stuff into the smooth chocolate or vanilla mix when the batch was partially frozen. This was a fairly new idea back then, and the results of their tests were often unbearably delicious. Of course, selling a frozen dessert in a place as cold as Vermont might not have been the smartest business idea, but they didn't have an alternative plan.

Ben and Jerry liked having fun and helping others have fun. In the earliest days, the board that listed their flavors described them as "orgasmic." Later, they switched to "euphoric." The point was to have days full of positive personal interactions with employees and customers. They wanted to make enough money to live on while they enjoyed themselves, but they didn't make much; in their first summer, they slept in the store. The following spring, to celebrate the anniversary of their grand opening, they spent a day giving away ice cream to anyone who showed up at the store, including dogs. Every day would have been Free Cone Day if they could have afforded it.

"We knew that we would only remain in business through the support of people in the local community," Ben said in an episode of the television show *Biography* that first aired in 2006. "I liked the idea of free ice cream for the people."[1] And the Free Cone Day tradition continues today, although dogs are no longer served.

Despite their images, though, Ben and Jerry were emphatically *not* hippies. They were smart and driven. They had been introduced to business by their families: Ben's father was an accountant, and Jerry's was a stockbroker. (Jeff's dad owned a small clothing store.) Jerry's original goal was to become a doctor, but all the medical schools he applied to turned him down after he graduated from Oberlin College in 1973.

Ben held a lot of different jobs after attending several colleges and dropping out of all of them. Before he went to Vermont he had been a potter, making stoneware bowls and pitchers. Some of Ben's work shows his sense of humor. He made a soup tureen with hands clasped across the front of the bowl, as if they were holding a full belly, and a ladle sticking out under the cover like a tongue. The pottery didn't sell, though, so he went looking for something else to do.

The original pint container from the early 1980s.

Ben was a brilliant marketer and salesman, with a fierce
competitive streak. He had a magical ability to connect to his
fellow baby boomers. He was a genius when it came to creating new flavors of ice cream, and he could be wildly funny,
warm, and kind. People followed him. "A lot of people come
up with crazy ideas," said Jeff. "But Ben would actually go
out and do the things he dreamed up. He would get me into
unbelievable situations. I wanted to support his craziness."

Jerry also enjoyed Ben's crazy energy, but he wanted a
quiet, orderly life. So Jerry decided to leave the ice cream business late in 1981, a few months after *Time* magazine began a
cover story with the sentence, "What you must understand at
the outset is that Ben & Jerry's in Burlington, Vermont makes
the best ice cream in the world."[2] Getting an endorsement
from *Time* was a really big deal in the summer of 1981. Ben &
Jerry's had started selling ice cream in pints just a few months
before the story ran, and they couldn't keep up with demand.
Jerry saw where the company was going, and he didn't want
to take the ride.

Ben knew that he had a chance to make it big. But the work was hard, and neither of them had intended to become business executives. With Jerry leaving, Ben didn't see the point of going on by himself. Then Ben delivered some ice cream to a local restaurant owner and artist and told him the business was for sale. The old restaurateur told Ben that the business was far too valuable to sell. He urged Ben to hold on to it.

Ben replied that he didn't want to run a business. "I said, 'Maurice, you know what business does, it's harmful to the environment, it's harmful to its employees,'" Ben said on *Biography*. "And he said, 'Ben, if there's something you don't like about business, why don't you just do it different?' That hadn't really occurred to me before."[3]

This photo of Ben (at left) and Jerry was taken in 1980 by Marion Ettlinger and has been printed on almost every pint container since.

Jeff Furman in his Ithaca office in July 1986, talking on the "grimy telephone."

Why Not?

The first thing Ben did after he decided to keep the business was to call Jeff Furman. Ben needed to turn Jerry's half of the company into cash, so Jerry could leave with whatever he would have gotten if the company had been sold. Jeff suggested that Ben sell some of Jerry's stock in a private offering to friends and family. He also drafted an agreement that would pay Jerry to stay on as a consultant, and he persuaded Jerry to retain 10 percent of the company's stock.

Jeff's next job was to find the money to expand the manufacturing operation out of a makeshift warehouse on Green Mountain Drive and into a real factory, one that was custom designed to produce ice cream with chunks in it. Commercial ice cream machines were designed to accept soft fruit, not hard chunks, so Ben & Jerry's ice cream makers had to use trial and error to figure out how to keep the machines from jamming. Jeff also had to make sure that the company complied with all relevant rules and regulations, particularly with regard to a growing number of franchised ice cream stores. The company's first independently owned Scoop Shop opened in Shelburne, Vermont, in the summer of 1981.

One early franchise owner remembers meeting Ben in those days. "His office was in a cold, grungy shed," he says. "We were alone, except for a kid in the back who was hacking up Heath Bars with something that looked like a machete." Heath Bar Crunch was the company's first breakout success. Everybody wanted some.

The second thing Ben did was to look for a general manager. Chico Lager was running a popular nightclub down the street from the gas station. In 1981, Ben was thirty. Chico was two years younger, and Jeff was eight years older, but they had all grown up in similar families. Chico had once considered opening an ice cream stand in Burlington. And when Ben approached him, he was trying to sell his bar and get into something new. The more Chico learned, the more interested he became, and Ben soon hired him as general manager. Chico and his family bought some stock in the private offering. Jeff and Chico were added to the board of directors, and Ben, Chico, and Jeff became the management team.

Jerry moved away from Vermont in 1982 to follow his future spouse, Elizabeth, to graduate school in Arizona. Just before he left, though, Jerry cohosted the shop's annual "Fall Down." This was a street party featuring contests in stilt walking, apple peeling, and frog jumping—and, of course, there was lots of free ice cream. The highlight of the proceedings was when Ben appeared shirtless, wearing a turban and diaper-style pants, playing the role of Habeeni Ben Coheeni, the noted mystic. "He is carried out by his devoted followers," Jerry said on *Biography*. "And Ben would go into this trance and would be laid across two chairs." Jerry, who had taken a class on carnival techniques in college, would then bring the festival to its climax. "A cinderblock would be placed upon Ben's ever-rounding bare belly, and I would lift a sledgehammer high above my head and bring it crashing down, demolishing the block."[4]

The poster for an early Free Cone Day featured two slogans: "Business has a responsibility to give back to the community," from Ben, and "If it's not fun, why do it?" from Jerry. Throwing parties by giving away huge amounts of inventory was not a full-blown social mission, but it wasn't business as usual, either.

Ben & Jerry's was ice cream for the people. And about the time that Jerry left for Arizona, the people developed an insatiable appetite. For a decade, the company often couldn't make its product fast enough. Annual sales grew from just under $1 million in 1982 to more than $58 million in 1989. In their 1984 prospectus, Ben, Jeff, and Chico had guessed that their sales in 1989 would be $15 million. This posed what a business consultant would call a "high-quality problem." As successful entrepreneurs, the guys needed to learn complex financial, legal, and management skills on the job as the number of employees grew from eighteen in 1982 to somewhere around three hundred in 1989, plus several hundred others working in franchised stores around the country.

For the three years after Jerry left, Chico focused most of his energies on protecting the bottom line. Ben handled sales and marketing, and Jeff did legal chores and whatever else needed doing. They managed the company in marathon monthly board meetings where, instead of voting, they discussed and compromised until the three of them agreed. Ben's generous, unpredictable spirit sometimes made Chico's job more difficult, but everyone was focused on the goal of managing the company's runaway growth. The growth allowed them to ignore smaller problems. And like Jeff, Chico enjoyed Ben's zaniness. He loved parties too, and Chico also recognized that Ben's crazy ideas were often masterstrokes of marketing.

Social Stirrings

Ben & Jerry's got serious about its "ice cream for the people" philosophy on April 26, 1984, the day the company made its first stock offering. That is when they really started sharing the company's wealth with the communities that supported it. That was the day the company went public—but only Vermont residents could buy the stock. Ben said the sale allowed Ben & Jerry's to give its best customers a piece of the action.

The company needed to raise $750,000 in equity to finance a $3.25 million ice cream plant in Waterbury, about twenty-five miles east of Burlington. Business was booming, and the prospects for expansion were bright. Or so the founders thought. Then Ben and Jeff tried to get a loan. Jeff remembers applying to dozens of banks before they found one that would even consider lending money to anyone who looked and acted like they did. And the bank officer added that he needed to see some equity first.

Ben came up with the idea to restrict the stock offer to people who lived in Vermont, with a minimum purchase of twelve shares at $10.50 apiece. Nearly everyone who heard the idea said that it was naïve and impractical. They told Ben that the stock offer could not reach its goal under those restrictions. But Jeff and Chico finally agreed to the plan because Ben would not back down. The fund-raising deadline was upon them. They needed to stop arguing and do something. Ben set the course, and they followed it.

The in-state stock offering was a classic Ben move, an idea that seemed crazy and exasperated his colleagues but then succeeded brilliantly. Chico and Ben made their pitches in rented conference rooms around the state. They sealed the deal by handing out free samples of ice cream after they finished talking. They easily raised the money, and that was just the beginning. The offer also generated a tremendous amount of publicity and goodwill. By the time it was done, nearly 1 percent of the households in the state owned shares of Ben & Jerry's.

Restricting the offer to one state also made it unnecessary to register it with the Securities and Exchange Commission, which reduced the banking costs. Giving ownership to a large number of people, each of whom held a small number of shares, meant that Ben could get the money he needed while retaining firm control of the company. And the sale went far beyond the standard business practice of making small donations to community organizations. It was more like a merger with thousands of patriotic Vermonters who would hassle the corner grocer if he ever ran out of Heath Bar Crunch. It was the first time the company found a big way to make its financial, social, and quality objectives move forward together.

Creative thinking and flexibility saved Ben & Jerry's more than once in those days. It came in especially handy when the company faced strong-arm tactics from Pillsbury, its chief competitor. Pillsbury, which spends millions on ads featuring a character called the Doughboy, owned Häagen-Dazs, the first super-premium ice cream in the United States. When Ben & Jerry's started selling in Boston, Pillsbury told its distributors there that they wouldn't get any Häagen-Dazs unless they agreed not to deliver Ben & Jerry's.

Pillsbury's move was blatantly illegal, but Ben and Chico didn't have enough time or money to rely on the courts. So they came up with a dual strategy. First, they sent Jeff out to interview lawyers. Jeff found one he liked at Ropes & Gray, an elite corporate firm based in Boston. "As I was talking to Howie, he leaned back and put his feet up on his desk," Jeff said. "He had a hole in the sole of his shoe. That sold me."

Howard Fuguet specialized in antitrust law because he liked working with entrepreneurs. "I had done quite a bit of work representing underdogs," he said. "I was intrigued by Ben & Jerry's, and I thought that we could win this." Howie became the company's lawyer, an important advisor to the board of directors, and, as the years went by, a storehouse of institutional memory.

Ben and Chico also crafted a non-legal strategy, in line with their philosophy of cultivating direct, personal relationships with customers. They put notices on their pints inviting customers to join a campaign called "What's the Doughboy Afraid Of?" They mailed out packets with bumper stickers and form letters customers could send to Pillsbury's CEO. They also flew Jerry to Minneapolis to stand in front of Pillsbury's headquarters with a picket sign. "I was very much in favor of this," Howie said. "I could see the marketing value of the lawsuit. I might have asked them to tone down a couple of their slogans, but it was a very interesting project."

Jerry always gets a laugh when he tells the Doughboy story in speeches now, mostly because he portrays himself as hapless and nutty. "Nobody had any idea of why I was there," he said at a talk at Cornell University in 2013. But that isn't quite true. Ben and Chico made sure that a photographer for the *Minneapolis Star Tribune* was there. The Associated Press picked up the story, and it ran all over the country.

The Doughboy campaign generated an avalanche of positive publicity for Ben & Jerry's, and it put so much pressure on Pillsbury that the big company was forced to back off. It also set a pattern the company would use, with spectacular results, for decades. Instead of doing traditional advertising or marketing campaigns, Ben & Jerry's would take their product directly to people. It would market to taste buds

In 1984, Ben & Jerry's asked the public to protest Pillsbury and Häagen-Dazs for illegally threatening the company's survival. Jerry's visit to Pillsbury's headquarters in April was widely covered by the press.

WHAT'S THE DOUGH BOY
AFRAID OF? 1-800-426-4604
in Vermont: 862-8286

through sampling, and also to an ordinary person's sense of fairness and justice by taking on social issues.

Ben & Jerry's commitment to linked prosperity deepened a year later when Jeff and Howie led the company through a national stock offering. Again, the company went directly to its customers first. It put a notice on each pint that encouraged customers to "Scoop Up Our Stock," with a toll-free number to call for a prospectus. "It was an unusual move," said Howie, "but once the Securities and Exchange Commission people understood it, they just laughed and said, 'Why not?' We kept trying to come up with things for Ben & Jerry's that were a little novel. I regarded it as a challenge, and they encouraged me."

As Ben, Chico, and Jeff worked on the prospectus for the national stock offering, they realized that they needed to tell potential investors exactly how much of their money the company planned to give away. Ben had been giving larger and larger cash contributions to local groups, while Chico had been trying to keep the giving at around 5 percent of pretax profits. So they created the Ben & Jerry's Foundation, an independent nonprofit organization funded by the company. Its goal was to support projects that were unlikely to be funded through traditional sources. The projects they were looking for would be models for social change, ideas that enhanced people's quality of life, and community celebrations. Jerry agreed to be the foundation's president. Jeff was the second board member, and Naomi Tannen, who had owned Highland Community, the school where Ben had met Jeff, was the third.

Ben endowed the foundation with fifty thousand shares of his stock, which was a little less than one-tenth of his equity in the company. He wanted to set the company's annual contribution to the foundation at 10 percent of pretax profits, or double the percentage that Chico had tried to maintain. Chico replied that giving this much away would make it impossible to fund future expansions without more stock offerings, which would further dilute Ben's ownership. The underwriters added that investors wouldn't buy into a company if it gave away so much cash, because that would reduce dividends. After a lengthy argument, Ben compromised on 7.5 percent of pretax profits, or nearly four times the national average.

Ten percent would have been fine with Jeff, though. Like Ben, he was enthusiastic about building a different kind of company. Jeff lived in Ithaca, a six-hour drive from Burlington, and he was a consultant, not an employee, so he was not involved in many of the day-to-day decisions. Jeff's work duties were not as intense as Ben and Chico's were. But as a board member and key advisor, he had a lot of influence. And Jeff often says he always looks for ways to make things more interesting, more political, and more fun.

Decisions and Consequences

The construction of the Waterbury plant went fairly smoothly because the guys got a gigantic lucky break. One day in 1984, Merritt Chandler, a recently retired business executive with deep roots in Vermont, walked into the office to get a prospectus for the in-state stock offering. Ben and Chico were just beginning to plan the plant's construction. In the best tradition of entrepreneurs, they were attempting to do a job for which they had not been trained. But building an ice cream plant is difficult, and this plant would be especially tough. It was going to make flavors with irregular-sized chunks, and those had never been produced in large quantities before. And the company was also going to start making its own mix, the smooth ice cream base, which meant that it was going to start mixing cream, sugar, and other ingredients itself.

Ben was "creative, bright, and a quick study, but he really didn't have the vaguest idea of what he was getting into," Merritt said years later in the employee newsletter. So Merritt, who had built plants for Xerox, offered to help. Within a month, he and Ben were working full time to manage the construction project. Merritt's engineering expertise was essential, and he also became an important role model for old-fashioned values like mutual respect, restraint, and discretion. These qualities are essential to managing a larger business, but they did not always come naturally to the employees or board of Ben & Jerry's, many of whom were proud to describe themselves as hippies, radicals, and misfits.

The plant's opening in the summer of 1985 was a major turning point for Ben & Jerry's. With close to a hundred employees in the building, Ben and Chico had to delegate authority, so they hired managers to direct sales, operations, and personnel. The atmosphere became chaotic as growth accelerated, because the managers didn't always agree or even know what others were doing—and also because the company's founder and CEO kind of liked things that way. Many companies develop a culture that mimics the personalities of their leaders. Everyone who worked with Chico says that he was a stable, no-nonsense kind of guy who liked a good joke. But Ben could be abrasive, and his wacky sense of humor sometimes baffled people. He had a habit of changing his mind without explanation, which made planning impossible. He was also maniacal about quality, and he worked very, very hard.

At the beginning of 1985, Ben & Jerry's ice cream was sold in Boston and New England, and the company had just started delivering to New York City. Other super-premium brands were emerging, and the board was eager to get into new markets before they did. Waterbury had quadrupled the company's production capacity to about eight hundred gallons of ice cream per hour. So the company's first sales director negotiated a distribution deal with Dreyer's, a California business that made premium ice cream and was looking to expand eastward. Dreyer's starting carrying Ben & Jerry's across the country in the summer of 1986.

The Dreyer's deal was an example of a sensible decision that also became a point of no return. It gave the company the ability to compete on a national scale with Häagen-Dazs, which was the only national super-premium brand in 1986. Without it, Ben & Jerry's would probably have remained a smaller, regionally focused ice cream business, with a much smaller impact on the world. But the deal also came at a price. By giving up control of the network that delivered its product from the factory to stores, Ben & Jerry's became dependent on others for its growth. The company also became more vulnerable to buyouts and mergers among distribution companies.

The introduction of a salary ratio was another casual decision that had huge consequences. One day in 1985, Jeff suggested that Ben & Jerry's borrow a tactic from the Mondragon Corporation, a confederation of worker-owned cooperatives in Spain. Mondragon's worker-owners determined the salaries of their managers by voting, and Jeff had read that the average ratio they settled on was three to one. In other words, the highest-paid Mondragon employee could not earn more than three times as much as the lowest-paid employee did.

Ben liked the idea of a salary ratio that was five to one. Chico hated it for several reasons, chiefly that the comparatively low top salaries would make it harder for him to hire talented managers. But even after the national stock offering was successfully concluded, Ben owned a little less than one-third of the company's shares, far more than anyone else, and he was still the president and CEO. Ben didn't throw his weight around often, but in this case he did. Ben announced that the company would follow a five-to-one salary ratio and, as one might expect, the line workers loved it. So did the media. Of course, every business school professor Jeff talked to told him that he and Ben were out of their minds. But with a new plant to open, new markets to enter, and interesting offers coming over the phone almost every day, there wasn't much time to debate philosophical questions.

In hindsight, it's easy to see the turning points. The stock offerings, the distribution deal, and the generous annual contribution to the foundation set the company's directions in finance, operations, and philanthropy. In the early years of public ownership, being controlled by shareholders wasn't much of a problem because Ben, Jerry, Jeff, and their Vermont fans controlled the majority of shares. But as the company grew, so did the number of owners, and balancing their needs with the founders' wishes became increasingly complicated.

The salary ratio shaped the company on a different level because it cut across every category of the business. Within the company, it caused endless arguments that sharpened the social mission, and it also defined the company's public image. It guided the company's fortunes, for better and worse, over the next nine years.

The Return of Jerry

The national stock offer had made Ben a multimillionaire at age thirty-five—at least on paper. But he was still working all the time. Eighty hours a week was not unusual. Ben's friends say that he has an exceptional ability to stay focused on a task and get to a goal. He had almost sold the company in 1982 because he didn't really want to be a business executive. And he still had the desire to get out in 1985. This time, he could have walked away with enough money to retire. But he didn't, because by 1985, Ben also had a compelling vision for his life's work. He was getting tired, but he was also determined to show the world that a socially responsible alternative to a traditional business could work.

Fortunately for Ben, one of the people he could turn to for help in 1985 was his best friend. Jerry and Elizabeth returned to Vermont just as the Waterbury plant opened, and Jerry started doing various jobs for Ben & Jerry's. He would pull an occasional shift on the production line, getting reacquainted with the employees. He also began attending board meetings. Jerry did not have an official vote, but that didn't matter much, because the board hardly ever voted. Ben, Jeff, Chico, and everyone else in the company were immensely relieved to have Jerry back in the mix.

Jerry was Ben's other half. Ben cultivated a laid-back public image, but when he was running the business, he was a taskmaster and a perfectionist who had the annoying habit of changing his mind without warning. "Working with Ben was, in plain English, a pain in the ass," wrote Chico in his entertaining memoir of the early years, *Ben & Jerry's: The Inside Scoop*. "Ben was usually so single-mindedly convinced that he was right about something that he often didn't even acknowledge the legitimacy of alternative points of view."[5]

Ben could burn people out. But Jerry was a peacemaker, calm and gracious and nurturing, and no one ever seemed to get mad at him. The two men have a deep friendship. They depend on each other, and they were surprising but perfectly matched business partners. They were like the raisins and pecans they mixed into chocolate ice cream to create Dastardly Mash, one of their first successful flavor combinations. No one else would have thought the combination would work, but no one could resist it, either.

Jerry led the founding board of the Ben & Jerry's Foundation, and with Jeff and Naomi Tannen, he set its direction. The foundation's first gifts in 1986 included a program at Goddard College that aided single parents on public assistance, a basketball court and ice rink in Waterville, Vermont, and other grants totaling $153,000. The foundation also launched a nine-month search for the best community celebration in the Northeast, with a first prize of $15,000. This was as much as they gave any individual grant. The foundation's big idea was to give small, targeted sums for groups that would not ordinarily apply to foundations, in hopes of maximizing the impact on actual lives.

The gifts fit with the company's policy of putting people first. They were good for business, too. Free publicity and word-of-mouth recommendations from passionate customers were more than enough to keep the growth train rolling. The board found itself managing a rapidly expanding food business whose identity was closely tied to its two charismatic founders, both of whom were passionate about social justice, inclusiveness, and grassroots decision making. They were not as passionate about the nuts and bolts of the ice cream business, however.

Ben and Chico encouraged employees to solve problems themselves, and the employees often found unusual solutions. "We didn't have an employee newsletter, and we needed one," said Lisa Wernhoff, who worked in the design department. "So a bunch of us started writing up items we thought were important. Once a month we would get together after work with scissors, tape, and a margarita blender. The later it got, the more risqué our jokes got. Around three in the morning, someone would go to the main office to photocopy, collate, and fold it. It was important to put it on peoples' desks before the day started, because we weren't supposed to do it during working hours."

As the Waterbury plant settled into a semichaotic routine, Ben and Chico reached an informal understanding. Ben would leave the day-to-day questions of running the business to Chico and the managers so that he could focus more on longer-term, strategic issues. Ben also said that he wouldn't mind if the company's growth slacked off a bit, because this would give the company's managers and employees time to grow into their new, bigger jobs. But, Chico writes, Ben had a hard time staying out of things. When he saw something that wasn't up to his standards, like a broken freezer door that wasted a lot of energy, he flew into a rage and insisted that it be fixed, now. When he saw an opportunity to go into a new market or was inspired to create a new flavor no one could resist, he plunged in. Sometimes Ben was in, and sometimes he was out, and no one could predict when he would change direction.

The company was struggling to make enough ice cream to meet demand. The factory was too small, even on the day it opened, and the complications of adding candy, fruit, and nuts to the mix meant that many batches didn't work. The production lines ran around the clock, with employees routinely pulling twelve-hour shifts, and accidents were a mounting problem. Ben, Jeff, and Chico found themselves running a fundamentally different kind of company. They were constantly hunting for experienced managers who were capable of handling the business issues caused by runaway growth. But they also needed managers who were inspired by the company's unconventional business practices—so inspired, in fact, that they were willing to take a substantial cut in pay. The company's search for mission-driven executives would continue for the next decade, and it would lead them to places they never thought they would go.

THREE

Progressive Sweatshop

The Bright Young Lad came up for his job interview in the fall of 1987. Charles M. "Chuck" Lacy was stuck in an unsatisfying job when a friend, Jeff Furman, told him that Ben & Jerry's needed managers. Chuck was twenty-nine, had an MBA from Cornell, and was newly married. He loved the Green Mountains, and he also liked what he saw at Waterbury. "They had courage," he said. "Also, they were hilarious."

Ben and Chico called Chuck "the bright young lad" and saved up jobs as they waited for him to arrive. Chuck spent his first day looking for the keys to the Cowmobile, a mobile ice cream stand, because it hadn't been started in a while. He asked Chico if he could see a copy of the budget, and Chico told him that they didn't really have a very good budget yet, and they definitely should, so why didn't Chuck write a better one? He was appointed director of safety on his second day, after a worker fell off a ladder and broke a bone. "It was a baptism of fire, but also exciting," he said. "Ben was intense and inspiring and also kind of mysterious. Chico had a magic touch—people would do anything for him. And the company was just exploding."

The Waterbury plant was already too small by the time it opened in 1985, so the company immediately began building additions, and construction did not stop for another three years. "Please continue to bear with us through the muck and mire," said the first issue of the satirical employee newsletter, the *Daily Plant* (slogan: "When properly potted, it grows like

Ben & Jerry's Ice Cream Factory in Waterbury, Vermont

By the late 1980s, the overburdened Ben & Jerry's factory in Water-
bury was also one of the state's top tourist attractions. (Left to right)
Toni Pratt, Diana Wells, Mary Messier (back to camera), and Kelly
Farrell staffed a production line.

hell!"). The article described plans for a suspension bridge to
get employees across the muddy field that led to the plant's
entrance, a hot tub and tanning booth for freezer workers
"who never get to see the light nor experience the warmth
of day," a meditation room for Jerry and others "who wish to
rise to even higher levels," and a pub "for those of you looking to sink to even lower levels."

Sales increased from $20 million in 1986 to $32 million in 1987, $48 million in 1988, and $58 million in 1989. The workforce more than doubled in 1987–88, to more than 250 employees. "Unemployment in Vermont was low, so we hired whomever we could get," said Chuck. "Our people were imperfect, and we loved them for it. A lot of us, including me, felt like we were getting a second chance." But it was a chaotic, inefficient operation. The company had eighteen "key managers" who all needed to talk to Chico, and it wasn't entirely clear who reported to Ben. "I encouraged Chico to pick his top five people and delegate," said Chuck. "We had to figure it all out as we kept working."

In the mid-1980s, opportunities came so easily to Ben & Jerry's that folks could be sloppy and still get away with it. One day in 1986, for example, the company received an anonymous postcard from two Grateful Dead fans suggesting a flavor named "Cherry Garcia" in honor of the band's guitarist, Jerry Garcia. Ben was inspired. He wanted to create an ice cream that would be like eating chocolate-covered

Cherry Garcia, a perennial bestseller since its release, as it appeared in 1987 (left) and in 2013.

cherries. He decided to add whole Bing cherries and small flakes of chocolate to a vanilla mix. Cherry Garcia was released on Washington's Birthday 1987, and it immediately became a perennial top-selling flavor. It kept the growth train rolling.

The problem was, Ben didn't ask Jerry Garcia first. And when he got a polite letter from Hal Kant, Garcia's lawyer, suggesting that Ben & Jerry's pay royalties for using his client's name, Ben did not reply directly. Instead, he wrote a letter to Garcia that said, according to Jeff, "Let's not deal with these idiot lawyers." The reply was a nasty letter from Kant threatening a defamation lawsuit and insisting that Ben & Jerry's immediately cease and desist. Ben promptly gave the cleanup job to Jeff, who Chico described as looking "a little like how Jerry Garcia might if he had been put in a dryer and shrunk."

Jeff flew to California and met Hal Kant at a coffee shop in Sausalito. Hal was in a good mood, Jeff says, because he had just won the Pot-Limit Omaha category at the World Series of Poker, where he was known as "Dead Man Kant." "We shared stories about representing weird people, I proposed a royalty, and we shook on it," said Jeff. "He mainly wanted to protect his client's name. It turned out that we saw things largely the same way. The Dead were the first band to allow their fans to tape their shows, and they had a grassroots foundation that was somewhat like ours." The ice cream royalties went to that foundation. The negotiation went so well that Jeff got six passes to any of the band's shows reserved for Ben & Jerry's, forever.

Publicity fueled the demand in those days. Journalists were infatuated with Ben & Jerry's, partly because the company was so good at offering them irresistible tidbits. Many of these had to do with the five-to-one salary ratio and a steady stream of clever marketing stunts that usually had a political subtext. The company's marketing director kept the legendary Newport Folk Festival from going under by writing a last-minute sponsorship check in 1988. A wave of adoring publicity followed, and for several years the gathering was known as the "Ben & Jerry's Newport Folk Festival." It was a typically shrewd use of promotional dollars that also reflected the values of the founders.

In 1989, the hitchhiker Jerry picked up in 1977, Rob Michalak, joined Ben & Jerry's to do public relations. He says that Ben & Jerry's was receiving an average of one hundred press clippings a week back then, and that almost all of them were positive. The media had found a new story, the "socially responsible business," and Ben & Jerry's was the poster child.

Scooper Evangelists

The socially responsible business movement had been building for a long time. Investors who opposed the Vietnam War or supported the civil rights movement had been organizing boycotts and drafting shareholder resolutions for decades before Ben and Jerry scooped their first cone. In the early 1980s, mutual-fund managers began catering to these folks by picking stocks that supported or avoided various causes. One of the most active "social investors" was D. Wayne Silby, who cofounded the Calvert Social Investment Fund in 1982. Calvert was one of the first funds to take a stand on apartheid by withdrawing from companies that did business in South Africa.

Silby belonged to a small group of investors, philanthropists, and entrepreneurs who were all dreaming the same dream in the 1980s. Another was Josh Mailman, an heir and philanthropist, who envisioned "a new paradigm: one in which business operates to add value to society, without compromising the well-being of future generations." Another was Marjorie Kelly, a young journalist who cofounded *Business*

Ethics magazine in 1987. In California, Yvon Chouinard was donating 10 percent of the profits from his outdoor products company, Patagonia, to environmental causes. In Maine, Tom and Kate Chappell were putting a strong proenvironment spin on their line of all-natural toothpaste and other products.

Just as Marjorie Kelly was publishing the first issue of *Business Ethics*, Wayne Silby and Josh Mailman invited Ben, Jerry, and Jeff to attend a meeting of six dozen socially minded investors and businesspeople in the mountains near Boulder, Colorado. The meeting launched the Social Venture Network, a loose-knit professional organization for those who wanted to merge business and social change. Ben made two valuable connections there. One was with Paul Hawken, a best-selling author and entrepreneur. He profiled Ben & Jerry's in his book *Growing a Business*, which was also made into a nationally distributed series for public television.[1]

The other connection was with Anita and Gordon Roddick, founders of the Body Shop. Their friends said that Ben and Anita were like twins separated at birth. Anita had opened her first shop in 1976, selling natural soaps and cosmetics, and had built it into a global success by "running in the opposite direction and breaking the rules," she wrote in her memoir *Body and Soul*. "I get a real buzz from doing things differently from everyone else."[2] The Body Shop had made a name for itself as a vocal opponent of testing cosmetics and other products on animals, by partnering with Greenpeace and other environmental and human-rights organizations, and by encouraging customers to bring in their own bottles and otherwise cut down on waste.

The Roddicks were preparing to open their first store in the United States, so they latched on to Ben and Jerry. The ice cream guys wanted to learn more about mixing business and social activism, so they were happy to share. The two companies became close because they shared the same passions and the same turbocharged work ethic. Anita told

Ben about how the first socially responsible businesses were owned by members of the Religious Society of Friends in the seventeenth and eighteenth centuries, and how the Philadelphia Yearly Meeting had started it all in the United States in 1758, when it prohibited its members from participating in the slave trade.

"I am still looking for the modern-day equivalent of those Quakers who ran successful businesses," Anita wrote. "[They] made money because they offered honest products and treated their people decently, worked hard, spent honestly, saved honestly, gave honest value for money, put back more than they took out and told no lies."[3] The Roddicks encouraged Ben to set ambitious goals, and they fueled his appetite for social change.

Ben and Jerry were frequently asked to speak at national conferences and meetings, and they turned out to be just as effective at selling corporate social responsibility as they were at selling ice cream. They became celebrities who were routinely characterized as either visionaries or naïve hippies, depending on the writer's point of view. But it's closer to the truth to say that they were preachers. They were trying to transform the way corporations did business because they believed it was the key to changing the world. Spreading this message was part of their job description.

Like everyone else in the company, Ben and Jerry were extremely hardworking, maniacal about product quality, and entangled in a workplace that operated like a slightly dysfunctional family. "Why do outsiders think that Ben & Jerry's is a haven for 60s flower children?" wrote an employee in the *Daily Plant*. "A local news anchor recently accused Ben & Jerry's of 'running on Grateful Dead time.' But the last time I saw Ben he had on a green and white striped button down shirt, baggy pants, and running sneakers. He looked like he was on his way to a prep school lacrosse game."

Ben & Jerry's was happy to use Grateful Dead images in

their marketing, but the company was anything but laid-back. Its style was more like what you would find in a restaurant kitchen during the dinner rush, if the rush lasted ten years. People who are under great pressure every day tend to blow off steam in weird ways, however, and with encouragement from Ben, the company regularly gave employees the opportunity to get freaky. At one meeting, Ben and the sales director stripped down to loincloths and wrestled sumo-style, slamming into each other to settle the question of whose belly was fatter. Long-time employees still carry fond memories of these foolish things.

Who Runs This Company?

In 1987, Ben, Chico, and Jeff recruited two older, more experienced businessmen to serve on the board of directors. One was Merritt Chandler, the retired Xerox executive who had led the construction of the Waterbury plant. The other was Henry Morgan, who had just retired as dean of the business school at Boston University. Henry had also been an executive at Polaroid, where he had established one of the country's first diversity training programs and led a campaign for businesses to boycott South Africa. Henry was on the board of South Shore Bank, a Chicago institution that offered mortgages to low-income people and emphasized the environmental impacts of its decisions. Ben & Jerry's kept some of its cash at this bank, and Jeff got to know Henry through those dealings.

When Henry and Merritt started participating in board meetings in the spring of 1987, the company's leadership style changed. Board meetings became slightly more formal. They made more decisions by voting, and the votes weren't always unanimous.

The company's managers were also moving toward the mainstream. A few days after Chuck Lacy reported for work in February 1988, he joined Chico and the other key managers at a three-day retreat. The facilitator was Phil Mirvis, an organizational psychologist who had worked with Henry Morgan at Boston University. Mirvis led the managers through team-building exercises designed to strengthen their ability to run the company. Ben and Jerry did not participate, except for one evening when they dropped by to talk about their vision. Their visit did not go well. "They basically told us we weren't weird enough," says Chuck. "I don't think many of us understood. We were trying to improve the way we made ice cream."

The confusion soon turned into an open confrontation with an absurd twist, in classic Ben & Jerry's style. It was a fight over peacemaking.

In the fall of 1987, Jeff told Ben and Jerry about a proposal that was circulating among peace activists. The idea was that 1 percent of the Department of Defense's budget (which would have been about $4.2 billion in 1988) should be redirected to cultural and economic exchanges between the United States and the Soviet Union. Ben was galvanized. He was so excited, in fact, that he startled Jennifer Henderson when he described the idea to her at a meeting in New York City—the meeting when Ben cheerfully agreed with Jennifer that he was insane (see chapter 1).

At the January 1988 board meeting, Ben unveiled plans for a new organization called One Percent for Peace. The board of directors included himself, Jerry, Jeff, Paul Hawken, and Jennifer Henderson, along with the president of South Shore Bank and other luminaries of the peace and social justice movements. At that time, the company was opening a plant in Springfield, Vermont, to make novelty products. The first product was going to be chocolate-covered ice cream on a stick, and Ben proposed that they call it a Peace Pop. The board agreed to that idea, but Henry, Merritt, and Chico were reluctant to support a group that didn't exist yet. They also worried that some retailers might refuse to stock products that courted controversy by advocating defense cuts.

Chico, Henry, and Merritt encouraged Ben and Jeff to find other companies that would sponsor One Percent for Peace and to come back with a more specific proposal. Ben and Jeff got right to work. They drafted a letter to potential supporters that said Ben & Jerry's was introducing Peace Pops, and that "the copy on these 2 million to 8 million packages will be used to alert the population to excessive military expenditures and to garner support for One Percent for Peace." The letter also said that the Ben & Jerry's Foundation would provide initial funding with an amount equivalent to 1 percent of the company's pretax profits.

The problem arose because Ben and Jeff mailed these letters before passing them by Chico and the other board members for review. The timing, coming so soon after the managers' retreat, could not have been worse. When they did see it, Chico, Merritt, Henry, and the managers mutinied. Ben had gone too far, they said. He was making commitments the board had not agreed to. The managers drafted a letter to the board that concluded, "We are either going to be an organization run by a management team, or an organization run by Ben. Which is it to be?"

After a lot more discussion, the board ultimately decided to endorse the plans Ben and Jeff had outlined. "I was against it at first. I thought Chico was right, that we'd lose business," said Chuck. "We argued on and on. Then, at one point, someone asked me, 'Why can't a company take a stand? Why not?' And I realized that I didn't have a good answer. So I changed my mind, and I think that had an effect."

Although no one had ever said so in public, the board had hired Chuck with the hope that he might become Chico's successor. Chuck had become a trusted advisor to Chico. When he changed his mind about Peace Pops, Chico went along with him. When that happened, Ben & Jerry's passed

One Percent for Peace was the company's first full-blown attempt to coordinate its social and financial goals. Ben, Jeff, and Jerry staffed a table at the Newport Ben & Jerry's Folk Festival in the early 1990s.

a watershed. It was the first time the company took a public position on a political issue.

Ben & Jerry's had always been extremely generous, giving 7.5 percent of pretax profits to its foundation and even more to the communities where it sold its products, and it had always treated its employees well. These policies were admirable but not unusual. After all, Andrew Carnegie gave generously to charity, and Henry Ford paid his workers well. But with One Percent for Peace, Ben & Jerry's went further.

Today, it isn't unusual for a company to put its marketing muscle behind a noncontroversial cause. Corporate social marketing takes many forms: Allstate encourages teenagers to sign a pledge not to send text messages while driving, and Home Depot pushes water conservation. But Ben & Jerry's was one of the first companies to do this, and in 1988 they went further than most companies would dare to go twenty-five years later. They started and funded their own not-for-profit organization, and they allied with a controversial cause (the peace movement) that would alienate potential customers—how many, no one could say.

The risks were substantial, but Ben, Jerry, and Jeff didn't care. "From our point of view, the risk of continuing the arms race outweighed any risk to the company," said Jeff. "We might have been scared of failing, but we were much more frightened of tactical nuclear warheads." The social mission was at least as important to them as profit and product quality, and maybe more. They were willing to bet the business on their beliefs.

Peace Pops and One Percent both launched that summer. The launch was rocky, but both efforts were ultimately successful. Jeff likes to say that the Soviet Union dissolved three and a half years after the launch, and there must be a connection. The launch did not hurt the company's image or sales, either; in fact, it helped. "People liked the idea that a business was taking a stand on issues outside of its own self-interest," wrote Jerry.[4] Inside the company, though, the cost was high. It took a long time for the board and management to regain trust in each other. And some managers never stopped resenting what they saw as the unnecessary complexity and loss of focus that came with social investments.

Henry's Memo

The core values that Ben, Jerry, and Jeff shared had not really changed all that much since the late 1970s. They were still suspicious of big business and Wall Street, and they dreamed of a world where profits and social justice could work together. But as the 1980s ended, they found themselves balancing social justice and profit in ways they had never imagined.

One moment of supreme weirdness came on May 9, 1988, when President Ronald Reagan named Ben and Jerry the National Small Business Persons of the Year. The guys sat in the White House Rose Garden, wearing suits and ties for perhaps the first time since they had graduated from high school, and basked in praise from the Pied Piper of free-market capitalism. They were deeply ambivalent about free-market capitalism. Weirder still, they were about to launch a product whose packaging attacked Reagan's defense budget and promoted peaceful citizen exchanges between Americans and Russians. Reagan had called the Soviet Union "the evil empire," and his idea of social justice was busting unions and giving tax cuts to rich people. And yet, he was saying such nice things about them. It was kind of confusing, like a scene from an absurdist play. It was just the kind of fun that Ben and Jerry liked to have.

Back in Burlington, the board meetings were not nearly as much fun. Henry Morgan, one of the two new members, soon found himself with an outsized influence on the board, as the division between profit and social mission deepened. On the five-person board, Merritt would usually side with Chico, Jeff would usually agree with Ben, and Henry would break the tie. Henry didn't like having this role, so he asked Phil Mirvis to sit in at board meetings and steer the discussion toward process.

Everyone on the board agreed that it was time to make the transition from a company controlled by its founders to one that was run by hired managers. Ben had even submitted a letter of resignation from his position as marketing director, effective March 1, 1988, which said that he looked forward to serving as an "outside director." Everyone also agreed that it was time to clarify the values the business lived by. If Ben & Jerry's was going to do more things like One Percent for Peace while also ceding control to professional managers, it needed to put the company's beliefs in writing. Ben & Jerry's needed a mission statement.

The meetings and interviews Mirvis facilitated did not end the division on the board, but they did shine a constructive light on the issues. As board members and managers took turns voicing their concerns, Henry Morgan noticed that they were saying the same things over and over. Many of them returned to an idea that one manager, Dave Barash, called "linked prosperity." The idea was that as the company grew, the benefits would be distributed not only to shareholders but to employees and the community. Each group's interests were intertwined with the others.

The idea of linked prosperity got to the core issue facing the company. Ben & Jerry's was looking for ways to advance a social mission and an economic mission simultaneously, without putting either of them first. As the social mission evolved over the next twenty-five years, Ben & Jerry's would struggle to integrate its financial and social bottom lines and to create synergy by combining profit-making with community building. Maintaining this creative tension was and still is the most challenging aspect of managing Ben & Jerry's, and it's also what makes the company different.

At the May 1988 board meeting, as the familiar arguments about social goals and operational efficiencies continued, Henry Morgan went into a side room to work on a mission statement. What he wrote was very close to the statement the company would use for the next twenty-five years:

> Ben & Jerry's is dedicated to the creation and demonstration of a new corporate concept of linked prosperity. Our mission consists of three interrelated parts. The PRODUCT MISSION is to make, distribute, and sell the finest quality all-natural ice cream and related products in a wide variety of innovative flavors made from Vermont

dairy products. The SOCIAL MISSION is to operate the company in a way that actively recognizes the central role that business plays in the structure of society by initiating innovative ways to improve the quality of life of a broad community: local, national, and international. The ECONOMIC MISSION is to operate the company on a sound financial basis of profitable growth, increasing value for our shareholders and creating career opportunities and financial rewards for our employees. Underlying the mission of Ben & Jerry's is the determination to seek new and creative ways of addressing all three parts, while holding a deep respect for individuals, inside and outside the company, and for the communities of which they are a part.

The success of Ben & Jerry's would depend on whether the tensions that would inevitably arise from balancing those three parts could be converted into creative energy. It would take another two decades of struggle before the company found a way to generate that creativity in a consistent way. Only one of those decades would include Ben and Jerry.

Do-Good Brownies

All boards of directors have the same job: to name the organization's mission, work with the organization's staff leadership to turn that vision into a plan, and encourage everyone in the organization to embrace the plan and reduce the gap between expectations and reality. When a mission has three interrelated parts, and one of them is changing the world, the expectations are much higher. This made the jobs of board members and CEO much harder than just selling ice cream.

The board held an all-company meeting in the fall of 1988 to unveil the three-part mission statement and invite reactions. "There were a lot of people going, 'Huh?' We were trying to figure out what they meant," said Lisa Wernhoff. "It got us thinking and talking."

"I was impressed," says Sean Greenwood, who was scooping ice cream and driving a company truck while attending the University of Vermont (UVM). "They were making us part of the decision-making process instead of just saying here are the rules, follow them. They were blowing out Ben's motto, that businesses have a responsibility to the community, and also what Jerry always says, which is, 'If it's not fun, why do it?' I thought, there's a real direction here."

At the end of 1988, the board appointed Chico president and CEO of the company, with Ben remaining as chairman of the board. The press release did not mention it, but Chico's promotion was actually part of his exit strategy. Chico owned a fair amount of stock in Ben & Jerry's, but his salary in 1988 was only about $75,000, or five times as much as a new plant worker. That was far below the market rate for a CEO of a company with annual sales of more than $50 million. And by the end of 1988, Chico was more than ready to leave. So when Chico was promoted at the end of 1988, Chuck became general manager. Both men had an informal understanding that Chico would gradually transfer the responsibility for day-to-day operations to Chuck over the next two years. Board members expected that Chuck would become the president and CEO in January 1991.

Still, the company's growth depended on the rain that came from Ben's brainstorms. He had another one late in 1988 when he learned about the Greyston Foundation in Yonkers, New York. The foundation operated a for-profit bakery that hired homeless people and others usually considered unemployable. Ben asked the group's leader if Greyston could make the thin, chewy brownies Ben & Jerry's used as the outside layers in their ice cream sandwich. Greyston said yes, Ben & Jerry's switched suppliers, and several dozen formerly homeless people got steady jobs. It seemed like a win-win.

But mixing business with a social mission is rarely simple. Greyston had never had a contract anywhere near as large as the one it signed with Ben & Jerry's, and Ben & Jerry's didn't check the company out thoroughly before the contract was signed. The bakery spent months trying to make brownies in quantity that matched the specs Ben & Jerry's needed. A lot of dough went into the trash, literally and figuratively.

Greyston nearly went bankrupt before it worked out the bugs, and production at the Springfield novelties plant was often delayed. Ben & Jerry's even sent several people to the bakery to help with the transition, including Jeff, who restructured Greyston's debt and worked out a new financial plan.

Eventually, the partnership was a success. In 2012, Greyston Bakery delivered $8 million worth of brownie pieces to Ben & Jerry's, accounting for the vast majority of Greyston's business. It employs about fifty people who were once homeless or chronically unemployed. Ben and Jerry wrote that the Greyston deal was "one of the best decisions the company ever made."[5] Still, it was a lot more complicated than just buying brownies. Customer complaints about the Chocolate Fudge Brownie flavor remained high for years.

Jeff accepts these rough patches as part of the deal. "We get involved in the operations of suppliers who have a social purpose, and that's fine. We should treat our social mission partners as if they are part of our family. If they're having problems, we should not give up right away. We should work with them, because it's more than an economic relationship."

Consorting with Communists

Shortly after One Percent for Peace launched, Ben got a call from a professor of Russian at Middlebury College. The professor suggested that Ben and Jeff go to Moscow and meet with activists there to try to establish One Percent for Peace in the Soviet Union. After several exploratory trips, Ben and Jeff decided to start a Ben & Jerry's Ice Cream Shop and factory near Moscow, with the goal of encouraging American and Russian scoopers to travel and get to know each other. It seemed like another simple idea. But the negotiations and planning took years, especially when the Soviet Union collapsed in the middle of things.

After several false starts, the Russia project finally started to move when Madeleine Kunin, the governor of Vermont, was establishing a sister relationship with the Russian state of Karelia. Kunin invited Ben to come along. Ben's seatmate on the plane was Kunin's chief of staff, Liz Bankowski.

"We talked for a long time about the salary ratio," said Bankowski. Ben was still caught between Chico, who argued that a cap on salaries made it too difficult to find qualified people for senior positions, and Jeff, who argued that the ratio was what made Ben & Jerry's fundamentally different from other for-profit businesses. "Ben had a lot of angst over it," she said. "I told him to keep an open mind."

Airplane trips give business executives a rare chance to sit and think without being interrupted. When he took that transatlantic flight in late November 1988, six months after the board endorsed the mission statement, Ben was struggling with the salary ratio, Greyston Bakery, One Percent for Peace, and several other initiatives. He was probably wondering how to advance the social mission without sitting through so many tough meetings. Fortunately, the trip was a success. And an even bigger win happened on the flight back, when Ben invited Liz Bankowski to apply for a seat on the company's board of directors.

FOUR

Staffing the Social Mission

Liz Bankowski was the first woman on the board of Ben & Jerry's, which was a big deal for a company that prided itself on having progressive values. But her value to the company went far beyond symbolism. She was just what Ben & Jerry's needed to take the social mission to the next level. She was a political professional who knew how to generate support for social initiatives, rearrange employee resources to push them forward, get them done in a focused way, and evaluate the results so that the company would do a better job next time.

Liz was one of several new faces who had a big effect on Ben & Jerry's in the 1990s. Another was Fran Rathke, a big-firm CPA who had graduated from the University of Vermont and wanted to settle in Burlington. When Fran showed up in April 1989, Chuck and Chico finally got someone who had the potential to become the company's first chief financial officer (CFO). Whenever something happened or a new idea emerged, Fran could give the board and top managers a realistic view of the financial impacts and options.

Another addition was Jerry. He had been involved as a consultant and employee since 1985, doing a little bit of everything. He opened the company's annual meetings with an inspiring story, gave interviews, took an occasional midnight shift on the production line, led promotions and celebrations, and generally spread positive energy around. Everyone loved him, and in 2014, they still do. Jerry's personal warmth and human skill, combined with his name on the label, made him the board's top diplomatic liaison to employees, the press, other businesses, and especially to his best friend.

Who Wants the Job?

In 1990, Jerry joined the board of directors as vice chair, and Liz and Chuck also became voting members. Fran attended the meetings in a nonvoting capacity as treasurer, but the board's informal style meant that her opinion carried as much weight as anyone else's. The group expanded from five to eight voting members, and all of them had their own understanding of the three-part mission.

Chico and Merritt still argued that as a shareholder-owned company, Ben & Jerry's needed to protect its profitability before it did anything else. Fran strongly supported this view. Henry agreed, but he was also fascinated by the innovations the three-part mission made possible. Ben and Jeff were always pushing. They wanted the company to be a laboratory for innovation and progressive business; they were more likely to be in favor of taking risks and going into uncharted territory. Jerry was always loyal to his best friend, but he was also a strong advocate for protecting employees' jobs and benefits. And Chuck and Liz were inspired by the company's courage. They wanted Ben & Jerry's to take risks for the sake of its values. But everyone also knew that the company could not survive without sustainable growth and profits.

Liz got her first glimpse of the board's informal style at the January 1990 meeting. "I thought it was a dinner to welcome me to the board, so everyone would try to make a good impression," she said. "But there was no pretense. There was a certain amount of tension in the air, so I listened, and it became clear to me that nobody wanted to run the company.

They were playing darts, and I remember they were saying, 'I don't want to run it.' And, 'I don't either.' And, 'I sure don't.' And I was thinking to myself, 'Hmmmmmmm.'"

The board was discussing Chico's departure. On New Year's Day 1991 he would no longer be an employee, although he would remain on the board. The problem was that Chuck wasn't willing to run the company unless he had daily access to Ben. Ultimately, Ben would do another stint as CEO, with Chuck becoming president. So Ben wasn't out of the daily grind yet, although he clearly wanted to be.

Chuck also turned to Liz, who became much more available to Ben & Jerry's when her old boss, Governor Madeleine Kunin, decided not to run for re-election in 1990. Liz did several projects for the company as a consultant in 1990 and 1991, focusing more and more of her energy on the social mission. She was the company's point person on a full-page ad that ran in the *New York Times* on December 31, 1990, to oppose America's imminent invasion of Kuwait. The ad was cosponsored by Ben & Jerry's and eighteen other companies in the Social Venture Network, including Patagonia, *Business Ethics*, *Utne Reader* (a bimonthly magazine, founded in 1984, that reprints "the best of the alternative press"), Working Assets (a telecommunications company that makes a donation to peace, human rights, and environmental groups every time a member makes a telephone call), and Stonyfield Yogurt (which began as an environmental education center and became one of the country's largest organic yogurt companies, donating $2 million a year to environmental groups). It was probably the first time a group of companies had ever used their logos to make an antiwar statement. "It was a modest way to suggest that businesses could use their voices in a different way," Liz said. "That was the core of what Ben & Jerry's was about."

In 1991, a worker at the Waterbury plant approached Liz and urged her to get the company involved in the debate surrounding the construction of a huge hydroelectric plant on James Bay, an Indian reservation in northern Quebec. The company sent seven employees, most of them line workers, on a fact-finding trip to the site, and it published their statement in a full-page ad in the *Burlington Free Press*. It wasn't a simple issue. Vermont utilities were considering signing up for the nonpolluting electricity, which was a clear environmental benefit, and the idea had widespread support. But the project had also flooded thousands of acres of Native hunting grounds, disrupting the traditions of an ancient community. The ad urged Vermonters not to export their environmental footprint. The state should spend more on energy conservation and alternative power sources, it said, and leave James Bay alone.

The political and social initiatives followed a hit-and-miss pattern. Ben, Jeff, or someone else would come up with an idea for a social initiative, Chuck would toss it to Liz, and Liz would take a swing at it. After a year or so of consulting while also serving on the board, Liz told her fellow board members she had noticed something funny. "We all agreed that the social mission was our point of distinction in the marketplace. I said that we had lots of people working on product quality and financial results, but no one on the staff was devoted to the social mission. And in true Ben & Jerry's fashion, the reaction was, 'That is a really good point. You should go do that.'"

Liz joined the staff as the company's first director of social mission in December 1991. She also remained on the board. This put her in a privileged position, because only Liz, Ben, and Chuck were both managers and voting board members. She was in the right place to push the social mission forward.

Liz set several goals for her new job. The first was to spread acceptance of the social mission throughout the company so that it could move beyond scattershot ideas from Ben, Jeff, and others. This was one reason why she decided

The *Daily Plant,* Ben & Jerry's unofficial employee newsletter, included this prediction in its January 1990 issue: "World peace will be achieved through cheap marketing stunts."

not to hire her own employees. "If the social mission was going to be at the core of our business," she said, "it needed to be owned and managed by the people in various departments, and staffed as needed."

"Liz was good at inspiring people," said Chuck. One reason is that she encouraged people to speak their minds. "It was exciting and challenging to work for a company that took out an antiwar ad, but also had employees who served in the National Guard," she said. "People knew what they were getting into when they took a job at Ben & Jerry's. Even if they didn't agree with the social initiatives, they liked that they were encouraged to talk about it." These debates were also an evergreen source of sarcastic jokes. One of the *Daily Plant*'s predictions for 1990 was "World peace will be achieved through cheap marketing stunts." Another was "Ben will change his mind."

Liz was particularly good at inspiring the company's sisterhood. Women executives were still unusual in 1990, and the female employees of Ben & Jerry's were thrilled to see a woman in the center of the action. They rallied around Liz, which further increased her power within the company.

By setting herself up as an internal consultant rather than a department head, Liz also advanced a second goal: keeping the social mission flexible so that Ben & Jerry's could respond to opportunities quickly. A third goal was to evaluate the results of social ventures so that the company could get a better idea of what kinds of tactics were most likely to succeed—or, just as likely, fail.

Liz spent much of her first year unsuccessfully trying to realize Jeff's dream of finding more diverse suppliers. Specifically, she was asked to look for African-American farmers who could provide the peaches the company used in Georgia Peach ice cream. It turned out that very few black farmers in Georgia raised peaches, and that even outside Georgia, the only not-for-profit organization representing black farmers was understaffed and couldn't handle the project.

In July 1991, Liz suggested that the company could have saved a lot of time and effort if it had asked a few strategic questions early on. She suggested that the old way of advancing the social mission—coming up with a cool idea and then plunging ahead to try to make it happen—should end. "We need to take a longer term view of projects like this," she wrote in a memo to Ben and Chuck. Suppliers who advance the social mission should be chosen based on "the feasibility of the idea, the availability of a good intermediary to make it happen, the resources available, the likelihood of the project becoming a success, and the commitment we wish to make to it."

Toward a Social Audit

Liz was stating the obvious. Any organization is more likely to succeed when it sets achievable goals and finds ways to measure its progress toward those goals. The trick would be finding a way to honor the culture of Ben & Jerry's, with all of its compassion, spontaneity, and fun, while also finding a way to express these qualities in numbers.

Today, many large corporations do some form of social reporting. They create frameworks to account for the social, environmental, and economic impacts of their operations. Their reports explain the company's efforts to minimize negative effects while maximizing positive ones, and some of them even suggest ways to improve. Yet many corporate social reports are not done independently. They are merely exercises in public relations, with little or no substance. Bank of America was fined $335 million for discriminating against people of color in December 2011, $1 billion for mortgage fraud in March 2012, and $2.8 million for overbilling customers in June 2012. But that didn't stop them from publishing a handsomely designed, 124-page *Corporate Social Responsibility Report* a few months later.

The first US corporations to hire independent auditors for the nonfinancial aspects of their operations did so because they were forced to. Regulatory amendments to the Clean Air Act in 1970, followed by the Clean Water Act in 1972, made petroleum and chemical companies liable for significant fines if they did not measure and contain emissions of a specific list of pollutants. The growth of environmental regulations, environmental law, and citizens' organizations in the 1970s encouraged more and more companies to audit and evaluate their environmental performance.

A social audit is a broader concept, and no laws force corporations to do them. Many corporate managers say that exposing their shortcomings in public has no upside, so they actively avoid this kind of publicity. Only a few for-profit companies published social assessments in the 1980s, and Ben & Jerry's was the first American company to do one. Part of its annual report for 1988 was a "stakeholder's report" that detailed the company's activities on behalf of five groups: employees, customers, suppliers, investors, and communities, which the company defined as "the entire world." The social auditor for 1988 was John Tepper Marlin, an economist who specializes in ethics. He visited Ben & Jerry's for two weeks, evaluated the accuracy of the company's claims, and pronounced them trustworthy.

John Marlin was an advisor to the Council on Economic Priorities (CEP), which did a lot to start the corporate social responsibility movement in America. The founder of CEP was his wife, Alice Tepper Marlin. As a stockbroker in the 1960s, Alice had done research for synagogues and churches that wanted to avoid investing in companies that made weapons. Her research was so popular, and so many companies were reluctant to cooperate with her, that she realized she had struck a nerve. Alice and her small staff produced dozens of reports that ranked corporate practices concerning the employment of women and minorities, pollution control, occupational safety, and other issues.

As John Marlin wrote his report on Ben & Jerry's, Alice was working on the first handbook on corporate social responsibility that was designed for consumers. The first edition of *Shopping for a Better World* came out in 1989. It investigated the performance of more than fourteen hundred companies that supplied American supermarkets. The book, which was essentially a long checklist, was small enough to fit into a purse or a pocket. It was hugely popular, selling millions of copies and going through many editions in the 1990s.

The book created a new consumer niche, as millions of shoppers began seeking or avoiding products according to the social policies of the companies that made them. Shoppers who are motivated by their social consciences tend to be college-educated women, and they often have lots of discretionary income. They are the same consumers that many companies are most interested in attracting. Marketers quickly understood that a good rating in *Shopping for a Better World* could give them an edge in the battle for market share.

Ben & Jerry's stakeholder's report for 1989 was written by employees and audited by William Norris, the founder of Control Data Corporation. In the 1970s, Control Data was among a handful of companies (including Stride Rite, Levi Strauss, and Herman Miller) that believed, as Norris had put it, in "addressing unmet societal needs as profitable business opportunities."

Ben liked William Norris, but he didn't like the stakeholder approach. There was too much self-congratulation, and the tendency would always be to promote the company's greatest hits without putting them in context. "Ben wanted to organize the report by department, and he wanted it to contain only data that were descriptive of the social mission," said Liz. "He asked me to establish measures we could report on over time that would clearly show if we were making progress."

In the summer of 1990, Ben handed Liz a copy of a "business responsibility checklist" written by a Stanford professor, Kirk Hanson, who had been working as a consultant in business ethics since the 1970s. The list, which was drawn from Hanson's decades of experience, went far beyond an internal audit. It listed more than two hundred specific actions that any socially responsible business might consider. Instead of just checking the company's progress against goals it had set internally, Ben was interested in setting new goals that proactively addressed social problems.

"We wanted to advance the social mission using all of the tools we had, including production, marketing, sourcing, retailing, and so on," said Liz. "This meant that we needed social reports from each part of the business."

Liz compiled the company's report on social performance in 1990 by sending each department a request for information on various subjects, then following up with interviews. The report discussed success and failure for a long list of activities in six categories:

- products and marketing (Rainforest Crunch, Greyston Bakery, buying all dairy products from the St. Albans Cooperative in Vermont, plus the unsuccessful search for African-American peach farmers)

- internal policies and operations (employee benefits; a mostly positive employee satisfaction survey; inadequate workplace safety; and leading-edge programs for women, minorities, gay men, and lesbians)

- resource management (recycling plastic buckets, struggles with wastewater treatment, and the lack of an energy conservation program)

- relationships with suppliers and franchisees (efforts to select suppliers that support the social mission, charity

events at franchise shops, and a new PartnerShop operated by people with psychiatric disabilities in Baltimore)

- philanthropy (the company's $363,000 donation to the
Ben & Jerry's Foundation, $60,000 more in donations
from the Employee Community Fund, plus donations of
ice cream and investments in socially responsible funds)

- "taking a stand" (a billboard opposing the licensing of the
Seabrook nuclear power plant in New Hampshire, the
Iraq War ad, opposition to bovine growth hormone, support for federal legislation guaranteeing unpaid leave for
new parents, and a boycott of coffee from El Salvador)

The report's auditor was James Heard of Institutional
Shareholder Services, a consulting firm that specializes in
corporate governance and shareholder research. His arrival
pushed the company toward getting results that were rigor-
ous and verifiable. "Ben always said that people don't value
what they can't measure," said Liz. Heard would audit many
of Ben & Jerry's social reports, which were published inside
the company's annual report, over the next fifteen years.

Ben & Jerry's 1990 report got noticed in the widening circles of socially responsible businesses. The Body Shop con-
ducted its first environmental audit in 1991, and it published
independently verified reports in 1992, 1993, and 1994.

It is hard to imagine how a company with 350 employees did so much in the early 1990s and still made great ice
cream. But somehow, it happened. Near the end of 1990,
Sean Greenwood gave a factory tour to the family of Dr.
Ruth Westheimer, a sex therapist who had become a television celebrity. Dr. Ruth expressed surprise that the company
was able to produce all of its ice cream in a factory as small
as Waterbury. "Why, Dr. Ruth," Greenwood replied. "You of
all people should know that it's not the size of the facility, it's
what you do with it."

Walking the Talk

It was always easier to balance the three parts of Ben & Jerry's mission when there was lots of money. And soon after he arrived, Chuck helped keep things going by putting together a team that put the growth train into high gear. The company's Burlington store sold flavors that were too hard to produce in bulk, and one of them, Chocolate Chip Cookie Dough, always sold out. Chuck picked a group of line workers, flavor specialists, and consultants and told them to figure out a way to make a dough that could be mass-produced and would remain soft at ice cream temperatures. When pints of Chocolate Chip Cookie Dough hit the market early in 1991, they became a national craze. They were a big reason why the company's sales increased from $77 million in 1990 to $97 million in 1991.

Chuck scored again in 1992, this time by seizing an opportunity that arose from failure. Grocers had been urging the company to address consumer demand for low-fat foods, and several big chains promised to give the company more freezer space if it would come up with a suitable product. So Ben & Jerry's introduced a "light" version of its ice cream in 1990. It was a contradiction in terms, and, predictably, it bombed. But Ben & Jerry's held on to that extra freezer space by quickly introducing several flavors of lower-calorie frozen yogurt that still had a rich taste and lots of add-ins. They were a hit, and the company's sales kept rising to $132 million in 1992, with 446 employees and 95 scoop shops.

The pay and benefits were impressive, too. They included health and dental insurance for employees and their families plus matching 401(k) contributions, profit sharing, and discounts on stock purchases. The company also offered these benefits to same-sex partners and was probably the first American company to do so. It threw in free membership in

The board of directors of Ben & Jerry's in 1994. Standing (left to right): Merritt Chandler, Fred Miller, Henry Morgan. Seated (left to right): Fred "Chico" Lager, Jerry Greenfield, Liz Bankowski, Jeff Furman, Ben Cohen, Charles "Chuck" Lacy.

a health club, free tuition for college courses, and an on-site day-care center. The pay for line workers was far above the market average, and the compensation problem for top managers was eased somewhat when the board loosened the salary ratio from five to one to seven to one at the end of 1990.

The salary ratio still cut both ways. It made it much harder for Chuck to find competent people for senior positions, but it also fostered an egalitarian spirit that made line workers more likely to suggest ways to improve processes. People felt that they could speak out, and that if they did, they'd be listened to. "There was a palpable energy that came from the company's success that kept everyone motivated," Chico wrote. "Most believed that the company had a genuine commitment to their welfare."[1]

Ben & Jerry's was still growing rapidly, but it was now a much bigger company with increasingly competent senior managers and a workable mission statement. Members of the board of directors still had differences of opinion, but for now, these differences were producing a kind of creative tension that drove the company forward. The director of social mission was a big reason why things worked as well as they did. With Liz's encouragement, Ben & Jerry's was pursuing social goals in a more disciplined way.

The board added a new member in 1992 when Henry Morgan persuaded a colleague, Frederick Miller, to join. Fred is a management consultant who works with businesses on diversity, team building, and leadership issues, and he had been tracking Ben & Jerry's for years before Henry asked him to get involved. Fred is also African-American, and his addition eased a sore point on a board that had been all white. About 95 percent of Vermont residents are non-Hispanic and white, so the relative lack of diversity among Ben & Jerry's employees was easy to explain. But a company with a national reputation for progressive political views needs diverse leadership.

The emergence of a competent management team allowed Jeff to step away from many of his consulting duties for the company in 1991. Things were going so well by the beginning of 1992 that Ben decided to follow Jeff and take a six-month "sabbatical." Ben bought a pickup truck and went back to making art, this time as a welder. Although the company's stock lost 10 percent of its value the day Ben made his announcement, sales and profits remained strong, and the company's fun, irreverent spirit kept chugging along.

Ben kept up his schedule of speeches for the cause of corporate social responsibility during his sabbatical. After a talk at the University of Pennsylvania, his hosts took him to the White Dog Café to meet its owner, Judy Wicks, who had been practicing her own version of caring capitalism since 1970. The White Dog was one of Philadelphia's best-known restaurants, and also a site for concerts, fund-raisers, and

Jeff Furman (pictured with delivery van and driver Eddie Krasnow) made thirty trips to Russia to assist a small team of Ben & Jerry's employees and Russian colleagues. They operated a store in Petrozavodsk, Karelia, from 1992 until 1996.

political events. Judy also invested in businesses in her supply chain that shared her values, such as farmers who grew organic food and treated their animals humanely. But she thought she was alone in this work.

"We were like two peas in a pod in terms of our philosophy," said Judy, who is about Ben's age. "Ben accused me of using good food and fun to lure innocent customers into social activism. He got it exactly right, mainly because he was doing the same thing. Suddenly, I didn't feel alone anymore."

Ben came back the next day for lunch to continue the conversation. "We couldn't stop talking," Judy said. Judy told Ben about a restaurant in the Soviet Union she had formed a partnership with in 1988, the same year One Percent was founded. The White Dog became Philadelphia's first member of One Percent for Peace, and Judy later hosted a talk by the executive director of Businesses for Social Responsibility, the new organization that absorbed One Percent. By that time, Ben and Judy had become close friends.

In July 1992, Chico, Ben, Jeff, and more than a dozen employees and family members traveled to Russia to attend the grand opening of the company's PartnerShop in Petrozavodsk, Karelia. Many of the travelers had never owned a passport before. It had taken four years, and Jeff had made thirty transatlantic trips. But they had done it. The plan was to send teenage scoopers from Ithaca, Russia, and other places on cultural exchanges. Within a few months of opening, the store was actually making a profit.[2]

A black-robed Russian Orthodox priest blessed the store at the opening ceremony. Later, while eating a surprisingly tasty Russian-made Ben & Jerry's ice cream cone, Jeff met a man who said he wanted to open a second shop in Russia, this time as a regular franchisee. Jeff said in an offhand way that it would cost about $80,000. The money was wired into the Ben & Jerry's bank account, with no signed agreements, a few days later. Things in Russia had certainly changed, although Jeff wasn't sure exactly how.

In the company's 1992 annual report, Ben wrote, "People ask me, 'Are you having fun?' And I stop and think and say, 'Yes, but the fun is different now.' It used to be serving and relating directly with our customers back at the old gas station. Now it's the fun of helping to create something new, something sustainable, that makes our lives and other peoples' lives better—especially those who have traditionally not been included in the world of opportunity."

The 1992 report mentioned that at the end of the year, the company had broken ground for a huge new ice cream plant in St. Albans, a small town on Lake Champlain about twenty-five miles north of Burlington. The old, crowded days of Waterbury were coming to an end. Chuck and the board were building a manufacturing facility that would be state of the art.

For Ben, Jerry, Jeff, and Chico, it seemed that the hard years were finally paying off. The company had defined its unique mission. Day-to-day decisions were being made by managers, not board members. After all the arguing, they were in a good place. And as 1993 began, it seemed like the company's growth might never end.

FIVE

Money Starts Talking

The Scooperdome went up in the winter of 1993. It was a glowing tent as large as a football field and as tall as an eight-story building. It made a huge bright spot in the subarctic gloom of St. Albans, Vermont, a hard-bitten village where one of the big employers was a state prison. Underneath the dome, dozens of construction workers prepared the foundation for an ice cream plant that promised two hundred new full-time jobs.

The employees of Ben & Jerry's could hardly wait. After eight years of hard, constant use, the Waterbury factory and its employees were badly in need of relief. Since 1989, some of the company's ice cream had been made at a Dreyer's plant in Fort Wayne, Indiana; more recently, the company had rented space at the St. Albans dairy co-op's facilities for a production line. But these were temporary fixes. The St. Albans plant was another watershed for Ben & Jerry's, which was planning to hire its five hundredth employee. They had been building and hiring to keep up with growth for more than a decade. St. Albans was going to get ahead of the growth. And while the ice cream plant at Waterbury was cramped and cobbled together, St. Albans was going to be sleek and up to date.

A design team led by employees had come up with dozens of ways to make the new plant safer and more efficient than Waterbury. They bought machinery that they hoped would decrease the time people spent in freezer rooms. They built drive-through receiving bays that would keep truckers' blood pressure down. "The days of everyone knowing everyone else are gone," wrote Jerry in the first issue of *Rolling Cone,* a biweekly employee newsletter that replaced the *Daily Plant* in February 1993. But, he added, knowing everybody by name wasn't the most important thing. Jerry wanted to ensure that as the new plant went up and the company grew, Ben & Jerry's remained a "joyful, participatory experience."

St. Albans did transform the company, but it didn't happen as Jerry hoped. In fact, it did the opposite. The plant took a year longer to open than planned, and it cost almost triple what was originally budgeted. At the same time, sales slowed abruptly in 1993 for several reasons, only some of which were within the company's control.

As Ben & Jerry's financial and operational problems deepened, however, the company became much more successful at encouraging progressive social change. It launched dozens of social initiatives in the mid-1990s, several of which had lasting international impact. As the decade wore on, more social projects were conceived and carried out by employees instead of by board members. And the more the social

The Scooperdome sheltered workers building a new ice cream plant in St. Albans, Vermont, during the winter of 1993–94.

mission came from the employees, the more successful it became. Employees, after all, understood the day-to-day realities of the business far better than the board of directors did. They were more likely to come up with ideas that could advance the goals of profitability and social impact at the same time.

"Ben & Jerry's helped create the field of corporate social responsibility," said Robert Dunn, the former president of Businesses for Social Responsibility. "They deserve tremendous credit for that."

Focusing the Social Mission

Focus was the main reason the social mission moved ahead in the 1990s. When Liz Bankowski became director of social mission at the end of 1991, she asked the board to name its number one priority for social investment. "The obvious choice was children and families," she said. "We make ice cream. Shouldn't we be identifying with children and families?"

In 1991, with the Soviet Union just a memory, Ben & Jerry's decided to change the social mission's focus. They merged One Percent for Peace into a new group, Businesses for Social Responsibility. Then they recruited other socially responsible businesses, including the Body Shop, Calvert Funds, Smith & Hawken, *Utne Reader*, Working Assets, Seventh Generation (founded in Burlington in 1988 to sell recycled paper and green cleaning products), and Rhino Records (a label specializing in reissuing oldies, based in a Los Angeles record store) to start a new organization. They called it ACT NOW and ran with the idea of combining each company's marketing and packaging efforts with information on political issues and resources for action. The first thing ACT NOW did was print up stacks of postcards asking for an increase in federal standards for fuel economy. Ben & Jerry's sent the cards to their shops and gave them to employees,

Ben & Jerry's used in-store kiosks to invite customers to become activists for the Children's Defense Fund in 1992–94.

with instructions to mail them to their members of Congress. The campaign did not get results. "Its goals were too broad," said Liz.

In 1992, Ben & Jerry's sharpened its focus. They decided to promote the agenda of the Children's Defense Fund (CDF), a leading national advocacy organization. The company took several actions, the most successful of which was to put informational kiosks in its ninety-five scoop shops. Each kiosk had a red telephone. Customers could join the CDF just by picking up the phone and giving their address.

The red telephone campaign increased the size of the CDF's mailing list by two-thirds. Customers who joined the list became activists, receiving alerts instructing them to contact their congressional representatives whenever bills affecting children were coming up for a vote. The campaign worked so well, according to CDF president Marian Wright Edelman, that members of Congress started begging her to "call the dogs off." Instead, Ben & Jerry's doubled down. It set a goal of turning one hundred thousand customers into CDF members in 1994, put red telephone stickers on all of its pint labels, invited Edelman to speak at the annual meeting of franchisees, and followed up with a monthly newsletter that encouraged franchise owners to come up with their own ideas.

Ben & Jerry's had 147 independently owned scoop shops by 1995, and many of them doubled as community centers for social activists. The stores donated about $750,000 that year in time, products, or money to local groups. Dave Bruno, the franchise owner in Albany, New York, who had met Ben in the Green Mountain Drive warehouse back in the early 1980s, had become a major donor to The Ark, an after-school program sandwiched into a housing project. In San Francisco, storeowners Brian Gaines and Roger Kaufman teamed up with Christmas in April, an organization that spruced up housing for low-income people.

As Ben is fond of saying, though, there are two kinds of social activism—direct actions that give short-term help to needy people, and advocacy that attacks the causes of social problems. Ben & Jerry's emphasized advocacy, and it encouraged its employees to speak out. The foundation made a $10,000 grant to a new organization called the Vermont Campaign to End Childhood Hunger, which was promoting the federally funded School Breakfast Program. The company and the campaign then encouraged Ben & Jerry's employees to address school boards in districts that hadn't signed up for the program yet. All the local officials had to do was ask, and the free breakfasts were theirs. Schools that signed up got an ice cream party as well.

When Ben & Jerry's started working with the hunger campaign in 1993, only 40 percent of the state's needy school children had access to a free breakfast. A year later, 60 percent did. In 2013, all but 21 of Vermont's 319 public schools offered this benefit. The company showed that small, well-targeted investments in advocacy make an enormous difference. Focusing on child welfare gave the company a noncontroversial label to use while addressing the controversial problems Ben, Jerry, and Jeff really care about: income inequality and the spending priorities of government.

The company's money got to work, too. Ben & Jerry's

usually had several million dollars in cash to invest in the early 1990s, so it looked for safe and legal ways to park those assets in places where they would benefit children and families. For many years it had been doing business with community banks that invested in Vermont and in low-income areas, as Chicago's South Shore Bank did. As the company's deposits grew, Ben & Jerry's also purchased tax-free bonds issued by schools, student loan funds, and hospitals. "If we have a choice between a highway and a hospital, we'll target the hospital regardless of the yield," said Tom D'Urso, who was hired as treasurer in 1994. The company also made direct investments in low-income housing, which offered the added benefit of a tax credit. D'Urso estimated that Ben & Jerry's earned a 12 percent annual return on its loan to Housing Vermont, a statewide not-for-profit for affordable housing.

"If we didn't take values into consideration, we could slightly improve our yield," said D'Urso. "But it's tough to say exactly how much." Besides, he added, he felt confident that most of the company's shareholders would support directing the funds in ways that were consistent with the three-part mission.

The integration of the social mission and marketing reached a high point in the One World One Heart festivals, which became larger and more elaborate during the 1990s. The festivals combined rootsy, diverse musical headliners with games, informational booths, and lots of free ice cream. At several festivals, a fleet of trucks arrived and dumped a pile of one billion grass seeds. Staffers let people play in the pile, then scooped the seeds into bags and gave them away.

"We dump the seeds to demonstrate how many a billion is, [and] to help people understand the magnitude of the numbers that get tossed around when we read about federal programs in the newspaper," wrote Ben and Jerry in a jointly authored book, *Ben & Jerry's Double Dip: How To Run a Values-Led Business and Make Money, Too*.[1] The bags were printed with a label that made Ben's point: that the US military budget was $300 billion, and that $20 billion of that could lift every American child from poverty.

The festivals were political and fun, but Ben and Jerry explained in their book that they were also cost-effective marketing. A festival in Minneapolis cost $150,000 and made nine million impressions through paid advertising and free publicity, for an average cost of 17 cents per one thousand impressions. That was a fraction of the cost of television advertising in that market ($6.92 per one thousand impressions) or a full-page newspaper ad ($34.15). And the festivals also gave Ben & Jerry's a chance to interact with perhaps fifty thousand attendees for six hours, turning many of them into enthusiastic fans.[2]

Ben & Jerry's did not do a lot of market research in the 1990s, but they did enough to know that a small segment of the total US population accounted for the vast majority of its sales. The company's core customers were well-educated baby boomers, especially those who were raising children. If the company offended someone who fell outside that segment, it wouldn't feel much pain. But it was critical to keep enthusiasm high among core customers, and growth depended on finding more people like them.

Calling Monsanto's Bluff

The company's Office of Social Mission—in other words, Liz Bankowski—emphasized flexibility as well as focus, so Ben & Jerry's could act quickly on opportunities to advance the common good that did not relate directly to children and families. These efforts ran the gamut from saving historic buildings to lobbying for the reform of corporate and foundation governance. "The idea was to integrate our concerns into every day-to-day decision," said Liz. "It wasn't to do some nice sponsorships or give away some money. We were truly looking to change the traditional model of business and show that a publicly traded company could also act in the public interest."

One integration strategy was to give employees power in the company's decision making wherever possible. In 1993, Ben & Jerry's was operating at five sites in Vermont: Waterbury, the St. Albans co-op, the plant under construction in St. Albans, a distribution center in Rockingham, and a plant making Peace Pops and other novelties in Springfield. The trustees of the Ben & Jerry's Foundation—Jerry, Jeff, and Naomi Tannen—invited a group of social activists to attend a retreat that would help them find new directions. "Our guests told us that if our goal was to encourage grassroots social change, we needed to walk our talk," said Jeff. "In other words, the trustees should give up their decision-making power."

The foundation organized employees at each of the company's five sites into community action teams and empowered the teams to give small grants to organizations throughout the state. Employees also elected a committee that advised the foundation's board on its national grant making. The plan worked so well that the foundation's trustees proudly started calling themselves a "rubber stamp board." The foundation was not particularly large. In 1993, it made 142 grants, totaling $808,000. But over the next two decades, under the direction of employees, it gave away more than $28 million.

Another strategy was killing three or four birds with one stone. "Chuck asked me to go down to New York and look at the Times Square Hotel because a friend of his, Rosanne Haggerty, was going to renovate it," said Jeff. "It was a huge historic building at the corner of Eighth Avenue and 43rd Street, one block away from the bus station. It had become a single-room-occupancy hotel, and it was filthy. The walls were yellow from tobacco smoke, and the ceilings were falling down. There was also an enormous amount of foot traffic outside. It took me about four minutes to decide that this was the perfect place for a not-for-profit to own a PartnerShop."

In 1993, Ben & Jerry's joined a group of investors to finance the hotel's renovation. They got their $1.3 million back with interest, along with tax credits of more than $1.9 million. Most important, the investment helped turn the building into another kind of landmark. Times Square became an award-winning 652-unit apartment complex for people who were formerly homeless, coping with chronic mental illness, or living with HIV/AIDS. The investment also helped launch Haggerty and her group Common Ground, an innovative not-for-profit that became a national model after building more than five thousand units of supported housing around New York City.

On April 15, 1994, a Free Cone Day, Ben and Jerry helped give away more than three thousand cones at the opening of a scoop shop on the ground floor of the newly renovated Times Square building. The company's fifth PartnerShop was owned by Common Ground and staffed by the people who lived upstairs, who operated the store successfully for the next fifteen years.

Other PartnerShops in 1994 were operated by a housing organization in Harlem, an organization for people with learning disabilities in Baltimore, a vocational school in Vermont, and the Learning Web in Ithaca. Not all of these were as successful as the Common Ground shop was. That was fine with Jeff, the shops' chief advocate. "These are experiments. The idea is to teach young people and disadvantaged people how to run a business," he said. "When you walk into a PartnerShop, if you think you're in a social service agency, we've failed. If you think you're in a normal ice cream shop, we've succeeded."

Sometimes, opportunities for the social mission came out of nowhere and acquired lives of their own. On January 11,

1994, Chuck received a letter from the International Dairy Federation warning that food processors like Ben & Jerry's were in danger of being sued. Chuck wrote "Doesn't scare me!" on the letter. Then he sent it around the office.

The letter was about recombinant bovine growth hormone (rBGH), a synthetic version of a hormone that enhances milk production by artificially extending a cow's lactation cycle. During the 1980s, Monsanto Corporation worked with other companies to develop it, and in 1986, the company's application to sell rBGH received preliminary approval by the US Food and Drug Administration. Consumer and farm advocacy groups objected to that decision for several reasons. The treatment had many destructive effects on the health of cows. Some scientists were also concerned that it might cause health problems in people, and economists warned that rBGH would drive small farmers, many of whom could not afford the treatment, out of business. Ben & Jerry's joined the debate in September 1989, when it put a sticker on each pint encouraging its customers to "Save Family Farms" and oppose rBGH.

On the day Chuck opened the letter, Monsanto was three weeks away from its first day of selling rBGH. The chemical giant was threatening to sue manufacturers who mentioned the product because it didn't want consumers to know that dairy farmers would be using the hormone. Few dairy farmers seemed concerned. But Ben & Jerry's decided to call Monsanto's bluff. They designed a sticker for pints that said, "We oppose the use of rBGH. The family farmers who supply our milk and cream pledge not to treat their cows with rBGH. The FDA has concluded that no significant difference has been shown, and no test can now distinguish, between milk from rBGH-treated and untreated cows." They paid farmers at the St. Albans co-op a premium to promise not to inject their cows with rBGH. And they released the new sticker on the same day Monsanto's salesmen started taking orders.

Ben & Jerry's became a go-to source for the media's coverage of the debut over rBGH, effectively raining on Monsanto's parade. As the years went by, the company also became a leader in the global movement against rBGH. The movement has effectively limited the hormone's use. Only 17 percent of cows in the United States were being treated with rBGH in 2007, according to the USDA, and every country in the European Union has banned it.

The rBGH campaign "went way, way out on a limb," said Liz Bankowski. "It wasn't going to increase our sales, and we took a huge risk by doing it. The only reason we did it was that it was the right thing to do. That is what made Ben & Jerry's different from other companies."

The Lively Dively Award

Ben & Jerry's was often the first company to take the plunge on an issue, and its willingness to take risks made following easier for other companies. In April 1992, for example, Ben & Jerry's became the first large company to sign a ten-point code of environmental conduct for businesses. The code had been drafted by the Coalition of Environmentally Responsible Economies (CERES) after a tanker, the *Exxon Valdez*, ruptured in 1989 and drenched the coast of Alaska with oil. Most of the early signers of the CERES code were churches and nonprofit groups. The endorsement from Ben & Jerry's gave the code momentum among private businesses. The following year, the oil giant Sunoco signed on. Today, CERES and Businesses for Social Responsibility (BSR) are global organizations whose members include corporate giants like Wal-Mart, IBM, and Royal Dutch Shell.

In April 1994, Ben went to Harvard's Kennedy School of Government to receive the George S. Dively Award for Corporate Public Initiative. It was as close to the Nobel Prize as he was likely to get. Ben's acceptance speech laid out his vision for business as a force for social change. "Corporations have been granted the right to become the major depositories and bestowers of wealth in our society," he said. "With all of this power, there is just no way businesses can walk away from the world's pressing problems ... the narrow view of maximizing profits is simply unacceptable when business is directly and indirectly responsible for so many of our problems ... business must be part of the solution, or there won't be a solution."

The Harvard elites squirmed in their seats, and Ben was delighted. He described the company's campaign to combat bovine growth hormone in the face of legal pressure from Monsanto. He cited one study that estimated the government spent more on welfare for corporations than it did on welfare to the poor, and that the social costs of white-collar crime rivaled those of crime in the streets. While Ben & Jerry's was far from perfect, he said, it was willing to take "a no-holds-barred look at ourselves" and publish the results for all to see. The company's social reputation, he said, didn't hurt its profitability—in fact, it was the key to its success.

"Could others do the same thing we are doing? Yes, and a growing number are," Ben said. "But the numbers of companies are too few, and their size is too small. We need more companies engaged in pioneering work, so that the frontier of social responsibility gets pushed out even further. And we need bigger companies to get into the act ... we need the Exxons, Toyotas, and Westinghouses."

After the speech, Ben and Liz drove to Boston's Logan Airport to get on separate planes. Liz was headed home, but Ben needed to go preach somewhere else. He gave her the engraved Tiffany crystal award, and halfway to her gate she dropped it. "I just laughed," said Liz. "It was so fitting, given what Ben had just said to the crowd. When Ben heard, he laughed too. So I put the cracked stump of it up in my office to remind everybody of several things. First, despite all the praise we were getting, we had to stay humble. Second, perfection isn't possible. And it also helps to have a sense of humor in tense situations."

Leading with Your Chin

As the company's social performance improved, something strange happened. Rob Michalak, the company's public relations director in 1993, found himself managing more and more bad publicity. One low point came in the summer of 1993, at the peak of ice cream season, when the Center for Science in the Public Interest named Ben & Jerry's one of the Ten Foods You Should Never Eat. They pointed out that a one-cup serving has as much saturated fat as a quarter-cup of lard. Yuk.

The publicity machine had turned on Ben & Jerry's. Joe Queenan, a writer who specializes in sarcasm, once estimated that he made $13,000 during the 1990s selling articles that attacked the company. Queenan's editors simply could not resist when he wrote that self-righteous celebrities like Sting, Ben, and Jerry "seemed completely incapable of scooping up a piece of litter or giving a blind dwarf a nickel without issuing a twelve-page press release appraising the general public of their awesome munificence."[3] Ouch.

In boxing, it's called "leading with your chin." Anyone who sets a public example for good behavior and invites others to follow will attract critics. And it was an easy decision for Queenan's editors at *Barron's*, *Forbes*, and other adoring journals of free-market capitalism to return fire on a company that was criticizing the status quo. In the mid-1990s, the mainstream media ran stories that were critical of Ben & Jerry's for using artificial ingredients in its "all-natural" flavors, for mistreating its suppliers, for not living up to the claim that its Brazil nuts came from a cooperative, for a high injury rate among employees, and for not protecting the price of its stock, among other reasons. "When we began, there were all those stories about 'Look what good they've done,'" Ben told the *New York Times* in 1994. "That stopped being news. So the new story is, 'Look what bad they've done.'"[4]

But the toughest and most persistent critics of Ben & Jerry's were its own employees, who often made it easy for reporters by agreeing with them. This surprised Milton Moskowitz, a San Francisco journalist Ben & Jerry's hired to write its "social performance report" for 1991. In 1993, Moskowitz wanted to include Ben & Jerry's in the second edition of his book, *The 100 Best Companies to Work for in America*. He was astonished, Liz says, when the board asked that the company not be included. "People were tired. It didn't feel like a great place to work," she said. "The managers felt like we were a bunch of idiots, and the employees got really worn down."

One reason for low morale inside the company was the lack of strong leadership, as Chuck struggled to get the St. Albans plant built and somehow restart growth. Another was the mercurial personality of Ben, who could be funny and inspiring in the morning and sullen and abusive in the afternoon. But the most important reason was that the employees were modeling the founder's behavior. Like Ben, they had set impossibly high expectations for themselves, and the company's public image reinforced those expectations. Rob Michalak remembers that it was common back then for reporters to be surprised that the sales figures for Ben & Jerry's weren't larger. "People thought we were a huge company," he says. "And in terms of advancing corporate social responsibility, we were."

The reputation of Ben & Jerry's rested on the company's annual social reports, so it was very important to prepare those reports carefully and to ensure the independence of their auditors. This became apparent when an investigative journalist tore into the Body Shop's reports in a 1994 article in *Business Ethics*. Jon Entine's article, which the Body Shop tried to suppress, blew a big hole in Anita Roddick's reputation. Roddick had made many statements about giving generously to charity—"We give most of our profits away," she had said—but Entine showed that the Body Shop had not made any donations between 1976 and 1986. In 1993, the company had given away less than 1 percent of its pretax profits, far below the overall corporate average for the United States. Entine also found that the Body Shop Foundation received only about 2 percent of its funds from the Body Shop's corporate headquarters or the Roddicks. Most of the foundation's funds came from franchised shop owners and a single donor, Richard Branson.

Entine found disgruntled employees who contradicted the Body Shop's environmental claims and disgruntled auditors who refused to return for a second year. He showed that the company's vaunted commitment to fair trade amounted to a tiny proportion of its spending with suppliers.[5] His investigation caused a crisis within the company, which ordered a much more ambitious and careful audit in 1994.

"We were shocked by what happened to the Body Shop, for several reasons," said Chuck. "First, we knew that Entine was not being fair. Second, we knew that Anita was not the only person he was after. But we had to keep going, and we had to make decisions. It takes courage to keep innovating when you know that you're a target."

Entine tried just as hard to nail Ben & Jerry's. He was known for debunking corporate claims, and a solid exposé about the Vermont hippies would have been an even bigger story than the Body Shop. He began investigating a deal Ben had made with an advocacy group for native people. Ben had connected with a Xapuri, native-owned co-op in western Brazil whose workers harvest nuts and other products from the rain forest instead of cutting it down. In January 1989, Ben decided to start a new company that would make candy from those nuts. As the sole owner of Community Products, Inc., Ben could do whatever he wanted with this company, so he planned to give away most of the profits to environmental groups and One Percent for Peace. He would sell some of the candy in gourmet food stores, but most of it would become add-ins to a new Ben & Jerry's ice cream flavor called Rainforest Crunch.

Ben & Jerry's bought $1 million worth of candy from Community Products in 1990, and more in subsequent years. Rainforest Crunch was a hit because it was delicious, but also because consumers felt that their purchases were supporting a sustainable business for indigenous people and slowing the deforestation of the Amazon. But there was a problem. The Xapuri co-op couldn't keep up with demand, so Ben & Jerry's ended up buying almost all of the nuts in Rainforest Crunch from conventional sources. The company tried to help the co-op, but developing a business in a remote section of Brazil turned out to be more than even Ben could handle. The co-op stopped selling nuts in 1994 and was quietly removed from the pint label. The failure of the Xapuri experiment gave Jon Entine his opening. He slammed Community Products and Rainforest Crunch in an article and was widely interviewed about it.[6] Ben & Jerry's admitted that Entine had a point in its 1994 annual report, and it soon retired the flavor.

New products often succeed for different reasons from those their creators intended. Each pint of Rainforest Crunch promoted the cause of sustainable development in the Amazon basin and encouraged customers to join the cause. It was one reason why public awareness of deforestation increased dramatically in the 1990s, and over the last two decades, the rate of deforestation in Brazil has slowed dramatically. In that sense, Rainforest Crunch was a success both financially and socially. Yet Ben & Jerry's had set its goals so high that

Entine was also able to portray Rainforest Crunch as a hypocritical scheme that never lived up to its stated goals.

In a larger sense, the company's encounters with muckrakers served an important purpose. Entine was an outside auditor, a particularly tough one, and Rainforest Crunch was the biggest mistake he found. His comparative lack of results showed that compared with the Body Shop, Ben & Jerry's produced social balance sheets that were comprehensive, transparent, honest, and held up to scrutiny.

Dropping Like a Rock

Chuck Lacy, as president of Ben & Jerry's, reported to Ben, the CEO. But Ben didn't really want to be part of the company's day-to-day operations. He spent most of his time advancing the company's social initiatives as part of its marketing activities. He was on the road a lot, making personal appearances and speeches, and he also was taking more time off. In June 1993, for example, Ben spent five days at a company-sponsored folk festival in California, flew back to Vermont to give a speech, and then left for a vacation in Alaska.

It was Chuck's responsibility to manage the construction project at St. Albans, even though he was not the company's single point of authority. But Chuck was distracted. A few pages away from Jerry's hopeful editorial in the February 1993 issue of *Rolling Cone*—the one about Ben & Jerry's remaining a "joyful, participatory experience" for employees —Chuck wrote that sales had fallen below expectations. Häagen-Dazs, the company's archrival, had introduced a new line of super-premium ice cream flavors that contained chunks. It was aiming directly at Ben & Jerry's. Worse, it was selling these new flavors at a discount.

"Two weeks ago, I got pissed off," Chuck wrote. "We can beat these guys." He outlined a plan that involved doubling the number of new flavor introductions in 1993 and ramping up on marketing and market research. The company had to keep coming up with blockbuster flavors because the production lines at St. Albans could produce a lot more ice cream than Ben & Jerry's was currently selling.

"Before St. Albans, we were building capacity behind our growth in sales," said Jeff. "That was safe in a financial sense, but it put a lot of stress on our employees. St. Albans was built ahead of growth. It was a big risk, and the execution was really poor."

Ben & Jerry's sold $33 million worth of stock and $30 million worth of bonds to finance the plant. Ben's share of the company's stock declined further, and the debt also made the company more beholden to creditors. These were not insurmountable problems, but large construction projects rarely go as planned, and things at St. Albans quickly started to go wrong. In March 1993, for example, the Scooperdome collapsed during a heavy snowfall. It was a total loss that set the construction schedule back a couple of weeks. As the costs kept piling up, the folks in charge didn't do much to control them.

Chuck had assigned overall responsibility for the plant to a married couple, both of whom had management experience, but neither of whom had any experience at building ice cream plants. He asked them to interview employees and others to get ideas about how to make the plant more efficient, and then supervise the design team as they worked in as many of the ideas as possible. Many problems arose because the team kept designing after the blueprints were done. Instead of agreeing on the manufacturing process and then building a structure to contain it, the team agreed on a structure and then tried to fit a manufacturing process inside it. The machines they chose did not fit, but the managers didn't tell Chuck about the problems. They just kept building.

"For a lot of that time, I wasn't even in Vermont," says Chuck. "I was traveling, doing the work a sales manager should have been doing, because we couldn't get a good sales manager for the salary we were offering. And we were in too many different businesses besides making ice cream. We were producing four big festivals a year, and our employees staffed these shows. Our factory tour was the most popular tourist attraction in Vermont. We doubled the number of franchised stores. We started a distribution company. And as a side venture, we took on the Cold War and started improving relations with the Soviet Union. We didn't just send someone over there, either. We started a new, international not-for-profit organization and recruited over two hundred businesses to join it. We were literally running five or six different companies. I was in charge of all of them, but no one was really in charge of each one."

The company was doing lots of great things, but it wasn't doing them in a way that could be sustained. Chuck was looking to Ben, the CEO, for leadership, but Ben was often out, and Chuck felt increasingly overwhelmed. So he ran from job to job as the problems in St. Albans kept getting worse.

"We had multiple problems," said Chuck. "I remember long meetings when we were dealing with the Jon Entine mess. We would just sit there in silence, trying to decide what to do. It stays light until 9 or 10 at night in Vermont in the summer. I remember that weak dusky light, and thinking about how our position in the market had changed. What we should do wasn't at all clear. We also had motion-sensitive lights in the offices, so after a while the lights would go out on us. They only went back on when someone moved."

As St. Albans bumped along, the rate of growth in sales started to slow down. It had been several years since the last big flavor introduction, and the company had also run out of big new markets to go into. Expansion into the biggest metropolitan areas in the United States was complete, but plans to expand internationally were still just plans.

A bigger, less definable problem was the national panic

In 1994, Ben & Jerry's promoted a line of ice cream "unfettered by chunks" with a poster honoring social activists (clockwise from top left) Pete Seeger, Michelle Shocked, Buffy Sainte-Marie, Dolores Huerta, Daniel Berrigan, Bobby Seale, Spike Lee, and (center) Carlos Santana.

attack toward fat. In April 1992, after a year of political wrangling, the US Department of Agriculture unveiled new dietary recommendations, which contained this fateful line: "Fats, oils, and sweets should be eaten sparingly." Sales of Ben & Jerry's frozen yogurt remained strong (despite its relatively high fat content), but the company's ice cream sales suffered. Tinkering with the formula was not an option, either. The company's attempt to sell a lower-fat ice cream had flopped a few years earlier. Of course it had. "Ben & Jerry's Light" is a contradiction in terms if there ever was one.

Since the mid-1980s, Wall Street equities analysts had been characterizing Ben & Jerry's as a growth stock. But a growth stock is like a jet airplane: it soars until the engines fail, and then it drops like a rock. Ben & Jerry's second quarter earnings in 1993 showed that growth in sales and income had slowed to an unremarkable 4 percent. The stock price fell from $30 in the spring of 1993 to $21 by August. Wildly successful new flavors like Chocolate Chip Cookie Dough had always worked before, but this strategy didn't work in 1993. Ben created a flavor named after the hippie icon Wavy Gravy, made with a caramel-cashew–Brazil nut base, a chocolate hazelnut fudge swirl, and roasted almonds. It was the company's great hope for the fall. But Wavy Gravy turned out to be a nightmare to make. Worse, the ingredients were so expensive that the company couldn't even be sure it made money by selling it.

In December 1993, Ben & Jerry's countered Häagen-Dazs's chunky flavors by releasing chocolate, vanilla, and other flavors that didn't have any chunks in them. Ben hired Spike Lee to direct a memorable television commercial and design a poster featuring "smooth" activist heroes like Pete Seeger, former Black Panther Bobby Seale, and National Farmworkers Association cofounder Dolores Huerta. Again, sales were disappointing. The ads did give the activists good publicity, however. "And the really good news was that Häagen-Dazs's chunky flavors also flopped," said Chuck. "We learned that consumers expected chunks from us, and smooth from them."

The fact was that in the United States in 1993, Ben & Jerry's ice cream had become a mature product in a category in which overall sales were nearly flat. The company's sales growth was just 6 percent in both 1993 and 1994. The news wasn't all bad. The company controlled 42 percent of the US market for super-premium ice cream, and it was the leader in super-premium frozen yogurt. But when the rapid growth ended, the stock tanked.

As the stock price dropped, Ben & Jerry's started looking like it might be vulnerable to a corporate takeover. This was not idle speculation either, because in the 1990s, the two giants of the global ice cream industry—Unilever and Nestlé—were racing each other to buy smaller companies. In 1993, they bid against each other to buy Breyer's, a nationally distributed premium brand. Unilever won, and Nestlé countered by purchasing more than one-fifth of the stock in Dreyer's, the Oakland, California–based ice cream company that bought and distributed a great deal of what Ben & Jerry's made. Industry analysts expected Nestlé to buy Dreyer's outright (and they eventually did, in 2003).

Board members of Ben & Jerry's had never paid much attention to quarterly earnings before, and they were disdainful of the short-term focus of Wall Street financial types. But Wall Street was certainly paying attention to them, and it felt uncomfortable.

Enough Already

It is fortunate that no muckraking journalists visited the St. Albans construction site in the fall of 1993, because they would have seen a disaster. The plant's construction team had purchased an untested system with the goal of sorting pints for distribution before the packages were completely frozen. The team was trying to solve what was a chronic problem at the Waterbury plant. Employees there had to spend hours inside a subzero-degree freezer assembling orders before they could be loaded onto trucks. That's dangerous and unpleasant work, and the new system was supposed to cut those hours dramatically. But it wasn't working.

As 1993 ended, the board was hearing alarming bits of news about what was going on at St. Albans. They sent Merritt and Chico to look at the operation and figure out what to do. Merritt and Chico were appalled by what they saw. Early in 1994, they reported to the board that the sorting and freezing system was a total loss, and that it was only one of many serious problems in the plant's design. The efficiency of the Waterbury plant had also deteriorated significantly, they said. More batches were being sold at cost or given away, and the company's cost of goods was skyrocketing. The board had been told that everything was going fine, but the truth was anything but.

In May 1994 the board went to a retreat in Maine. They heard that the financial situation was deteriorating rapidly (ultimately, the company would post a loss for 1994). Then they heard Merritt and Chico's recommendations, which were convincing. As discussions continued over the long weekend, more and more board members, including Ben and Chuck, came to agree that it was essential to find an experienced CEO who knew how to turn a profit. "Chico came on strong at a time when we were getting desperate," said Jeff. "And I didn't have an alternative idea."

The board approved a plan that would have Ben and Chuck resign from their positions as CEO and president. They appointed a transition team consisting of Chico, Chuck, and Liz to turn the company around while the board searched for a professional CEO. And the salary ratio had to go too, because it would be impossible to find a qualified candidate if the total compensation could not be more than seven times what an entering plant worker made (in 1994, about $17,000 a year).

Chico had been opposed to the salary ratio since the board adopted it in 1985, and most of the other top managers weren't fond of it either. "It made my job impossible," said Chuck. "As the company grew, the jobs at the top kept growing and changing, while the scooper jobs at the bottom never changed. After a while, we couldn't hire qualified people for the top positions. During most of my tenure, half of those jobs were not filled. We doubled the size of the company with no head of sales. Liz was pinch-hitting on human resources, while Jerry, Fran, and I were pinch-hitting as head of sales. Of course, we had trouble maintaining focus. But at the same time, we had a high public profile, and the social mission defined us. I knew that abandoning the salary ratio would be a public relations disaster."

For Ben, giving up the CEO job might have been an admission of failure, but it was also the fulfillment of a dream. "It is a position I was never really meant to have," he told employees in a special issue of *Rolling Cone* that announced the decision on June 13. The company needed "a single point of authority" with more management experience than either Ben or Chuck could muster. The salary ratio "was an experiment that worked for us when we were a younger, smaller company," he wrote. Eliminating it "is the hardest decision that our board has ever made." But, he added, the decision was unanimous.

Ben would continue as chairman of the board, with Jerry as vice chair. Chuck would stay on the payroll for another year, until the new boss settled in, but he lost his authority at that meeting in May. Chuck was thirty-eight when he left the company, and he had worked there since he was twenty-nine. "It was essentially my only professional experience," he said. "It was a great ride. But the whole situation got to be bigger than I was."

The company's annual sales were less than $46 million the year Chuck arrived and more than $155 million when he left. But that number alone doesn't do justice to his contribution. Between 1990 and 1992, Chuck led the company as it introduced several blockbuster flavors. By the time he left, Ben & Jerry's had become a powerful national brand. The power of that brand was based on wildly creative flavors of ice cream with chunks in them, and also on public enthusiasm for its three-part mission. Over the years, consumer loyalty to the brand would carry the company through troubled times again and again.

The days following the decision to abandon the salary ratio were especially stormy, as a media deluge hit just as employees were processing their angst. "People were saying it was the end of the company," said Sean Greenwood, the public relations manager. "I thought that was kind of silly. We weren't losing our jobs, or even getting a pay cut, and we still had great benefits." In fact, the benefits got even better. All regular full- and part-time employees were awarded the option to buy stock at $16.75 a share. Half the options were exercisable in two years and half were eligible in four, with the number of shares depending on salary and tenure.

The company awarded stock options for two reasons. First, they wanted to give employees a stake in the company's success. As *Rolling Cone* explained, someone who was awarded four hundred options at $16.75 could gain $2,600 by selling half their shares in 1996 and another $2,600 in 1998, as long as the stock price returned to $30. But the idea backfired because of the second reason. The company also started awarding stock options so that they could make competitive offers that would attract top managers.

Senior managers got far more options than the rank and

file. In 1995, for example, the new CEO of Ben & Jerry's negotiated a salary of $226,000 plus another $100,000 if he hit performance targets, as well as 180,000 options at $10.81 a share. This meant that he could make a capital gain of $3.6 million if he was able to sell those shares at $30. It didn't matter how he got the stock price back up. In fact, a bidding war between parties that were trying to buy the company was probably the quickest way for that "professional" CEO to make the most money. And the money started talking, immediately.

Ben & Jerry's social performance report for 1994 was mailed to all shareholders in April 1995. Paul Hawken, whom Ben had met at the first meeting of the Social Venture Network, wrote it. Hawken's 1993 bestseller, *The Ecology of Commerce,* was inspiring hundreds of entrepreneurs to pursue socially responsible ventures.[7] Hawken wrote a candid ten-thousand-word essay on the relative successes and failures of a bewildering number of initiatives, policies, and plans at Ben & Jerry's. It was published, unedited, in the annual report.

Ben & Jerry's managers lacked focus, said Hawken; morale was a serious problem, mistakes were being made, and a lot of things needed improving. "But what they cannot be faulted for," he added, "is their steadfast commitment to beliefs about how businesses can and should interact with the greater community. Here, they continue to be on solid ground, a constant and fun-loving reminder that businesses can do things differently, even brilliantly."

According to Jeff, Ben was technically correct when he told the employees that the board's decision on the salary ratio had been unanimous—but Ben wasn't telling the whole story, either. "Abandoning the salary ratio triggered a lot of changes," he said. "I never really wanted to get rid of it. The big idea at Ben & Jerry's has always been linked prosperity. If the shareholders do well, everyone should do well, starting with the employees and moving outward to the customers and neighbors. Linked prosperity means linking your livelihood to a sense of purpose. When we abandoned the salary ratio, we started going down a different path."

SIX

Yo, I'm Not Your CEO

In the summer of 1994, the transition team—Chico, Chuck, and Liz, with help from Merritt and others as needed—began unwinding the problems at the St. Albans plant and working on solutions. Meanwhile, Jeff and Liz ran the search for a new CEO. In May, at the same meeting at which the board decided to abandon the salary ratio and conduct the search, they had come up with an idea that smacked of pure, old-fashioned Ben & Jerry's style. It was distracting, inefficient, hilarious, and brilliant.

Ben unveiled a poster that was modeled on the army's Uncle Sam Wants YOU design, with a photo of a scowling Ben and Jerry pointing, wearing top hats, and saying "We Want You To Be Our CEO." Anyone could apply by sending in a one-hundred-word essay. "I believe this is the first time in the history of corporate America that a CEO has been recruited on telephone poles," Ben wrote.

Loyal customers jumped at their chance to show Ben and Jerry their stuff. The company received another avalanche of free publicity and more than twenty-five thousand entries, including:

- a rubber hand, because "you need a hand";
- a rubber foot, "to get my foot in the door";
- an application accompanied by 150 lids for Mint Oreo Cookie ice cream;

Robert Holland at the press conference announcing him as the winner of the "Yo, I'm Your CEO" contest on February 1, 1995. The poster is behind him.

- an entry wrapped in a Superman cape and tights, with a note saying the applicant was looking for a better day job;
- several cakes, with the application written in icing;
- several framed artworks; and,
- an application from Jim the Wonder Dog.

"Ben was an amazing person," said the man who got the job. "Whenever you turned the kleig lights on, he would go into gear and whatever came out of his mouth was golden. He was incredibly good at seizing opportunities." One day, for example, Oprah Winfrey said on her show that she had a hankering for Ben & Jerry's. *Oprah* might have been the most influential show on television in those days. Two days later, Ben showed up at her studio bearing several pints. He became an impromptu guest on the show. "How much was that worth? A lot," said the CEO.

Ben speculated that most of the job applicants were going for second prize, which was membership in the elite Free Ice Cream For Life club. That prize went to an eighty-five-year-old

Vermonter. Everyone else got a certificate, suitable for framing, with this message: "The bad news is, you didn't get the CEO's job. The good news, however, is that you didn't get the CEO's job. Whew! You're just too valuable to the world to be peddling ice cream." It was the opposite of a typical CEO search, topped off with a backhanded insult to the man who got the job.

The contest was a head-fake to the media, and it worked. Instead of focusing on how the company was abandoning the cornerstone of its progressive values (the salary ratio) and looking for a buttoned-down CEO to save it, reporters happily focused on the wacky company that thought anyone could be its leader. And the contest sent the right message about the company's values, even though no one on the board expected the winning entry to come in the mail. "We felt that we had an obligation to cast as wide a net as possible," said Jeff. "I actually refused to pay the search firm we hired for a while because they were not bringing us enough women and people of color. We got a ton of free publicity. And Ben & Jerry's is supposed to be about having fun. The search was fun, at first. But there was also a dark side. Everyone, including me, expected that the search would bring us some kind of superhero. No one could live up to our expectations."

The differing expectations of board members had always been the problem, and the board was still unable to get past its own disagreements. Perhaps a "professional" CEO could somehow thread the needle.

A corporate headhunter found Robert Holland, an engineer who had started his career as a management consultant for McKinsey & Company. Holland had experience as a troubleshooter, had done lots of charity work, and was an open, friendly kind of guy. He supported the three-part mission. And he was also African-American, which probably made a difference to a board that was acutely aware of its own lack of diversity. Bob's salary—$226,000 plus a performance bonus and stock options—was below the average for the CEOs of American corporations with sales of $150 million, but it was still upsetting to many of Ben & Jerry's employees.

In 1992, 72 percent of employees had said they were satisfied with the fairness of the company's salaries. In 1994, after the salary ratio was abandoned, only 53 percent were satisfied. After all, the definition of success or failure depends on your expectations, and the company had always set its expectations extremely high. "Bob felt like the beginning of a new era," said Sean Greenwood. "It was a step change."

Do the Tighten Up

Bob reported to work on February 3, 1995. Three months later, Ben and Jerry signed employment agreements that delineated their positions as chairman and vice chairman of the board of directors, respectively. They were each paid $132,745 a year plus benefits, or about seven times what the lowest paid employees made. Yet they also received several benefits that other employees did not get, including performance bonuses and company cars.

The end of the salary ratio meant that for the first time the company could make competitive salary offers to managers who had the capabilities and experience the company needed. They weren't cheap, though. In 1996, the company's chief operating officer had thirty-five thousand stock options, and the head of human resources had twenty-five thousand. CFO Fran Rathke received thirty thousand options in 1995; Liz Bankowski received five thousand plus another twenty thousand in 1996.

The only job Ben was required to do to draw his pay was running the board of directors. Jerry's only job was to back him up. They could do other things too, but only if the board gave its permission. This was not a difficult transition for

Jerry, who had always been comfortable with collaborative decision making, but it was a huge change for Ben. "I'm fairly autocratic," Ben told the *New York Times* just before Bob Holland was hired. "I'm hard to please, not very communicative. People perceive me as intimidating. I tend to be more conceptual, and Jerry tends to be more practical. I tend to be more independent, and Jerry is better with people. I am not able to do the routine things Jerry is."

"Ben is the creative one, the risk-taker," Jerry continued. "Ben has often told me that he would rather fail at something new than succeed at something that has already been done before. That's a shocking concept to me. Also, as a team, we have a good sense of the absurd. The most immediate absurdity is that our business was started by two non-businesspeople and it has reached such an exalted status in the ice-cream world."[1]

Ben and Jerry were not the only ones who stepped away from the day-to-day routine after Bob arrived. Jeff became much less involved in the company's operations, although he stayed on the boards of the company and its foundation. Chuck stayed for a few more months, but he was not in the office. Instead, Chuck helped launch Ben & Jerry's in the United Kingdom. In 1994, Ben had decided to ship a few pallets of ice cream to London and sell them at gourmet shops. He did it for the same reason he had signed the national distribution deal with Dreyer's in 1985. Häagen-Dazs was succeeding in Europe, and Ben & Jerry's needed to stake its claim before someone else took the number two position. Once again, Ben was seeking growth.

The company hired Helen Jones, a marketing executive with three young children, to manage the brand in the UK. "Chuck would come over to my house and we'd do our planning over a take-away curry, while my kids crawled around at our feet," said Helen. "The company had no problem letting me set up the UK business in my home, and they knew

I was doing it while raising three children. I am enormously grateful to them for that." But the company did not give Helen a lot of resources. "One problem was that a lot of people in Burlington did not agree with Ben and were concerned about the decision to go into the UK," she says. "Another was that the Ben & Jerry's folks really did not know much about how to do business over here, so even the people who wanted me to succeed didn't know how to help." After Chuck left to take another job, Helen says, she was pretty much on her own.

Bob did have several experienced advisors. Liz Bankowski stayed on as director of social mission. Fran Rathke was still the CFO. And Chico, who had come back temporarily to chair the transition team, stayed on until he found Bruce Bowman, who became chief operating officer in August 1995. But Liz and Fran were busy running the company, and Chico was focused on turning St. Albans into a working ice cream plant as fast as possible. He did it, too, with the assistance of a consultant who had a lot of experience building ice cream plants. So as the winter of 1995 melted into a muddy Vermont spring, Bob often found himself trying to keep up.

Bob had been hired to make the company profitable again, so he went looking for ways to tighten things up. He did not need to look far. "The people at Ben & Jerry's were incredibly smart, focused, and right-minded, but they had zero experience relative to the rest of the business world," he said. "Their cost of goods was incredibly high, and they didn't know why. Meanwhile, their competitors had nailed down the cost of goods to a gnat's eyelash."

One reason for the high cost of goods was that the company's production standards had slipped. If a run of Chunky Monkey ice cream was "off-spec"—for example, because it had the right banana-flavored base but not enough chocolate chunks—it was sold at a loss or given away. And remember, Ben had been a potter. Ceramic artists tend to be manic about quality. Any batch that was even a little off was put in the seconds freezer. The Waterbury plant gave away thirty-seven thousand gallons of ice cream in 1995 and sold even more below cost. This was a big reason why Vermonters loved the company. They were happily eating lots of free ice cream that was all monkey and no chunky.

Another problem was that production planning had gotten sloppy. "It was like the wild, wild west of ice cream," said Debra Heintz, who was hired away from a big firm in 1994 to become the company's first director of materials management. "I remember reading a report that said we produced too much of a flavor and it expired, so we had to destroy it by incineration, which produced energy, and the energy we created was seen as a partial success."

Another reason for the high cost of goods was that the company gave away a lot of coupons that could be redeemed at any store for one free pint. "They wanted people to try the ice cream, which was good," said Bob. "But nobody could tell me how many coupons had been given away. The coupons didn't expire, and they didn't track how many of them were being used. I assumed it was all of them. There were just too many happy faces out there."

While the transition team and Bob worked to decrease the company's cost of goods, Chico was finding all kinds of things at the St. Albans plant that also would have been funny if they hadn't cost so much. The employee teams had come up with all kinds of worthy ideas, but no one had knit them together in a sensible way. For example, the ceiling in the administration space was three stories high, so it wasted huge amounts of heat. And the plant had a glass-block wall to let in sunlight without losing heat, which was smart, but they put lockers in front of it.

The big problem at St. Albans was the freezing system. Chico and the engineer he hired persuaded Bob to pull the plug on it in early March, and Bob approved a $6.7 million write-down that caused the company to officially post a loss of $1.8 million on sales of $149 million in 1994. (In 1993, the company's profit had been $6 million.) Then Chico's engineer ordered a spiral-style hardener that matched the one in use in Waterbury. To install it, they had to cut a hole in the roof, lift the unusable equipment out with a crane, lower the new equipment into place, repair the roof, and build a new system around the spiral hardener. Production lines were running in St. Albans by September, but it took another six months to get them fully debugged. The elapsed time to get the St. Albans plant built and running smoothly was three and a half years.

Social Metrics

Bob said that what he was trying to do was simple: "First you set the metrics for success, and then you fine-tune them over time." He was following a strategy the company had tried to follow for years, and in some departments, it was succeeding. Late in 1995, for example, Liberty Mutual sent Ben & Jerry's a check for $500,000. It was a partial refund of the company's insurance premium. Chuck had worked for years to empower an employee-led safety committee, and the committee had reduced the number of lost-time accidents enough to push the insurance rate down. After years of being unacceptably high, the accident rate was finally headed in the right direction.

Ben & Jerry's had also been taking steps to reduce its environmental footprint almost since the company began, but it didn't start setting environmental goals and measuring its progress toward those goals until the mid-1990s. Andrea Asch, the company's manager of natural resource use, surveyed the company's practices and measured its environmental impact in six areas: packaging, energy, transportation, product waste, dairy waste, and chemical use. Her survey gave the company baselines it could use to set measurable goals. It committed to reduce solid waste by 30 percent and dairy waste by 20 percent in 1995. Working toward these goals required Andrea to think creatively and use persuasion. She worked with suppliers to replace disposable containers with reusable ones. She persuaded Waterbury's line workers to find ways to clean the equipment by using less water. She even worked with a local not-for-profit to compost the dairy waste from making ice cream.

Even so, it took years for the company to meet these environmental goals. "The hard part was putting projects in place," said Andrea. "But it was a start. We were putting a stake in the ground and starting to do something. We would learn along the way. If we waited until our system was perfect, we would never start."

In the fall of 1995, Liz persuaded the board to hire a consultant to expand the company's commitment to social metrics. The consultant's job would be to identify key elements of the social mission in every aspect of the company's operation and express them as measurable goals. Simon Zadek of the London-based New Economics Foundation (NEF) supervised a team of employees who interviewed franchisees and employees. He then set internal performance indicators and tried to compare them to external benchmarks. For example, the team found that the company's entry and middle-level salaries in 1995 were higher than the averages for manufacturing jobs in Vermont or the United States.

Zadek wrote that Ben & Jerry's annual social reports prior to 1996 had been "assessments," because they did not involve accounting practices; rather, independent observers had been invited to investigate and report on social performance in any manner they chose. By contrast, a true social audit, like a financial audit, had to be comprehensive, comparative over time, externally validated, and transparent. The procedure, rather than the investigator, had to be in charge.[2]

Starting in 1997, the social report was written by employees using the guidelines NEF had set, under the direction of Liz and the board of directors' new social mission committee. "It took hundreds of years to develop a set of what are called generally accepted financial accounting principles," wrote the finance department manager who headed up the team that did the social audit of 1996. "These standards are continually evolving. The same process needs to happen in social accounting. In order to be useful, information on corporate social performance needs to be understandable (standardized) and believable (audited)."

The report on the company's social performance in 1996 was a statistics-laden almanac that claimed fifteen pages in the company's annual report, with dozens of measurements in the areas of workplace, operations, environment, marketing/sales, finance/shareholders, foundation grants, and political positions taken by the company. (The company gave the foundation $768,000 from its profits in 1995, but retained $255,000 to pay off the loan it had made to the foundation when the company lost money in 1994.) The outside auditor was again James Heard, the president of a consulting firm that served institutional shareholders. Heard had audited the company's social report in 1990, when it had been a much simpler operation. He would return as auditor every year from 1996 until 2004. And for the next four years, the report grew increasingly detailed.

"Ben & Jerry's made itself a target when we said that our social and environmental activities were as important as our business results," said Liz. "The audits were our defense. We were a public company, so we had to report our business results. Whenever someone criticized the company, the chances were good that we had already covered that subject in a social report. People would ask, 'Why did you put the St. Albans plant so close to Lake Champlain, where any spill of wastewater could get into the bay?' I could point to the section of our report where we said that St. Albans was an economically depressed area with a large Native American population. We wanted to provide them with good jobs. We were advancing a social goal despite an environmental risk. Maybe we were wrong, but that was our decision.

"The audits allowed us to stop saying, 'We're doing good things,' and to start saying, 'Here are the goals we're working on, here's the progress we've made, and here's where we're still having problems.' We were trying to demonstrate a different way of running a business. It required us to have a huge amount of honesty and integrity. People always expected Ben & Jerry's to be the best employer, the best for the environment, the best of the best. Well, the only way we could attempt to be the best is to define what it meant."

Ben & Jerry's switched to a social-auditing approach just as the idea was being taken seriously by bigger companies. Late in 1995, companies like Disney and Nike started responding to pressure from human rights organizations by seeking a truce. The big companies agreed that they bore some responsibility for the working conditions at companies in the developing world from which they bought products, and they asked for guidance on how to evaluate those working conditions. "This was an immensely important breakthrough in the history of corporate accountability," Zadek writes. In the resulting scramble to develop those labor standards, the work Ben & Jerry's was doing suddenly got a lot of attention.

"People find themselves in the right place at the right time, applauded for advancing ideas that would have been (and often were) dismissed as lunatic ravings just moments before," writes Zadek. "Mainstreaming ideas can best be understood as an associational process, a sort of institutional poetry rather than a linear, scientific transmission. One thing does indeed lead to another."[3]

Tougher Problems

"When I started at Ben & Jerry's, I told them I saw two problems," said Bob. "The simple one was, how do you make money? I thought we could fix that reasonably soon. The other one was, how do you compete in an industry driven by marketing? Solving that one would take a lot of teaching. My mistake was, after I got the first problem solved, I kept going."

Ben & Jerry's did make money in 1995. It netted a little less than $6 million on sales of $155 million, and sales increased 4 percent. But 1996 would be tougher, wrote Bob in a January letter to employees. The external pressures on the company had grown because its chief competitor, Häagen-Dazs, had made drastic cuts to its administrative expenses. The brand had been consolidated into the marketing department of Pillsbury, which itself was a division of a British multinational named Grand Metropolitan. With lower overhead costs and much deeper pockets, Bob said, Häagen-Dazs could now spend more on advertising, marketing, and launching new products like sorbets and no-fat frozen yogurt.

Ben & Jerry's internal problems were just as serious, said Bob. He was finding it hard to get the employees to work together. People talked back to him and told him he was wrong. But what Bob saw as insubordination was actually something else. The company's employees had been told for more than a decade that they should speak freely. They had been told that the company hired people for their passion and trained them into their jobs. Also, almost every employee was also a shareholder, and they took their ownership stakes seriously.

"What I loved about Ben & Jerry's, the whole time I was there, was that you could be brutally truthful," said Liz. "You could go up to anybody and say, this is where we're okay and this is where we're not, and you didn't have to worry about recriminations. We might have been the only company with more than five hundred employees that behaved in this way. We told very tough stories about the company, and it led to real change."

Ben & Jerry's matched Häagen-Dazs by coming out with its own line of sorbets in March 1996, and then it raised the stakes. It used the social mission, which was a point of difference from the competition, to make an ordinary flavor special. Since 1990, the company had been buying its coffee beans directly from a co-op of Mexican farmers, paying a small "fair-trade" premium over the market price so that the co-op could improve living conditions in the farmers' villages. In 1995, they made a similar arrangement with a co-op of vanilla farmers along the Pacific coast of Costa Rica. With 60 percent of the vanilla extract sourced through this deal, Ben & Jerry's relaunched its vanilla flavor as "World's Best Vanilla" and put the fair-trade story on the label. It didn't hurt that in the fourth quarter of 1996, they sold the flavor in quart containers for the price of a pint.

The sorbets and World's Best Vanilla were both hits. By September 1998, the Costa Rican farmers had been able to fund several reforestation projects and build health clinics and schools because of the Ben & Jerry's contract. This track record helped them find other sources of support and move forward on their own.

Working the social mission into a flavor could be tricky, though. In 1993, the company had launched apple pie–flavored frozen yogurt, with La Soul Bakery supplying the pie. La Soul was a New Jersey not-for-profit that employed recovering addicts. Its mission was similar to the mission of Greyston Bakery, which had been supplying brownie pieces to the company more or less successfully since 1988. Ben & Jerry's bought $1.5 million worth of apple pie from La Soul, but the flavor didn't sell, and in 1995 Ben & Jerry's stopped making it. This left La Soul with debts it couldn't pay, and it left the recovering addicts jobless. La Soul's director sued, and Ben & Jerry's settled out of court. The episode left everyone feeling uneasy.

"La Soul was a hard lesson, but a good lesson," said Bob. "If a person adopts a child, it's theirs until they teach it how to survive on its own. It was the same with Ben & Jerry's. If we adopt a not-for-profit, we should not cut them loose until we teach them how to find their own customers. If we haven't taught them how to get customers, then they belong to us. That seemed obvious to me, but Ben and I argued about it for a while."

As 1996 wore on, Bob and Ben were having more and more trouble communicating. "I can remember in one discussion, Ben asked me, 'Where did you get your data?' I had gotten it from a big market research company called IRI," Bob said. "So Ben said, 'This explains why you're wrong. They get their data from supermarkets. Most of our customers buy from mom-and-pop stores.' I told him he was living in an idealized world. Our sales were coming from supermarkets. If it weren't for supermarkets, we wouldn't be in business. He just threw up his hands and said that couldn't be right. He didn't want to hear it.

"Eventually, I decided that Ben was more important to Ben & Jerry's than I was. Clearly we couldn't coexist. But who was I to chase him out of the company? So I told the board that either Ben needed to go or I would go, knowing that they would not let go of Ben. He was the company."

Board members say that Bob didn't have any real defenders by the summer of 1996. "Everyone agreed that we needed a different guy," Jeff said. But those who wanted the company to run along more traditional lines were inclined to agree with Bob's advice. Those who wanted to pursue more unconventional strategies, including Ben and Jeff, were now at a loss. "We were sitting there trying to figure out what to do next, and not coming up with much," said Jeff. "We were out of ideas.

"I remember one time, Merritt said to me, 'You and Ben are like seagulls. You fly in, shit all over everything, and fly away. We have to clean it up.' I could see his point. So around that time, I stopped talking so much."

The Distribution Dilemma

Just then, a new kid showed up. Merritt Chandler retired from the board in May 1996, and he was replaced by Jennifer Henderson, an original board member of One Percent for Peace who had been working with the Ben & Jerry's Foundation for almost a decade. Jennifer was an organizational development consultant and an activist at the Center for Community Change, a not-for-profit in Washington, DC, that organized low-income people and communities of color.

Jennifer does not have a traditional business background. She is lively and has an easy laugh, and she often compares her colleagues to characters from *Star Wars*. Like Bob and Fred Miller, who joined the board in 1992, she is also African-American. "Bob was my first contact when I came on the board," she said. "He picked me up at the airport, and he drove to the meeting at about 15 miles an hour so he could be the first to tell me his side of the story. He was demoralized. Half the board felt that he was giving the company good advice that the company was refusing to take. Fred was leading the faction that was trying to push Bob out. And I was like, what the hell is going on here?"

Jennifer says that, like Liz, her first job on the board was to act as the referee for arguments between male board members. "Eventually I came to believe that Bob's business advice was right, but that he didn't understand the company's culture," she said. "He was a consultant, not a CEO. And the first rule of consulting is, leave when the client still wants you to stay. If Bob had left before he wore out his welcome, he would have been a hero."

Bob was affable, and he went along with the social mission, but he didn't inspire people. "He was used to managing from thirty thousand feet. That was his background and his style," said Sean Greenwood. "I liked Bob, but like a lot of employees, I never felt like I could connect with him." Bob needed to dig deeply into the complexities of a company that was dedicated to an unconventional way of doing business, and he didn't do it. Every Friday at 5 p.m. he would run to the airport to fly home to his family.

Bob's choice for marketing director, Jerry Welsh, was a pioneer in cause-related marketing. In 1981, Welsh had led campaigns for American Express that gave not-for-profit groups small donations each time the card was used. The campaign was a big win-win—it sent a lot of money to the not-for-profits—and helped renovate the Statue of Liberty, among other things—as it boosted traffic for American Express. Cause-related marketing became a big deal, and now it's a traditional way of doing business. But Ben & Jerry's was not doing cause-related marketing.

"Jerry Welsh thought we needed a cartoon character, like a talking ice cream cone," said Lisa Wernhoff, the designer and contributor to *Rolling Cone*. "He was very boisterous and friendly. But he didn't get it. We know that the social mission boosts sales sometimes, and it costs us money sometimes, but that isn't supposed to be the point of it. We have a social mission because it's the right thing to do. Sometimes the social benefit alone is enough."

Bob Holland was also aware of a deeper, more serious threat to the company's health. In January 1996, he wrote that the next six months "could be the last opportunity for the company to dictate the terms of its existence." Ben & Jerry's had done a brilliant job of creating irresistible flavors and promoting them in creative ways, but that was not enough to become a truly national brand of ice cream. Distribution, which had long been the company's weak point, now threatened to become a full-blown disaster. And if Ben & Jerry's did not have good distribution, it could make the world's best ice cream and still go broke.

Since the early days, Ben & Jerry's had outsourced its distribution to a network of companies. These distribution companies, not consumers, were the ones that actually bought the ice cream Ben & Jerry's produced. Distributors drove trucks loaded with all kinds of frozen food directly to grocery stores and other kinds of retailers. They were "direct store distribution" companies, and they made more money if they delivered lots of different products. It didn't matter much if the products they delivered were competing with each other.

Most of these distributors carried either Ben & Jerry's or Häagen-Dazs. It was important to have one of these brands on the truck, because super-premium ice cream was in high demand—all grocers wanted it—and to have a complete line of it, you had to have both brands. The distributors loved Ben & Jerry's because it was highly profitable, and it also helped them get all their frozen food into stores.

There was another way to get products into stores. Ben & Jerry's could drive its ice cream in its own trucks, and send the trucks directly from the factories to warehouses owned by grocery store chains. The chains would then deliver the ice cream to the stores. But warehouse distribution made it more likely that consumers would buy ice cream that had melted and refrozen, which ruined the texture. Ben & Jerry's also rejected warehouse distribution because it gave them less influence over the contents of grocery freezer cases.

In 1996, the ice cream business was changing. Ben & Jerry's biggest distributor, Dreyer's, was buying up more and more small distributors. They were becoming the number one ice cream distributor, with near-national reach, and there wasn't a clear number two. In 1993, Dreyer's had competed with the world's two biggest ice cream makers, Nestlé and Unilever, to purchase the ice cream division of Kraft Foods (which included Breyer's Ice Cream). Unilever won that contest. A few months later, Nestlé bought 22 percent of Dreyer's. Nestlé got two seats on the Dreyer's board of directors, but Nestlé also promised not to increase its stake beyond 35 percent for another decade.

One reason for that alliance was that Nestlé and Dreyer's both used direct-store distribution. Unilever used warehouse distribution, so it had less of a need for Dreyer's profitable direct-store distribution business. But the bigger reason was that Dreyer's was coping with forces it could not control. William Cronk, who was president of Dreyer's in 1993, says he realized that the ice cream industry was consolidating and that sooner or later Dreyer's would have to sell to either Nestlé or Unilever. The multinationals were simply too big to resist, Cronk said, so he arranged for Dreyer's and Nestlé to have "an eight-year dating relationship." As a minority owner, Nestlé had time to learn about the way Dreyer's did business, and particularly how it treated its employees.[4]

Most of the folks at Ben & Jerry's scoffed at the idea that a sale to a multinational was inevitable. But the pieces were moving around on the chessboard and there were lots of potential end games, most of which were bad for Burlington. There were also ominous indications that Grand Metropolitan might put Häagen-Dazs up for sale. If Dreyer's and Häagen-Dazs were both purchased by Nestlé, it would be a disaster for Ben & Jerry's, because the company's only viable distributor would also become its archrival. Several board members believed that the only way to stay independent in the long run was to find or build an alternative distribution system. Whether or not the company could do that wasn't clear.

Bob announced his resignation on September 27. The company's sales remained sluggish, the stock price was stuck below $15, and competitive threats were growing. "It was a desperate moment," said Jennifer. "We had failed with Bob, we were facing huge problems, and we needed to find someone new fast."

They didn't look long. Shortly after Bob resigned, Fred Miller suggested that the board consider replacing Bob with Perry Odak, who was then CEO of the company that made Winchester guns. It seemed like an outrageous suggestion for Ben & Jerry's, which used a peace sign in its marketing material. But Fred said that he had been working with Perry for over a year, and he thought this might be the right guy. Perry had superior skills at financing and valuation, and he had a track record of turning troubled companies around. So Ben contacted Perry, and before long they were talking terms.

"I think a lot of us knew in our gut that this was not the right path for us to take, but we didn't have a good alternative," said Jennifer. "So we agreed to hire a turnaround specialist. That was a huge mistake. For the second time, we hired the wrong kind of leader."

SEVEN

The Gulf Was So Wide

W hen Perry Odak became the CEO of Ben & Jerry's, the media crowed that the peaceniks had hired a leader from a company that made guns. They also said that Perry was a down-to-earth guy from a Hudson Valley farm who had worked his way through Cornell by milking cows. They got the facts right, but they buried the lead.

Perry was a turnaround specialist. He was the man Fred Miller had suggested in the days following Bob Holland's resignation, and he did what he was hired to do. Starting in January 1997, he executed a plan that worked brilliantly for shareholders. The company's financial condition began improving shortly after he arrived. He brought focus and skillful planning to every aspect of the operation, and he gave the social mission the resources it needed to keep moving ahead. But that isn't all he did.

Perry's career had followed a pattern. He had spun off companies for sale when he worked at Atari in the 1980s. In the 1990s, as a management consultant, he helped a holding company cut its debt by selling fifteen companies in just nine months. He even merged two dairy companies just two years before he arrived at Ben & Jerry's. "The best predictor of future behavior is past behavior," said Pierre Ferrari, who joined the board of Ben & Jerry's in 1997. "Perry took on organizations that had run into some kind of trouble, turned them around, and then sold them. He approached everything with that kind of attitude. You know, every problem is a nail if you're a hammer."

115

Clash of Principles

Perry signed a three-year contract. His base salary was not unusual, compared with the CEOs of other companies that had annual sales of $167 million: $300,000 plus a bonus of $100,000 and relocation costs of $25,000. But he also got the option to buy 360,000 shares of Ben & Jerry's at $10.88 a share. This meant that if the company's stock went to $30 and he sold it, he would pocket $6.8 million.

"We feel incredibly lucky to have found a person of Perry's caliber," said Ben at the press conference to introduce the new CEO. Jeff, Pierre, and Jennifer weren't so sure. "I didn't have a good feeling about him at all," Jeff said, "because of the way he negotiated his contract. I thought his demands were outrageous, and he made them in a take-it-or-leave-it kind of way. But I also felt like I should keep my mouth shut, because I had suggested Bob to the board just two years earlier. Everybody shrugged and said that if Ben is okay with hiring Perry, we should do it."

Perry looked the part of a CEO. He was tall and reserved, with a neat haircut and moustache. He always dressed well, which stood out in a company where the dress code was anything goes. The board had done only a perfunctory, informal search before hiring him. Ben and Jerry had courted Pierre, a former marketing executive for Coca-Cola who was working for the relief group CARE. Pierre had grown up in a middle-class European family that lived in the Belgian Congo. "They were interested in me because I had jumped from the corporate world to the do-gooder world," Pierre said. "I felt a strong, immediate connection to both of them." Pierre didn't want another executive job, though, so Ben and Jerry offered him the board seat Chico was vacating. Perry countered Pierre's appointment by nominating Andrew Patti, an old colleague who was just leaving his job as president of the

Dial Corporation. "This guy didn't fit in at all," said Pierre. "He thought he was going to be doing philanthropy." Perry's board pick resigned after eighteen months.

The clash of principles began almost immediately. Perry and some of the people he hired acted as if making a profit and using business to create social change were two separate goals, and that mixing them only made sense if it sold more ice cream. Ben and others on the board believed that they needed to hire a turnaround expert who would tighten up the business, and that these changes would not damage the three-part mission. Jeff and other decision makers also thought that Perry's track record of selling companies didn't matter, because Ben & Jerry's had safeguards in place that meant it could never be sold. How could they all have been so wrong?

People have an amazing capacity to deny the obvious when the facts clash with their cherished beliefs. Ben, Jerry, Jeff, and everyone who believed in the three-part mission, as smart and talented as they were, simply could not grasp the serious trouble they were getting into. They came from small-business backgrounds. They had never seen this particular style of trouble before.

Ben and Chico struggled for sixteen years to agree on how to advance the three-part mission, but both of them believed in it. They both started out running businesses that were rooted in their communities. In their first decade of running the company, the differences between Ben, Chico, and the Rotarians who met for lunch every Monday at the Burlington Hilton were differences of style and degree, not of kind.

The idea that businesses should invest in the financial and social health of the places where they operate has deep roots in the United States. It goes back to 1728, when a Philadelphia printer started a civic improvement club for middle-class merchants and tradesmen. The club was organized around a series of questions, such as, "Do you think of anything at present, in which we may be serviceable to mankind?" The printer's name was Ben, too. Ben Franklin.

Perry Odak's business philosophy was foreign to the three-part mission and also hostile to it. During a long career, he had repeatedly demonstrated his belief that board members and managers of publicly traded businesses should be laser-focused on boosting financial returns to shareholders. Employees, customers, suppliers, and the community at large are all lower priorities, according to this view. Because shareholders own the company, it would be immoral for managers and board members to allocate profits to any other group.

The idea of shareholder primacy is also all-American, and many of the people who believe in it—people like J.P. Morgan and Carl Icahn—make lavish charitable gifts. But they don't bring their generosity into the office.

Shareholder primacy is a flawed doctrine for several reasons, according to Lynn Stout, a legal scholar and author of *The Shareholder Value Myth*. One reason, she says, is that shareholders do not actually own corporations. Corporations are independent legal entities that own themselves, just as people own themselves. And, Stout adds, no coherent body of case law exists to show that corporate directors have a legal obligation to maximize returns to shareholders. In fact, there is another doctrine in corporate law, the "business judgment rule," that says courts should not interfere in the rulings of corporate boards if the boards are free of conflicts of interest and are reasonably well informed.[1]

Shareholder primacy is really just an idea, but in the late 1990s, the idea was especially fashionable. Think tanks and the media made heroes of Milton Friedman, Alan Greenspan, and other experts who attacked the foundations of community-oriented capitalism. These opinion leaders argued that corporate managers and board members who invested more than they needed to in their businesses, or paid their employees more than they had to, or gave away too much to the community, were simply doing it wrong.

The employees of Ben & Jerry's had been taking fire from these people for years. They had been struggling for more than a decade to show that a for-profit, shareholder-owned business could have more than one bottom line. But now they were working for a true believer in shareholder primacy. Perry Odak's career was a clear warning that all the work they had done might be dismantled. Incredibly, board members crossed their fingers and hoped everything would turn out fine.

"We Gotta Buy!"

A lot of people were happy to see Perry join the company. "I thought he was an excellent CEO," said Howard Fuguet, the company's lawyer. "We had large, complex economic issues to deal with, and the industry was consolidating, and he was skilled in these areas. I remember a number of meetings where Perry and I were alone. We would talk about where we wanted to be in a year, and then work backwards to see what we had to do to get there."

Perry was good at disciplined, strategic thinking, something Ben & Jerry's sorely needed. He was also extremely smart and hardworking, and he made his expectations clear. "He was a good leader," said Liz Bankowski. "If you had a good idea and you made the business case for it, he would support you." In April 1997, Perry wrote that his goals were to "optimize the outstanding equity that Ben & Jerry's continues to have in its brand name, and to ensure steady, sustained growth in earnings and earnings per share while attempting to contain our costs."

Ben was also happy to leave matters in Perry's hands—at first—because he was absorbed in another new venture. On the page of the annual report facing where Perry stated his goals, Ben and Jerry glossed over the company's business problems. Instead of addressing them, they proudly unveiled Ben's new group, Business Leaders for Sensible Priorities, which was dedicated to redirecting the federal budget away from military spending and toward education, job training, and crime prevention.

"What we continue to learn at Ben & Jerry's is that there is a spiritual aspect to business just as there is to the lives of individuals," they said. "As we give we receive, as we help others we are helped in return." How would the company hold on to that generous spirit while simultaneously cutting costs and boosting sales? "It all comes down to how well we manage ourselves," they wrote. In other words, that's up to Perry.

By conventional measures, Perry was a first-rate CEO. He moved decisively on several fronts at once, and he got results. He set a clear course, although he did not say more to the board or employees than he was legally required to say. This was a jolt to staffers, who were accustomed to having bosses whose doors were always open. "Perry was not a warm and fuzzy guy," said Carol O'Neill, franchise site selection manager. "He certainly was not an aging hippie."

Employees quickly adjusted to Perry, however, because if they did their jobs well, he would leave them alone. This was a big improvement over Ben, who was infamous for barging into people's offices and changing their job descriptions. And it was also better than Bob Holland, because Perry was a man with a plan. Yet something was missing. "Ben was inspiring, and Bob Holland was like your dad," said public relations manager Sean Greenwood. "They hugged people. I don't think Perry ever hugged anybody. He was an outsider. He was here to do certain things, and he did them."

Perry brought in several top hands with mainstream corporate backgrounds, and that was when Rob Michalak, the head of public relations, who had known Jerry since 1977, decided to leave. "The environment was getting more serious, the business was being challenged, and my job was in transition," Rob said. "I felt like the work I had been doing was complete."

On May 4, 1997, the board held a meeting via conference call. Ben, Jerry, and Jeff did not attend, and the board attained a quorum without them. They voted to increase the limit on stock options from five hundred thousand to nine hundred thousand. With the board's approval, Perry offered most of these new options to his direct reports, including eighty-two thousand options for a long-time colleague he hired as director of business development; seventy thousand for the sales and distribution director; fifty-two thousand options to the newly hired marketing director; fifty-two thousand to the chief operations officer (Bruce Bowman); and forty-five thousand to the chief financial officer (Fran Rathke). The board also awarded Perry another sixty-seven thousand options, at $24 a share, in 1999. Rosalie Vitrano, Perry's wife at the time, bought another fifteen thousand shares.

Most of the company's employees owned at least a few shares of stock, and some of them owned a lot. Liz Bankowski, for example, owned 28,766 shares in 1998. In October of that year, as potential buyers circled around Ben & Jerry's and the stock price started to climb, *Rolling Cone* began publishing the price in a box in every issue. Almost every employee focused on it. A person who had bought one thousand shares at $12 a share would see a capital gain of $18,000 if they sold the stock at $30.

"I bought as much stock as I could," said Pierre. "I am a brand guy, you know, coming from Coca-Cola. I believe in the Ben & Jerry's brand. The stock had been trading above $30, and the brand was still strong. When the stock was at $12, I thought Ben & Jerry's was the best value in town. I kept telling the board, 'Either somebody's going to buy this sucker or we're going to emerge from this mess and the stock is going to go back to the thirties. Either way the opportunity is unbelievable. We should buy back as much stock as possible, as quickly as possible. A brand like this, and it only costs $12 a share? Oh my God! We gotta buy!' I thought the board should buy the company back and get its stake over 50 percent, so we wouldn't be vulnerable to predatory investors."

The company was clearly in a crisis when Perry arrived. "But the crisis could have been managed differently," said Pierre. "Perry managed it the wrong way. He managed it to make the most money for the people who owned stock options, starting with himself."

Massive Misunderstanding

The whole Ben & Jerry's family—employees, customers, shareholders, suppliers, dogs, children, and some beings who were harder to describe, totaling about thirty-five thousand people—gathered on June 28, 1997, for the annual free festival the company called One World One Heart. It was sunny and so hot that employees gave away more than a thousand gallons of water, tens of thousands of ice cream cones, and several cases of sunscreen. People played games, swam, danced to big-name musicians, and filled out postcards to send to their congressional representatives on all kinds of issues. Before the party started, Ben lured twenty-two hundred shareholders into a huge tent by chanting, "The meeting is starting, the meeting is starting" over and over, while Perry looked on in amazement. It was one of the happiest, smoothest-running festivals in the company's history, partly because it started with good news.

According to *Rolling Cone,* Ben introduced Perry to the community by saying, "Folks, this is the kind of guy you want minding the store. I believe that our revitalized board and management team is building on the foundations of those who came before and will enable us to realize the Ben

& Jerry's of our dreams. So here's the star of our show, Mr. Perry 'Show Me the Money' Odak!"

"Thanks, Ben," said Perry. "I've been to a lot of annual meetings, and so far this one tops them all." Perry said that he'd "sat around way too many meetings of boards and bankers where everybody was clawing at the corporate carcass, and I was the sole person hollering about people's lives and jobs, and I gotta tell you it's refreshing to come to a company where I don't have to say that anymore."

Perry performed. He told the shareholders that plans were in the works to redesign the pint labels to make them easier for shoppers to understand; that he was working to get the product into more convenience stores, cafeterias, airlines, restaurants, "you name it"; that expansion into other countries was going well, with deals in Japan, Canada, and Southeast Asia supplementing existing operations in the United Kingdom, Belgium, Luxembourg, the Netherlands, and Israel; that the company's first national radio advertising campaign was yielding good results; and that Ben & Jerry's was making its first big foray into market research. The company had also teamed up with Vermont's best-known rock band, Phish, to release a new flavor called Phish Food, and it was proving to be a blockbuster. The band was donating its licensing fee toward the cleanup of Lake Champlain. A month after the festival, for the first time ever, the St. Albans plant ran all three of its production lines simultaneously.

Perry had also been presenting this happy story to financiers. And he was getting results on that front, too. In 1997, the stock of Ben & Jerry's was a value play. The price was low, the brand was valuable, Perry's track record was clear, and word started getting around on Wall Street: buy Ben & Jerry's now, and you'll make a bundle. One mutual fund bought 797,500 shares of Ben & Jerry's in 1997. Another fund bought 745,800 shares in 1998. By the end of 1999, mutual funds owned 17 percent of the company's stock. Perry owned another 5 percent; managers and directors who weren't founders owned another 3 percent. This was far greater than Ben (13 percent), Jerry (3 percent), and Jeff (1 percent) put together.

The founders were not overly concerned about being out-numbered, however, because the company had a dual share-holder system. The mutual funds and managers owned A shares, each of which had one vote. But Ben, Jerry, and Jeff owned three-quarters of the company's B shares, and each B share had ten votes. So if a hostile takeover attempt was made, the founders could easily vote it down. And the dual shareholder system did hold buyers at bay, for a while.

But the balance of power was shifting, and when the shift became apparent, the tension turned to antagonism. "Perry was focusing on margins and insisting on discipline," said Pierre. "No question, he was a good manager. But this cre-ated tension, too. Ben would get an idea for a new product, Perry would question whether or not it would be profitable, and Ben would get angry.

"It got worse when Perry started trying to identify the incremental costs of the social mission. Some of this was easy. All you had to do was look at the annual payment we made to the foundation. But other parts of the social mission became very complicated. If we make fair-trade agreements with our suppliers, what is the added cost of that? What is the added cost of paying a living wage? What actual benefits accrue to the company when we pay more so that the chick-ens who lay our eggs are treated humanely? What do we get for those added costs?

"Ben just hated it when Perry did this. But the act of cal-culating these costs has interesting philosophical aspects. Should you even do it? It opens up a debate about whether or not the social mission is worthwhile. Most people on the board said that people should live a dignified life, period.

Some of them said that we should make these things happen right now, no matter what it costs." Others, including Perry, argued that spending related to the social mission should be at least as disciplined as any other kind of spending. But if you couldn't prove the benefits on a spreadsheet, did that mean it was waste?

Since 1988, the board had been trying to perfect a three-part mission. When they succeeded, it was usually because of the talented people they hired. In 1997, they were succeeding more and more often. And insisting on accountability and results wasn't a bad thing. But it often seemed to the board that Perry and the managers he hired were speaking a completely different language.

The misunderstandings flew thick and fast, producing moments that would have been funny if they hadn't been so sad. At one board meeting, Perry's sales manager proudly announced a new social mission initiative he had thought up. The managers traveled a lot, he said, so they were going to collect all the shampoos and soaps from their hotels and give them to the local homeless shelter. "They were very proud of that," said Pierre. "I was sitting there with Ben, Jerry, Jeff, and Jennifer. Nobody laughed, because the guy was serious. But our jaws were on the floor. The gulf that separated us was so huge."

EIGHT

Leading with Progressive Values

Perry Odak and most board members of Ben & Jerry's had huge differences of opinion about how to run the business. But Perry also put the business back in gear. Each component of the three-part mission did well under his leadership. Nobody disagreed about the ice cream: it was still delicious, people still loved it, and they ate more and more of it. The social mission was doing fine, too, as employee execution of social initiatives continued to improve.

Perry's attitude toward the three-part mission was "Let's make the economics work first. Let's find the right product and the right format," he told a class at Cornell in 2000. "And then with that, how do you practice in a caring way to minimize impact on the environment, to give back to the communities where you operate, to make sure that people are paid properly, and so on. We put the economic mission ahead when we start something new, and then bring the social mission up alongside of it as we go."[1]

The approach Perry described sounded close to the vision that Ben, Jerry, Jeff, Jennifer, and Pierre had, but there was a crucial difference. The founders and their allies insisted that the three parts of Ben & Jerry's mission had to be equal. The company's breakthrough successes would come from taking risks other companies were not willing to take, they said.

The careful, risk-averse strategy Perry followed was not what they were used to, and it also wasn't what they wanted.

The disagreements between board members hardened as Perry advanced his agenda. The board separated into factions and squared off. And as they attacked each other, the clock kept ticking. The ice cream industry continued to consolidate. More and more, it seemed that selling out to Nestlé or Unilever was the only way for Ben & Jerry's to secure its future as an international brand.

Cost-Effective Activism

Perry understood that the social mission was like putting chunks in the mix. It set Ben & Jerry's apart from other brands of ice cream, and it was a big reason why the brand was so valuable. So if a social initiative seemed cost-effective to him, he'd support it.

In June 1997, the company was running ads on Don Imus's nationally syndicated radio show. People listened to Imus because he made crude jokes, and one morning, after reading a Ben & Jerry's ad, Imus said, "Don't be a fairy, buy some Ben & Jerry's." Perry was in Los Angeles at the time. He canceled his meetings and immediately flew to New York to register a protest with Imus, who promised not to mix homophobic slurs with the brand again. The Associated Press picked up the story, and it ran all over the country. Ben & Jerry's kept buying ads on the show, too. Perry believed in public "impressions" first, social impact second.

Perry acted as if the social mission were part of the cost of marketing. This meant that employees who pitched social initiatives to Perry in the right way could still get the support they needed to make a difference. Liz Bankowski did this in the winter of 1997. The company had been working on the fight against bovine growth hormone (rBGH) for years, and it had been a priority ever since Chuck had written "Doesn't scare me!" on the letter from the dairy association. Now the campaign was at a tipping point, and Liz needed $250,000.

The money was to fund a lawsuit that had begun in 1996. Ben and Jerry had announced the suit at a press conference at the Whole Foods store in Chicago, with the CEOs of Stony-field Farms and Organic Valley standing next to them. Ben announced that the three companies were suing the City of Chicago and the State of Illinois. Although rBGH had been on the market for two years, the Food and Drug Administration had not published any guidelines for the labels of products that contained hormone-enhanced milk. They had left that decision up to the states. So Liz contacted the offices of the attorney generals in all fifty states, and four of them—Illinois, Nevada, Hawaii, and Oklahoma—said that they would not allow the sale of products whose labels mentioned rBGH. The lawsuit challenged those statements.

The decision to file the suit was a "wonderful moment, a classic moment," said Liz. "Ben and Jeff and Jerry and I were saying, 'Yes! Let's sue them!' And the chief financial officer and the sales manager were saying, 'My God, do you know what will happen if we can't sell our product in Illinois?'"

A year later, the lawsuit's costs were mounting. Ben & Jerry's was the lead plaintiff, and the other plaintiffs were not obliged to pay. Liz told Perry that the four states were likely to back down if they thought the plaintiffs were serious. Perry agreed and gave Liz the money, and Liz turned out to be right. Illinois settled, the other states followed, and the anti-rBGH label stayed on the pints.

"We established the right for a nationally distributed product to say that it did not use rBGH," said Liz. "I think it was the most effective action the company ever took to truly change the world.

"What other company would have put themselves in that position? The whole point was that Monsanto and rBGH would prevail as long as they could keep labels off of packages, because people would not know that the hormone had been used to make the milk. As soon as people understood the issue, they didn't want anything to do with it." Today, it is common for dairy products sold to consumers in the United States to carry hormone-free labels.

"This was an example of a corporation doing something that the political system could not do," said Liz. "The activists couldn't generate enough buzz. Politicians were never going to do anything unless we, as a company, took action. We showed that a corporation acting in an unselfish way to advance the public interest can do big, important things."

Stating the Values

Liz supported Perry's insistence on precision and accountability. She wrote that the social mission works best "when we have a definable outcome, set realistic goals, and stay with an issue for the time it takes to have an impact, like we did with the Children's Defense Fund. The results are better when we hold an issue campaign to the same high standards of any marketing initiative."

Liz had been arguing for years that the company's informal style had to adapt to the reality of hundreds of employees and a product whose future was overseas. "Ben & Jerry's had a history of blurry lines between functions," she said. "Meddling was expected, and decisions never seemed to be final. That was part of the culture." So when Perry asked Liz to define exactly what the social mission meant, what the company should do to pursue it, and equally important, what it should not do, she was happy to oblige. In fact, she had already been working on that question for several years.

Four years earlier, Liz had written a detailed chart summarizing the company's values and how they were expressed in four broad areas: the workplace, business practices, the environment, and social mission projects. "The workplace was on the chart because it was essential for the company's social values to be consistent," she said. "If we advocated for a social change, that change had to exist within the company."

Some of the items in the document known as "Liz's Chart" reflected actual conditions in the mid-1990s, but some of them didn't. Under the workplace section, she had listed the company's generous benefits, its dispute-resolution policies, and its commitment to safety. Yet the company's accident rate remained above the average for American food plants. The chart was really an unsorted wish list of goals and strategies, but it did put everything on paper for the first time.

In 1997, the board's social mission committee asked Liz to lead a discussion at the annual retreat in September. She gathered several previous attempts to talk about the social mission and tried to boil them down into one concise statement. "Some words came up over and over again," she said. "What I always liked about the company was that we went out and did things before we put them into words. We also had endless arguments about what our values were. So I wrote a statement to say, these are our values, with the hope that it would end the arguments."

The board worked on Liz's draft over the next two months, putting it through several iterations. In November, they titled it "Leading with Progressive Values Across Our Business" and approved it as "the company's definition of its social mission." The version they passed read as follows:

> We have a progressive, nonpartisan social mission that seeks to meet human needs and eliminate injustices in our local, national and international communities by integrating these concerns into our business activities. Our focus is on children and families, and the environment.

- The gap between the rich and the poor is wider than any time since the 1920s. We strive to create economic opportunities for those who have been denied them.

- Capitalism and the wealth it produces does not create opportunities for everyone equally. We practice caring capitalism by integrating concern for the disadvantaged in our day-to-day business activities, and by advancing new models of economic justice that can become sustainable and replicable.

- Manufacturing by definition creates waste. We strive to minimize our negative impact on the environment.

- The growing of food is increasingly reliant on the use of toxic chemicals. We support socially and environmentally sustainable methods of food production and family farming.

The U.S. continues to spend $265 billion [a year] on its military. This is four times what we spend combined on child health, welfare, education, nutrition, housing, job training, and environmental programs. We seek and support nonviolent ways to achieve peace and justice.

We strive to manifest a deep respect for human beings inside and outside our company and for the communities in which they live.

The progressive values statement was a big hit with Ben, Jerry, and Jeff. Today, the company still relies on a slightly modified version of the statement to define itself. It is an expansion of the three-part mission statement of 1988, which is actually painted on the wall of the CEO's office. But among the employees, Liz says, "there was never a complete buy-in, and that was fine. As long as you knew when you came in the door what we stood for, that's all we owed you.

"For example, when I was interviewing senior executives,

I would walk them around and point out that we invited people to bring their real selves to work. There were a lot of family pictures in the offices, and we had a good number of same-sex couples, and nobody had to hide their children or the fact that they were gay. So one good thing about the statement was, nobody came in surprised. Maybe you didn't share the company's commitment to progressive social change, but you knew what you were getting into."

The values statement was also part of a larger effort to balance the social mission with the profit imperative. As the board was mulling it over, Perry and Liz met with each department head to review their social mission objectives for 1998. Perry balanced those objectives against costs, and the social mission didn't always win. For example, the company abandoned an effort to make organic ice cream after research suggested that the product would be too expensive to sell. Ben was extremely disappointed, said Liz. And lots of old-timers were disappointed when Perry decided to stop making Peace Pops. But One Percent for Peace no longer existed, Perry told the *New York Times,* and "we said to ourselves, where is the equity? It's in the Ben & Jerry's name, not in the name Peace Pop."[2]

Creativity, and the ability to move quickly to seize opportunities, continued to be important elements of success in the company's social initiatives. Liz saw an opening on October 10, 1997, when the Nobel Prize committee announced that a Vermonter would be sharing the Peace Prize with her organization, the International Campaign to Ban Landmines. When that announcement came, the company had about forty thousand Peace Pops it didn't want. So Liz arranged for the pops to be shipped free to stores that agreed to collect signatures on an anti-landmine petition. The company delivered thousands of signatures to President Bill Clinton encouraging him to sign an international treaty banning land mines. Clinton didn't sign the treaty (and neither did Bush or

Obama), but more than 125 nations did send representatives to a signing ceremony in Ottawa, Ontario, on December 3. Thanks to Ben & Jerry's, Peace Pops were the most visible snack in the halls.

The Right Ingredients

Fair trade was another area where the company's efforts were paying off. Back in 1989, the expiration of an international agreement between coffee-producing countries had given American companies an opening to deal directly with coffee farmers. Ben & Jerry's was one of the first companies to do this. In 1990, they began buying coffee from a farmer's co-op in Oaxaca, Mexico, called Aztec Harvests. In the initial years of the contract, Ben & Jerry's accounted for more than 60 percent of Aztec Harvests' sales. In 1997, buying roughly the same amount of coffee, they accounted for just 20 percent.

Ben & Jerry's purchasing manager visited the coffee-growing village of Pluma Hidalgo in 1997. He reported in *Rolling Cone* that the village was at the end of a seven-mile jeep track that took him an hour to drive. Most of the farmers there were members of Aztec Harvests. But, he said, conditions in Pluma were middle class by Mexican standards. Unlike in neighboring villages, the children wore shoes.

Aztec Harvests succeeds as a "values-led supplier" because it has good answers to three important questions, according to Debra Heintz, who arrived at Ben & Jerry's in 1994 with experience in materials management, production, and systems analysis from larger companies. "First you have to ask, how consistent is our demand for what the supplier makes? Aztec Harvests worked well because we use coffee in several flavors, so if we stop making one of the flavors, we don't have to stop buying their coffee."

Ingredients the company doesn't use as much of are

riskier. "We have several uses for the brownies we buy from Greyston Bakery, too," said Debra. "But some ingredients, such as the apple pie we bought from La Soul, were for just one flavor, and the flavor didn't sell.

"The second question is, how many other customers does the supplier have? Aztec Harvests worked better because we went through a middleman who was successfully marketing their coffee to other businesses as well as ours. Also, we only bought half of their output for the first few years, even though we could have bought it all. It would have felt good to buy it all, but we didn't want to make them too dependent on us in case we had fluctuations in demand.

"This is a big contrast with Greyston. We have been buying brownies from them for twenty-five years, and in 2013 we were still buying more than three-quarters of the company's output. We and they would both like for them to diversify, to make their business more stable.

"The third question is, what is the quality and depth of the firm's leadership? The Aztec Harvests people are great partners because they have support from several organizations, but this isn't always the case. And these are just a few of the criteria we need to review before we leap into a relationship with a supplier.

"Of course, we also had some issues with lack of skills at Ben & Jerry's at that time. When we signed those contracts, we didn't have robust skill in purchasing or logistics. Those partnerships led us to some wonderful things, but in our enthusiasm, we also made some avoidable mistakes."

The people who built Ben & Jerry's had an abundance of passion and an incredible work ethic, and that worked well for fifteen years. But as any company gets bigger, its processes become more and more complicated, and past a certain point, hiring for passion doesn't work anymore. The St. Albans plant was a disaster because the company's leadership went into it believing that their employees were so talented that they could handle anything. They didn't consult an expert who actually knew how to build a big ice cream plant. The plant is running now because Chico hired that expert, Dave Vancura, who sorted it all out. Good intentions are not enough.

"Ben & Jerry's works best when we find ways to get both expertise and passion," said Debra. "People with specialized skills are essential. But if they don't have the passion, the company loses the thing that makes it so special. We need experts, and we also need people who are constantly challenging us and making us think outside the box. After all, we wouldn't even have a company if Ben had not found a way to mass-produce ice cream with chunks in it."

Outside the Box

Thinking outside the box is a specialty of Jeff Furman's. It has to be, because he advises small businesses on how to add social values and social benefits to their structures. The PartnerShops, the contract with Greyston Bakery, and other initiatives Jeff was involved with took enormous amounts of work. This wasn't a problem for Jeff because, like Ben, he is happiest when he is working for a start-up business or small advocacy group.

Jeff likes jobs that reward improvisation and quick action, and he doesn't like going through stages and channels to get things done. After the Los Angeles riots of 1992, for example, Jeff looked for ways to encourage young people in the South Central neighborhood to become entrepreneurs. He got a grant to turn a refrigerated truck into a mobile ice cream stand, and he arranged to staff it with teenagers from a neighborhood high school. The idea was to drive the truck a few miles north, to the campus of the University of Southern California, and sell ice cream there as a mobile Partner-Shop. Although USC backed out of the deal and the ice cream truck never rolled, Jeff kept working in LA. He later served on the board of a successful not-for-profit group, Food from the Hood, which awarded more than $250,000 in scholarships to Crenshaw High School graduates during its first two decades.

Ben & Jerry's paid Jeff as a business development consultant through the end of 1997. By the time his contract ended, he had supervised the launch of eight PartnerShops, including three in New York City, two in San Francisco, and one each in Ithaca, Baltimore, and Johnson, Vermont. He had also spent years launching and maintaining the shops in Russia. Each project was unique, and employees often found themselves in situations that few franchisers experience. The company's involvement in Russia ended abruptly in February 1996, for example, after organized criminals threatened to kill the employees and take over the stores.

The company's San Francisco partner was Juma Ventures, a start-up that offered jobs and stability to homeless youth. Franchise Site Selection Manager Carol O'Neill has fond memories of walking around at night in the Tenderloin neighborhood with the staffers of Juma Ventures, handing out condoms, donuts, and coffee to homeless teenagers. Juma has since become a far bigger operation. It works in three cities and employs more than 150 at-risk young people who put their earnings into college savings accounts. The money they earn is matched by other donors two to one.

The company opened four new PartnerShops in 1999. The most ambitious was in the lobby of the newly renovated Lawson House YMCA in Chicago. Lawson House is one of the largest single-room occupancy hotels in the state, and many of its residents were formerly homeless. The shop was part of a program that helped people move toward self-sufficiency, and it operated for five years. The Lawson project was similar to the successful shop operated by New York City's Common Ground, which expanded the roster by opening a satellite facility in Rockefeller Center. Two more shops were franchised to youth employment groups in Minneapolis, Minnesota, and Sarasota, Florida.

Jeff didn't do those deals, however. He had taught Carol O'Neill and other people how to do them, and they were taking the lead. In September 1997, Carol and a surprise guest, Rosanne Haggerty of New York City's Common Ground, traveled to Ithaca for the tenth anniversary of the first PartnerShop. The mayor

Jeff Furman hugs Carol O'Neill at the tenth-anniversary party for the Ithaca PartnerShop in 1997.

and other politicians served free cherries jubilee to more than two thousand people, and in true Ben & Jerry's fashion, there were musicians, jugglers, clowns, and prizes. The party peaked when Carol and Rosanne unfurled a scroll signed by Ben and Jerry that proclaimed Jeff the "Grand PooBah of PartnerShops" and awarded him the company's ultimate honor—membership in the Free Ice Cream for Life club.

In 1998, Jeff's only involvement with Ben & Jerry's was occupying seats on the boards of the company and its foundation. He left with a lot of satisfaction, but he also had an uneasy feeling. "You can't express all of the benefits of a social venture in a spreadsheet, especially in the beginning," said Jeff. "Social ventures are like any other start-up. It can take years to see their benefits. You have to be committed to the idea, and you have to keep pushing."

Jeff did keep pushing. But starting in 1998, a lot of his efforts went into other organizations. Managing a business as big as Ben & Jerry's required skills he did not have, and a lot of other groups wanted the skills he did have. It seemed like a good time to move on.

NINE

Unacceptable Choices

The employees of Ben & Jerry's thought it was kind of strange that their CEO, Perry Odak, didn't have a computer in his office. He had an inbox and an outbox and a desk, but he didn't keep much stuff in there at all. His wife and stepson had not moved to Vermont, and neither had several of the top managers he had hired. As one person who worked with him regularly put it, "He didn't want to leave any bread crumbs." So it's hard to say exactly when Perry decided the company would be better off sold.

He wasn't the only one with that idea, though. Any company that has a strong brand and a depressed stock price is a candidate for a takeover, and the stock of Ben & Jerry's had been depressed for several years.

In 1997, the two global giants of the ice cream industry—Unilever and Nestlé—were jockeying for position to buy the number one and number two American super-premium brands, Häagen-Dazs and Ben & Jerry's. Nestlé had an inside track because of its minority stake in Dreyer's, which was the major distributor for both brands in the United States. Unilever had spent the last few years acquiring ice cream companies in other countries, including Mexico, East Asia, and Thailand, under the direction of Kees van der Graaf. But if Unilever was going to get to the next level, they needed to acquire new skills. "We were very good in many aspects of the business but not very good in super-premium ice cream, and we also didn't know how to run ice cream shops," said Kees.

Two American companies knew how to do those things well. Häagen-Dazs had an advantage because it was an established brand outside the United States, but buying it wasn't practical. The big American company that owned Häagen-Dazs (Pillsbury) had been purchased by an even bigger British conglomerate (Grand Metropolitan) in 1988. Nine years later, as Unilever and Nestlé maneuvered, Grand Met merged with Guinness to form Diageo (an even bigger conglomerate). Diageo didn't want to sell any of its holdings until the dust settled.

The other choice was more than acceptable to Unilever, and it also looked like it might be headed for a sale. "We liked the way Ben & Jerry's did business," Kees said. "We thought they had a superior product, and they ran great stores." The three-part mission statement also intrigued the company's top executives, he added, although "I don't think we realized how important it was at first."

Dreyer's (with Nestlé standing behind them) was already deeply involved in the operation of Ben & Jerry's. Every year since the mid-1980s, the lawyer for Ben & Jerry's, Howie Fuguet, had helped negotiate their distribution agreement. "It was quite complex," he said. "It was more like an operating agreement." And, he adds, it was always clear that if Ben & Jerry's was ever interested in selling, Dreyer's would be interested in buying.

Several of Perry's coworkers believe that he did not want to sell the company at first. But Perry certainly knew how to sell companies and, as the offers came in, he listened. At some point in 1997, he took it a step further. "Perry reached out to me," said Richard Goldstein, who was the director of Unilever's North America operations. "He was shopping the business, although it clearly wasn't for sale. Neither Ben nor Jerry, if they knew about this, approved of it."

Perry's actions were mainstream behavior for top corporate executives in the merger-mad 1990s, and they would not have raised eyebrows at many other companies. But thirteen years after the sale, long-timers at Ben & Jerry's still resent what they call Perry's deceit. "No question, he was a good manager," said Pierre. "But his objectives were not in line with what the board would have preferred. I think if he had just come out and said he was setting the company up for a sale, most of the board would not have agreed. In fact, we didn't."

Yet board members have the ultimate authority in any company. They hired Perry, and they could have fired him or countered his moves. So why didn't they? According to Jeff, Perry was free to make his moves unnoticed in 1997 because the board was inexperienced. They believed that a professional manager like Perry should not require close supervision—in fact, they thought that it would be irresponsible to get too involved. "The phrase we used was 'nose in, fingers out,'" Jeff said. "We were trying to be more like a real corporate board. We thought that our job was to set the direction, and we should leave the execution to others."

Ben and Jerry, the board chair and vice chair, also had several other jobs. They were the company's chief spokesmen as well as full-time leaders of the movement for corporate social responsibility, and the two roles were intertwined. They spent several months in 1997 on a promotional tour for their book. They had collaborated with a writer to explain how the three-part mission worked and advise others on how to get started on their own versions of it. All profits from the book were going to a campaign to get corporate donations out of politics.

Ben also had a pivotal role at the Social Venture Network (SVN), according to Judy Wicks, the owner of Philadelphia's White Dog Café. Judy and Ben became close friends shortly after they met in 1992; Ben nominated her for SVN membership in 1993, and a few years later she was vice chair of the board. Judy says that in the 1990s, Ben and Anita Roddick, cofounder of the Body Shop, were SVN's box-office draws. "Back then, the goal was to get big so we could take on the big bad corporations and show that large companies could be led by their values," she said. "Ben and Anita were our heroes. They taught a whole generation that there is a caring way to do business. The movement that SVN serves has evolved a great deal over the last few decades, and they helped us do that."

In April 1997, Ben went to Washington because his group, Business Leaders for Sensible Priorities, was sponsoring a street performance by the Vermont-based Bread and Puppet Theater. He put on a costume the troupe called Uncle Fatso—a huge and distorted version of Uncle Sam. "I'm here because the country is giving the Pentagon more than it even asked for while it's cutting programs for kids in school, for health care, for women with children," he said in *Rolling Cone*. "It ain't right." Jerry was also in Washington that day, attending a press conference where business leaders and environmental groups called on the Clinton administration to regulate paper mills so that they would no longer produce dioxin, a potent carcinogen that is a by-product of the manufacturing process.

With so many invitations and so many urgent social problems, it was hard for Ben and Jerry to say no to an open microphone. The founders and Jeff were a lot better at organizing protests and pushing the social mission than they were at managing the problems of a business with almost seven hundred employees and multinational competition.

At the end of July 1997, Ben, Jerry, and Jennifer attended a meeting in Vermont with Perry and other employees. Perry called the meeting to assess the company's competitive position and generate new ideas. The group talked at length about the distribution problem. The company was now selling 55 percent of its ice cream to Dreyer's, and that share seemed likely to increase as Dreyer's continued to buy up small distribution companies. Ben & Jerry's desperately needed to find a new distribution partner, or some new way to get its product to customers, because, as Jeff puts it, "It's like selling shoes to Wal-Mart. When your company has just one customer, that customer owns you."

Two of the guests at the off-site meeting in July 1997 were from the Gordian Group, an investment bank that describes itself as "providing financial advisory services in distressed and complicated situations." "They did valuations," said Howie. "They determined how much a company was worth." It should have been clear to everyone who attended that the bankers were probably preparing the company to be sold. So at some level, the board must have known what was going on. Employees were warning them, but the board was still deadlocked. Board members who thought a sale made sense countered those who were opposed to selling. The company desperately needed to decide on a long-range strategic plan, but the board was stuck.

The managers considered developing new product lines, because 85 percent of the company's revenues came from pint sales. They kicked around the idea of selling cakes and pies, beverages, and yogurt. But Perry decided that the company's best bet was to stick to the original product and try to sell more ice cream. With the St. Albans plant, "the company had grown its production capacity way beyond its needs," he told a class at Cornell University in August 2000. "We had about 50 percent excess production capacity. So the incremental cost per gallon was relatively low, because all that overhead was sitting there anyhow."[1] Häagen-Dazs already had big, rapidly growing businesses in Europe and Japan. So Perry decided that the future of Ben & Jerry's depended on international markets.

There were also indications that Ben & Jerry's could succeed in Europe. As the Vermonters were wondering what to do, Helen Jones negotiated a deal that put Ben & Jerry's scoop stations inside a chain of about twenty movie theaters throughout the United Kingdom. "It worked like a spring-board," she said. "People tried the product and demand started to build. We were able to go to supermarket chains with pent-up demand on our side, so they would agree to our terms."

The social mission was also proving a viable export. "We looked for ways to establish the brand as fun and irrever-ent, with a social conscience," said Helen. It was important to emphasize showing the company's commitment to the social mission instead of just telling people about it: "The Body Shop had taken a terrible beating in the press over here, so I was wary of preaching."

Helen sent employees out to hold ice cream parties for volunteers who would do neighborhood-level activities like cleaning up a park or building a playground. She also bought a surplus American school bus and turned it into a mobile PartnerShop called the "Flying Friesian" (Friesian is the Eng-lish term for the black-and-white dairy cow Americans call a Holstein), which drove around the UK in the summer to raise funds for a child-advocacy organization. "We wanted to fit in," she said. "We weren't going to act like an arrogant Amer-ican company."

Shark vs. Anchovies

The final battle over the company's independence was joined early in 1998, when Perry told the board that Dreyer's had proposed a merger. He advised them to take the offer seri-ously. Henry Morgan, Fred Miller, and Andrew Patti agreed with Perry; they wanted to negotiate. Ben, Jeff, and Pierre were outraged by this suggestion. Liz, Jennifer, and Jerry also wanted the company to remain independent, but they were increasingly concerned that an independent Ben & Jer-ry's might not be able to compete. If the company's market share declined, people would lose their jobs, and that was unacceptable.

Perry and the board's executive committee (chaired by his old colleague and ally, Andrew Patti) drew up each meeting's agenda, which was somewhat unusual. Typically, the board's chair sets the agenda, but Ben had given this function away. In March 1998, Ben objected to his own committee's agenda, which included a discussion of anti-takeover provisions, a proposal for an executive committee that could act when the board could not be convened, and a proposal to ask shareholders to approve one million new shares of stock at the annual meeting. At one point, the board had to ask Ben and Perry to leave the room so discussion could continue. The board finally approved the proposals, with Ben, Jerry, and Jeff voting against them. Perry also blocked several social mission proposals made by the founders.

At the next meeting, in June, the board split over a proposal to amend their policy on stock options. The proposal allowed managers to vest all of their options, regardless of the original exercise dates, if the company had a change of ownership. At the meeting, Howie Fuguet said that the merger proposal from Dreyer's had "changed the assumption that the company would never be sold."

Looking back on that meeting, Howie explained that "accelerated vesting" proposals were fairly common. "They either protect management or enrich management, depending on your point of view," he said. "Sometimes, but not always, the top managers lose their jobs when control changes." Accelerated vesting was definitely not in the Ben & Jerry's stylebook, however. The motion passed 5 to 4, with Liz abstaining.

"I think that once Perry understood how divided the board was, he seized the opportunity," said Jennifer. "He saw a chance to sell the company and dissolve the board in one stroke. And the dynamic on the board was really weird. It started when Bob Holland was the CEO. Bob identified several things we needed to fix to make the company viable.

He was not a good fit for us, but he gave us good advice. We refused to take it. So we brought in Perry, and his ideas turned out to be similar to Bob's." The company needed to cut costs and invest more in long-term efforts to increase sales and solve the distribution problem. The only realistic way to do that was to cut salaries and benefits.

"We did not want to hear that," said Jennifer. "We wanted the answer to be something else. But the thing we really didn't like about Perry was his corporate style. It was so non–Ben & Jerry's. He used to say, 'It is what it is.' He was really telling us that we all have to fend for ourselves. If the board couldn't agree on a plan, by God, Perry was going to be the big dog and win, even if it meant taking the company down. That became clear in Lake Placid."

The Lake Placid Lodge is a resort in the style of grand Adirondack mountain camps, with a granite-and-timber mansion surrounded by cabins and outbuildings. The board gathered there on Sunday, September 13, 1998, for its annual three-day retreat. On Monday, Perry derailed the proceedings when he threatened to sue the board for violating the terms of his employment agreement. Ben's interference was making it impossible for him to do his job, he said. He also brought along a lawyer to show that he was serious. The meeting became a free-for-all between the pro-sale and anti-sale factions, with small groups forming and re-forming in an attempt to reach some solution that would satisfy both sides. Things got heated and personal. "It was god-awful," says Jennifer. "It was the beginning of an eighteen-month trail of tears."

The board eventually settled with Perry by agreeing that Ben and Jerry would switch roles and move. Jerry would become chair of the board, Ben would be vice chair, and both of them would move out of the company's South Burlington headquarters and into an office the company would rent for them downtown. "Ben and Jerry were waiting outside, and the board sent me out to tell them," said Jeff. "It was late afternoon and the guys were sitting on a porch swing, looking at the lake. I sat down with them and the three of us just marveled at the whole thing. They were fine with it. Actually, it was a beautiful moment." The three men were moving through their third decade as partners in a cause. Their friendship went deeper than the company.

Although love endured between Ben, Jeff, and Jerry, there wasn't much left on the board. "Perry was a command and control guy," said Jennifer. "He told me once that he had hired a private detective to check out each board member." The climate changed in the office, too. "Ben had always been adamant that we pay our farmers fairly, and I admired him for that," said Debra Heintz, who oversaw relationships with suppliers. "But the direction now was for us to negotiate tougher with farmers."

"His [Perry's] style was a lot less collaborative," said Dave Stever, the company's brand manager. "It was more like, 'This is what we're doing and this is how we're moving and this is where we're going.' There was less room for discussion."

"Perry was a shark in a sea of anchovies," said Tom D'Urso, the company's treasurer. "I don't think he did anything that was illegal, but I do think he betrayed the mission of the company. I always thought that our mission was to maximize value by optimizing the three equal parts of our mission—profit, product quality, and social change. Our definition of value was greater than net income. Perry either missed that, or he ignored it."

Employees have a story they like to tell to sum up the discomfort they felt with Perry. The company's annual meeting of franchise owners always ended with a big costume party, and one of the managers always came to the party in an outrageous drag outfit. But Perry refused to wear a costume. He showed up in his regular outfit of business casual clothes and cowboy boots because the party, for him, was clearly an obligation. As the party raged, Perry went into the men's room and encountered the manager, wearing his big frilly dress, at the urinal wall. The two men eyed each other in mutual disdain as they relieved themselves, both convinced that the other guy didn't belong there.

Social Mission Integration

Despite the turmoil on the board, there is ample evidence that working conditions at Ben & Jerry's improved as financial conditions improved. Surveys taken in 1997 and 1998 showed that employees were more likely to express confidence in the company's future, to say that their managers cared about what they thought, and to see the social mission as a critical part of the company's success. Every employee was awarded both company stock and stock options in 1998, too. As far as linked prosperity goes, Ben & Jerry's was walking the talk.

In 1997, the board's social mission committee asked Liz Bankowski and every department head to set social mission goals for the following year. They were ready to take things to a new level. Ben, Jeff, and other board members wanted to integrate the social mission horizontally by adding it to policies in every department, from manufacturing to human resources, operations, waste disposal, franchise operations, philanthropy, and finance. They also wanted to integrate the mission vertically by adding social metrics at every stage of the supply chain. This sometimes meant re-engineering the way the product was made.

One of the company's projects for 1998 involved shrinking the environmental footprint of the paper it used. Most paper mills in the 1990s used elemental chlorine to bleach their wood pulp from gray to white. The wastewater from this process was laced with several toxic chemicals, including dioxin, an extremely potent carcinogen. Ben & Jerry's pint cartons, like many food containers, were made of paper coated with white clay that made them impermeable on the inside and ready to take ink on the outside. The product would be just as appealing to consumers if the containers were made out of coated paper that wasn't bleached. By eliminating chlorine from the process, this switch would also eliminate a significant amount of dioxin from the waste stream. Ben was on the board of Greenpeace, and chlorine bleaching was one of the group's major concerns. But no one had ever made a food container out of unbleached paper before.

The "eco-pint" was unveiled in February 1999 after several years of development. By the end of that year, one-third of Ben & Jerry's packaging was made out of unbleached paperboard. The company had gone forward with its original plan despite the government's approval of a less-polluting alternative in 1998. A standard-size mill that adopted the new process, using chlorine dioxide as its bleaching agent, would produce between seven and ten tons of organochlorine-laced sludge a day, according to the Worldwatch Institute. This was a big improvement over the thirty-five tons a day produced by elemental chlorine. But the company's goal was to transform the process, not just to improve it.

Sticking with unbleached paperboard was more expensive. But "our goal was to eliminate the use of chlorine bleach to whiten paper," said the company's environmental impact guru, Andrea Asch. "Our hope was that if we made the change, other companies would be encouraged to join us." Ben & Jerry's had been a corporate leader in environmental impact reduction in 1992, when it signed the CERES principles, and again in 1994, when it added a label certifying that it did not use ingredients produced with bovine growth hormone. The company hoped that with the eco-pint, it might happen again.

Ben & Jerry's also made changes at the other end of the supply chain, launching a long-term effort to reduce the environmental impact of dairies and other livestock farms. Feed, manure, and fertilizers are loaded with nitrogen and phosphorus. These chemicals become pollutants when they wash out of agricultural soils in large amounts and end up in rivers and lakes. In 1999, Ben & Jerry's joined with a grain company, experts at Cornell University and the University of Vermont, its main dairy supplier (the St. Albans co-op), and two pilot farms to look for ways to reduce runoff in small, practical ways.

The goal of the dairy initiative was to make a more significant impact by encouraging people to think in broader terms. Ben & Jerry's had considered and rejected the idea of producing organic ice cream because of its expense, despite its social benefits. Instead of staying out of the discussion, however, the company decided to double down. They broadened the discussion by committing to something their academic partners called "sustainable agriculture." This field was almost unknown in 1999. It does not define success in terms of avoiding all synthetic chemicals. Instead, its goal is broader, using farming methods that follow the principles of ecology.

The company's commitment to job training was also changing. It had set a goal of opening five new PartnerShops in 1998, but various barriers and complications kept it from opening any. Even though a new program coordinator (Martha Lunbeck) helped Ben & Jerry's open four shops owned by nonprofits in 1999, Liz was rethinking the whole idea. "The PartnerShops worked best when they trained teenagers," she said. "The jobs they created weren't as suitable for a single mother with two kids." One problem was that Ben & Jerry's ice cream stores worked best in places with a lot of upscale foot traffic, and the rent for these places was often expensive. Small not-for-profit groups often couldn't sustain the substantial effort and resources needed to keep a shop alive. Liz decided to start seeking partnerships with local economic development agencies instead.

Ben & Jerry's also took steps in 1999 to integrate the social mission into its overseas operations. It adopted global operating guidelines aimed at protecting the brand's image and the three-part mission in other countries. The company said it would look at each country's human-rights record and take steps to address any issues, and it would also try to express its activism in ways that respected local cultures. "We tried to imagine how we would translate the mission to other countries back then," said Helen Jones. "We had so few resources that we didn't really have a chance to test our theories. But we talked about all kinds of things."

At the end of 1999, the company tried to tie all these ideas together at a higher level. Senior employees from the international division joined others from marketing, purchasing, public relations, research and development, information systems, finance, human resources, retail operations, sales, environmental, and the Ben & Jerry's Foundation in an interdepartmental values council, which was charged with reviewing the company's progress on social initiatives, generating new ideas, and encouraging cross-departmental cooperation. The council's first quarterly meeting happened in December.

Also in 1999, a national survey found that Ben & Jerry's was one of the best-regarded companies in the United States. The public gave it the fifth-best reputation in the country, which was particularly significant because the top four finishers (Johnson & Johnson, Coca-Cola, Hewlett-Packard, and Intel) were so much larger. Coca-Cola probably spent more on public relations than Ben & Jerry's spent on salaries. Ben & Jerry's was a small company whose impact was huge.

In the 1999 annual report, social auditor James Heard said, "Ben & Jerry's most impressive achievement regarding its social mission is the way in which it has institutionalized the company's values into decision-making. The company's values are reflected in matters small and large ... Social mission objectives are part of every manager's job, from the Chief Executive Officer on down, and these objectives have also been incorporated into the company's strategic and operating plans.... While the company may sometimes have fallen short in achieving its social mission goals, it demonstrates a commitment to progressive values that few companies can match." Heard didn't know it, but he was writing a sort of eulogy. He submitted his audit in March 2000, just a few weeks before the company was sold.

Chairman Jerry

Jerry has said that he spends most of his time just following Ben Cohen around, and he often describes himself as an ordinary, uninteresting person. His friends disagree. Jerry's eighteen-month term as chair of the board was exceptionally demanding, and he bore the burden with grace and skill. He was the one person everyone trusted, with superior diplomatic abilities and an unfailingly positive approach. And "he also got results," said one board member. "If he hadn't stepped in when he did, the company might not have survived."

Jerry started chairing board meetings in November 1998. The company's options were narrowing and Ben was, once again, out. Ben had a tendency "to either be extremely overinvolved in the company's business, or to be completely withdrawn from it," said Pierre. "This kind of behavior went on for years, and it created chaos." In April 1999, Ben did not contribute to the annual report; in June, he skipped the One World One Heart festival; and in September, he didn't go to the board's annual retreat on Cumberland Island.

Jennifer says she and Jerry became a two-person caucus because they were both undecided about the sale and, unlike Liz, Perry was not their boss. "Jerry was weary of all the fighting," she says. "He believed that Ben would leave if Ben could not get the company the way he wanted it to be. So the question was, what would the company be without Ben?"

The meetings were endless and exhausting, and the directors were legally prohibited from saying anything unless they reported it to all the shareholders. "They wouldn't ever talk to employees about what they were doing in the boardroom," said public relations manager Sean Greenwood. "But it was obvious that these meetings were intense. They would come out of them looking like they had been in a fistfight.

"They always said the same words to us. Eventually they printed their mantra on buttons that they wore, and they handed them out to us to wear, too. The buttons said, 'No decisions have been made, no conclusions should be drawn, we remain hopeful.'" Even at the end, Jerry kept trying to make things fun.

One of the board's tasks was creating legal barriers to discourage hostile takeovers. For years the founders had controlled about three-quarters of the company's B shares, each of which had ten votes. In 1998, they took two more precautions. They successfully lobbied the Vermont legislature to pass the "Ben & Jerry's law," which authorized the directors of corporations chartered in the state to consider issues beyond shareholder wealth when making decisions. The law's intent was to defray lawsuits shareholders often file when a board does not say yes to the highest bidder. It authorizes directors to consider such matters as "the interests of the corporation's employees, suppliers, creditors, and customers; the economy of the state, region, and nation; [and] community and societal considerations, including those of any community in which any offices or facilities of the corporation are located."[2]

In August, the board also passed a shareholder rights plan

to block "creeping takeovers." If any party bought a large block of stock, the board could immediately issue enough new shares to existing shareholders to dilute the interloper's position. The key word in these anti-takeover measures, however, is "hostile." "The whole purpose of anti-takeover laws is to leave the decision power with the board of directors, and not with whoever wants to take over the company," said Howie. "That is why the special voting power of the B shares was revocable by a simple majority vote of the board. The board has ultimate legal authority, not the founders or anyone else."

Ben brought his lawyer to the November 1998 meeting and proposed that all directors should have the right to hire and invite their own lawyers at company expense. Soon thereafter, a small crowd of sober, well-dressed men started lurking silently outside board meetings. "If you said something in a board meeting in late 1998 or 1999, you would be held to what you had said, even if you were just thinking out loud," Jennifer said. "Informal discussions became impossible."

Meanwhile, the industry's freeze on Ben & Jerry's was starting to harden. During the summer of 1999, Perry told the board three pieces of bad news. First, Dreyer's would soon announce the launch of "Dreamery," their own super-premium brand. Second, Unilever might be developing its own super-premium ice cream. And, worst of all, Nestlé's and Dreyer's were becoming the coowners of a new venture, Ice Cream Partners LLC, which would hold exclusive rights to produce and distribute Häagen-Dazs in the United States.

These were serious threats. If Dreyer's had equity in Häagen-Dazs, it would give that brand priority over Ben & Jerry's in its distribution network. Häagen-Dazs would get more space in the nation's freezer cases and better deals with grocery store owners. If Ben & Jerry's could not find an alternative distributor to Dreyer's, it would not be able to compete. Dreyer's was also pushing Dreamery, which could force Ben & Jerry's down further—instead of the number two brand nipping at Häagen-Dazs's heels, the company would be stuck at number three. And if Unilever, which had its own distribution system, added a super-premium brand, Ben & Jerry's might end up with the low spot on the totem pole. In an industry where overall sales were not growing quickly, this was not a viable place to be.

"Ben kept saying let's just keep going, keep trying things," said Jeff. "We had beaten Pillsbury, we had beaten Monsanto, and somehow we would beat these guys too. But the board was getting tired of fighting. They were also concerned about their responsibilities to shareholders and employees."

"Henry Morgan kept telling Ben that it was not his company any more, and that he had given it up on the day he sold stock," said Jennifer. He spoke for a growing number who framed the issue as Ben playing with other people's money. As the crisis deepened, people turned away from Ben because he couldn't offer a compelling solution. "It just seemed like a terrible situation with no good answers, no options," Ben said on the 2006 episode of *Biography*. "And I find those things very difficult."[3]

Ben's unwillingness to compromise was his greatest strength, but also his greatest flaw. It's a general rule in governing bodies that once a coalition is irretrievably broken, its leaders should resign and give other folks a chance. Only one member of the board of Ben & Jerry's followed that rule. In June 1999, Liz resigned from the board, although she kept her job as director of social mission. "I felt that if we really wanted this company to survive, we needed to let other people take the reins," she said. Her departure left the board with eight voting members. Perry, Henry, and Fred wanted to sell. Jeff, Ben, and Pierre didn't. Jennifer and Jerry were the crucial swing votes.

The Gathering Storm

Jeff sat on the porch of the Greyfield Inn on September 13, 1999. He was looking out at the ocean, searching for signs of a hurricane. The Greyfield is a colonial-style mansion on Cumberland Island, Georgia. It was built for Andrew Carnegie's niece, who owned the entire island before the family donated it to the National Park Service, and it is now a four-star hotel. The beach was secluded and spectacular. But Jeff was miserable.

The board of Ben & Jerry's was having its annual retreat at Greyfield, and its members had just voted to begin sale negotiations. They had spent years fending off potential buyers, and now Jeff feared that they had given up. The board was also considering closing one of the company's plants, which meant that seventy-five employees might lose their jobs. At the same time, some of Jeff's colleagues were talking about vesting stock options, awarding bonuses to top managers, and following legal tactics that Jeff, a lawyer, didn't think were necessary or even ethical.

Jeff's family was far away in New York, many of his allies were even farther away in Vermont, and Ben himself—the company's cofounder, muse, and vice chair of the board—was nowhere to be seen. Jerry, the other cofounder and current board chair, was gamely running things. Every once in a while he and Jeff would make eye contact, and Jeff noticed that Jerry looked just as sad as he was. Both of them feared that they were losing the social mission and the soul of Ben & Jerry's—in other words, their life's work.

Twelve years before, the board had committed Ben & Jerry's to three equal and interrelated goals: making the world's best ice cream, promoting progressive social change, and providing decent financial returns for employees and, oh yes, shareholders. Now the last of these, the shareholders, were speaking the loudest. How had it come to this?

The rest of the meeting hadn't been any fun, either. The company was losing market share to Häagen-Dazs. Dreamery was expected to take away more market share, starting immediately. The company's distribution agreement with Dreyer's had just expired, and after thirteen years, it was not renewed. The stores Dreyer's had serviced would be covered temporarily by Ice Cream Partners, but this was not a viable long-term plan. The company's sales director had been researching alternative forms of distribution. He reported that a patchwork system of smaller distributors would have big gaps, and filling in those gaps would be expensive. Switching to a warehouse distribution system would probably mean significant declines in product quality, as well as a 40 percent decline in sales.

Richard Goldstein, the chief of Unilever North America, said that the social mission and the split on the board of directors "came up in my early discussions with Perry. When he explained to me the complexity of the situation, and the social mission, and the this and the that, I had to go through an educational process. I really had to spend some time understanding what we were talking about."

Goldstein knew that the company's value would be greatly reduced if he could not gain the support of its charismatic cofounders. "Without Ben and Jerry, the company would not be worth buying," he said. But he also needed to craft a deal that would get past his bosses in London and Rotterdam. "I did a considerable number of acquisitions for Unilever," he said. "The Ben & Jerry's acquisition was fairly small, relative to the other companies we bought, but it took me almost two years. I never did another deal that was remotely like it."

TEN

The Sale Agreements

Richard Goldstein's office was on the twenty-first floor of Lever House, the landmark mid-twentieth-century skyscraper in midtown Manhattan where Unilever executives ran their North American operations. The first time Ben and Jerry met him there, "They had to walk down a corridor to get to our conference room," he said. "And they took their time, chatting with everybody. They stopped at each desk and gave all the secretaries coupons for free ice cream.

"They were dressed in T-shirts and jeans, just like they dressed in Vermont. To them, nothing had changed—they just happened to be in New York. The staff never forgot them, though, and Ben and Jerry did the same thing every time they showed up. But then the meetings would start, and there were many, many meetings. This wasn't a quick deal."

Goldstein says he charmed and reassured Ben and Jerry until they decided they could trust him. At the same time, he worked to narrow their options until the price of holding on to the company became too high. Although Ben and Jerry tried to put a good face on the deal, it was intensely painful for both of them. Ben summed up their feelings about the sale when he said, "It was just about the worst day of my life."[1]

It was also a painful time for Jeff and others on the board of directors. A narrow majority of board members struggled to support a plan that would take the company private, preserve the three-part mission in its original form, and keep Ben in some kind of senior management role. The private equity

deal stayed alive until five days before the board signed the
company over to Unilever. The private deal meant round-
the-clock meetings for the people who were trying to put it
together, and it was an exasperating sideshow for those who
didn't want it to happen.

Even after the sale, Ben, Jeff, and Pierre wanted to believe
that going private could have succeeded. Ben & Jerry's had
beaten Pillsbury in 1984 and Monsanto in 1996, and perhaps somehow they could have found a way to beat Unilever and Nestlé, too. They were trying to go back to the old
days, when they were underdogs who somehow succeeded
at things everyone told them were impossible.

"It's classic Ben," Jerry said in the *Biography* profile. "I
mean, he's thinking outside the box. He isn't deterred by
other people and so-called experts telling him that he doesn't
know what he's doing."[2] For twenty-two years, the company had been gleefully thumbing its nose at the experts. Its
beloved brand—the very thing Unilever wanted—was built
around that spirit.

Perhaps Ben could have done it again. He came close.
But this time, he couldn't get enough people who were willing to join him in battle. The company had gotten too big.
With hundreds of jobs and several hundred million dollars of
shareholder money on the table, the stakes were too high.
"I remember, just after the sale, the three of us were sitting
together, feeling incredibly depressed," said Jeff. "I tried to
say something to make us feel better. The best I could do
was, 'We failed because we succeeded.'" They were in the
same place that Chuck Lacy had been in 1994. They lost control of the company because it got bigger than they were.

The media gave Ben & Jerry's another drubbing after the
sale. Ben, Jerry, and the company they founded would never
regain the esteem they enjoyed when Ben & Jerry's was
independently owned. Yet the social mission did endure,
and so did the company. Ben & Jerry's still exists today as a

Vermont-based corporation, and Unilever does not control every aspect of its operation. Ben & Jerry's has a three-part mission, and Unilever controls the economic part. The product quality and social missions are still largely controlled by the independent board of Ben & Jerry's Homemade, Inc.

It's a unique arrangement and a hard one to describe, which is why almost everyone missed it. It was much easier to believe the standard story of a big soulless company gobbling up a small, plucky firm, belching contentedly, and continuing on its relentless path. After all, that is what happened to the Body Shop, Aveda, Horizon Organics, Odwalla, Cascadian Farm, and many other socially responsible businesses founded in the 1970s and 1980s. But the people who work for Unilever are not soulless, and Ben & Jerry's did not surrender unconditionally. They kept trying.

Soap and Margarine

"The only reason we were successful in this acquisition is because Ben and Jerry became convinced that Unilever would honor its word," said Goldstein. "There was no point in buying the brand unless we could get the founders to agree that this is what they wanted." So in those early meetings, he listened and kept his position flexible.

Goldstein and Unilever had several advantages over Dreyer's, their chief rival in the competition for Ben & Jerry's. First, the long business relationship between Dreyer's and Ben & Jerry's had not exactly been warm or friendly. "When Dreyer's first made their offer in 1998, their guy read to us from a sheet of handwritten notes on a yellow pad," said Pierre Ferrari. "He made promises about the social mission that were very specific." But they didn't ring true. After more than a decade of haggling over distribution agreements and fact-checking business practices, Ben and his allies were convinced that a merger with Dreyer's would be strictly business. The social mission would be abandoned. They said no.

Another advantage was Goldstein's considerable skill as a negotiator. "I never saw the man read from a piece of paper," said Jennifer. "He not only remembered everyone's name, he also remembered what each person's last thoughts had been. He was like a soap opera writer. He'd remember and say that Fred had glared at Jennifer while she was looking at Jeff to see what Jeff's reaction would be. The guy was so smart that I suspected he was not from this planet. I wanted to trail his ass after the meeting to see if he got on a spaceship."

Goldstein and other top Unilever executives of the 1990s needed to have superior diplomatic skills. The company had two chairmen—Antony Burgmans, who ran the company's offices in the Netherlands, and Niall Fitzgerald, in London. This meant executives often had to guess which man would be in charge in any given situation. "It was sort of like being a child in a family," said Goldstein. "There were certain things where you'd turn to your dad, and other things where you would go to your mom, and then there were some issues where you knew darned well you had better talk to them both."

Diplomacy was also important because Unilever does business in over a hundred countries. It is the second-largest food company in the world, behind Nestlé and in front of Kraft. Running something this large requires as much statecraft as it does traditional business management, which is fitting: in 2013, Unilever's market cap was slightly bigger than the GDPs of Bangladesh, Angola, or Morocco. And size has its advantages. To Unilever, spending more than $300 million to acquire Ben & Jerry's was small potatoes.

The company also has its own version of a social mission. It was founded in 1930 when two European companies, Lever Brothers in England and Margarine Unie in the Netherlands, joined forces to gain greater control of palm oil plantations and other farms in Asian and African colonies. The Dutch family-owned firms that merged to become Unie had been instrumental in developing margarine in the late nineteenth century. William Lever, founder of the English company, was the first grocery wholesaler to cut large blocks of soap into small, prepackaged cakes that were inexpensive and ready to use.

Both companies were founded in the spirit of doing well by doing good. Margarine was a longer-lasting and more sanitary alternative to butter, which was an important source of calories but was often too expensive for working-class families. Lever's innovation put better hygiene within reach of working-class families while also making him rich. But Lever's legacy came from his decision to increase the loyalty and productivity of his workers by paying them well and also offering them pensions, unemployment benefits, company cafeterias, and an eight-hour day. Benefits like these were almost unheard of in Victorian England, but Lever Brothers prospered. Lord Lever (he was raised to the peerage in 1917) even built a model village, Port Sunlight, where his factory workers lived in relative luxury with their own medical clinic, school, and art gallery.

Unilever's public relations folks like to say that their company's commitment to humane and ethical behavior goes all the way back to its origins. They are not as eager to add that one reason for Lever Brothers' profitability was its reliance on forced labor in the Belgian Congo, or that Lord Lever was directly involved in enforcing that horrific system, but nobody's perfect.[3] In 2000, Unilever contributed about $60 million (€44 million) to local groups for education, arts and culture, environmental protection, health, economic development, sports, and disaster relief in seventy-eight countries. Its giving amounted to 1.37 percent of the company's profit after taxes that year. And the company characterized more than $20 million of its giving as long-term "social investment," or sustained involvement in a social issue that related to Unilever's business interests.[4]

Unilever executives say that the company's size gives it leverage to advance social goals in ways that go beyond philanthropy. "Their strategy is to work from within," said Kees van der Graaf, who served on Unilever's board and held a variety of top-level positions. "And therefore you shouldn't be afraid to go early into suspicious countries. You should go right in and help establish better ways of working there. Unilever never stopped operating in South Africa, for example, although they were against apartheid right from the beginning. They made it clear to the regime that Unilever employees had equal rights inside their factories and if you don't like that, we will leave your country." The threat had teeth, because Unilever's direct and indirect employment accounts for about 1 percent of South Africa's workforce.

Ben & Jerry's would never have chosen to make ice cream in South Africa during apartheid, and Unilever's corporate giving ratio might have seemed puny in comparison to the 7.5 percent of pretax profits Ben & Jerry's contributed. But both companies subscribed to the 250-year tradition that started when Quaker merchants used private-sector tools to advance social goals. "I wasn't troubled by the social mission," said Goldstein. "Giving to charity and choosing suppliers because of their good practices was not terribly unusual for us. We did it around the world."

Jerry's Decision

Ben & Jerry's sale negotiations officially began on August 4, 1999, when a Unilever banker made a telephone call to the Gordian Group to start putting together an offer. Ben & Jerry's had considered and turned down an offer from Dreyer's the previous year. Perry Odak had been in regular contact with both Unilever and Dreyer's since then. But that was just talk. In August, as the company's distribution system was falling apart, the board had to take all offers seriously.

The negotiations began in earnest after the board and senior managers returned from Cumberland Island. Ben & Jerry's proposed to Dreyer's that they create a joint venture for distribution that would have similarities to the partnership Dreyer's and Nestlé had formed to make and distribute Häagen-Dazs. The board abandoned this idea by the end of October. They asked Dreyer's if it was interested in resuming merger discussions, but Dreyer's said no. Ben & Jerry's also proposed a similar distribution scheme to Unilever. Goldstein also said no, but he added that Unilever was still interested in buying Ben & Jerry's outright, for cash.

Ben and Pierre also asked Perry to investigate and respond to ideas about how to keep the company independent. Ben submitted a long list of ideas and questions, including forming strategic partnerships with other socially responsible food companies, choosing a limited number of licensed retailers, offering home delivery (with marketing through a website or email), and putting pint vending machines (which could be maintained by local not-for-profit groups) outside high-traffic locations like post offices, video stores, and volunteer fire departments. He also suggested that the company appeal directly to its customers, as it had in the Doughboy campaign. The campaign should inform loyal Ben & Jerry's customers about global consolidation in the ice cream industry and the company's efforts to remain independent, he said. It should implore them to buy the product and demand it from their retailer. Ben and Pierre recommended that the company make small investments in all of these ideas, then increase their stake in the ones that succeeded.

Pierre added that some of the potential business combinations being discussed might create antitrust issues, which he asked the company's lawyer, Howie Fuguet, to address. He also suggested that the company take aggressive steps to counter the launch of Dreyer's super-premium brand (Dreamery); explore sales through institutional food service; try an aggressive, risky "values-led" initiative to "re-energize the brand"; and, most of all, don't rush to a deal. It was important to test these ideas in the marketplace before deciding the company's future, he said.

Perry responded to each of Ben and Pierre's points at a board meeting on November 18. He had investigated all the food companies Ben mentioned and had concluded that partnering with them would be too expensive and risky. Licensed retailers would be a legal nightmare, he said—and besides, products that are bought on impulse, like ice cream, need to be as widely available as possible. Home delivery, Internet marketing, and vending machines might be significant in the long run, but they wouldn't save the company over the next few months. Howie added a memo saying that he did not see any antitrust issues that would block a deal.

The board decided to hire a management consultant and appoint Jeff and Pierre to work with them on realistic ideas for remaining independent. But after Perry's convincing smackdown of Ben and Pierre, the prospects were not encouraging. And the mood didn't get any lighter when the Gordian Group presented its financial analysis.

Earnings as a percentage of sales would almost certainly decline if the company remained independent, said the bankers. Sales in supermarkets and convenience stores in the United States were already declining, with no turnaround in sight. If the company increased sales in other countries and through its franchisees, the overall effect would be a wash. In other words, if the company executed its present strategy perfectly, there would be no growth and eventual layoffs. If anything went wrong and sales declined, the layoffs would happen sooner.

Two offers were on the table on November 18: Unilever's and a surprise all-cash offer from the European ice cream firm

Roncadin, which started the bidding at $32 a share (although this offer was quickly withdrawn). On November 30, Goldstein said that Unilever was prepared to pay $33 to $35. Also on that day, Dreyer's said it was ready to reopen discussions of a merger or some other arrangement. The board met on December 1 to consider the three offers and also draft a press release because someone had let the cat out of the bag. Ben & Jerry's stock was trading heavily, with its price headed up. The board would be vulnerable to charges of mismanagement if it didn't say something.

On December 2, Ben & Jerry's issued a press release saying it had received "indications of interest to be acquired at prices significantly above recent stock closing prices." The share price rose from $21 to over $27, and another media deluge began. "We were under siege," said Jennifer. "We couldn't meet in Vermont anymore because it would attract too much attention. We were legally prohibited from talking to anybody, but strangers kept calling me at home. We all put our spouses through hell."

What Jennifer couldn't say was that the most important decision had already been made. According to several people who were involved in the meetings, at some point during the fall of 1999, probably during one of those tense, endless sessions, Jerry decided that selling the company was the lesser of two evils. Ben, Jeff, and Pierre still wanted to remain independent, even if it meant shrinking the company. But Jerry became convinced that an independent Ben & Jerry's could not succeed, and when he changed his mind, Jennifer did too. The vote became five to three.

This break was painful to everyone, especially the founders. "Seeing the strain on their friendship hurt me more than losing the company," said Jeff. "It was this awful combination of rage and despair. It was the way you feel when someone you care for is in danger and you can't do anything about it. I remember telling people, 'If Ben and Jerry lose each other over this, I don't care what the number is. It's not worth that.'"

Employees say that at the end of 1999, they felt like children watching their parents head for divorce. "It was a helpless feeling," said brand manager Dave Stever. "We weren't part of the process, so we didn't know what was going to happen. But a lot of us had friends who had gone through stuff like this, and typically it doesn't turn out well."

So the company would be sold. The question was, to whom?

The Dark Horse

When Terry Mollner heard that Ben & Jerry's was for sale, he got so upset that he smacked his hot tub. "I had finished a training session for the men's group I belong to, and afterwards a few of us jumped in to relax. I told them about it and I got so angry that I started slapping the water. This was horrible. This could not happen. So then one of my friends said, 'Why don't you do something about it?'"

This was not an idle taunt. Terry was prominent in the world of socially responsible investing. As a cofounder and board member of Calvert Social Funds, he had been active in the field since it started. He was acquainted with most members of the Social Venture Network, including Ben. "Still in the hot tub, I get an idea," he said. "Ben & Jerry's could use all the publicity around the sale to raise money to buy out its shareholders and go private. The holding company that owns Ben & Jerry's would be the beginning of a conglomerate that would buy all the other socially responsible companies that are headed for the block, like Stonyfield Yogurt, the Body Shop, and Honest Tea. It would be a socially responsible Berkshire Hathaway.

"I called Ben the next day. He remembered who I was, although we weren't friends. I told him my idea and he said, 'It's too late. The board has decided to sell the company to Dreyer's. They meet in a few days. It's all over.' He was really depressed.

"I asked Ben if he wanted to stop the sale and he said that of course he did, but they had already agreed on a price—$265 million. Neither of us had any idea of where we could find that much money that fast, but Ben agreed to let me try." Terry and Judy Wicks, the founder of Philadelphia's White Dog Café and a close friend of Ben's, spent the next few days on the phone. They persuaded twenty-five prominent socially responsible investors and business owners to form an investment group, with Terry as the spokesman. Their banker was a friend of Terry's who had just set up an investment group called Meadowbrook Capital, with Terry on the board.

Ben took Meadowbrook's proposal to pay $265 million "or best offer" to the board and asked for more time to get the money together. The group didn't have any significant equity, said Terry, "so it still seemed impossible. But people said we were crazy when we started Calvert, too, and today Calvert is managing $12 billion. Doing the impossible is where the fun lies!" Terry gets a gleam in his eye when he says this. He is a fairly large man with a salt-and-pepper beard, and he wiggles in his chair like an excited boy. He is the kind of person you could talk to for hours. Needless to say, Ben was galvanized.

"I remember once, long ago, I asked Ben why he was always so confident that his crazy ideas would work," said Jennifer. "He said, 'It's a funny thing. The more I believe in an idea, the more creative I get.' That comment changed my life."

As the board considered Ben's request for more time, interesting things started to happen. Protestors gathered outside the company's store in Burlington. They spray painted "Don't Sell Out Vermont!" on the wall outside the store. They suggested new flavors called "Chubby Bureaucrat," "Funky Money," and "Two-Faced Swirl." Congressman Bernie Sanders and Mayor Peter Clavelle attended the rally. Governor

Howard Dean also joined the fight because, he said, Ben & Jerry's needed to stay in Vermont. It was one of the state's most important ambassadors.

Garret LoPorto, a web designer in Massachusetts, put up a site to encourage people opposed to the sale to buy shares so that they could vote against it. LoPorto also put the company up for sale on eBay, with a starting bid of $10 million. "Ben & Jerry's has been one of the few truly noble businesses of our time," he wrote. But now, he added, giant corporations "want to skin the company alive and use its gentle lamb-skin brand identity to fool unsuspecting consumers into purchasing their soulless profit driven products."[5] Maybe Dick Goldstein was right. If the founders did not stay around to reassure their customers that it was still Ben & Jerry's, the brand might not be worth buying.

Jennifer voted with Jeff, Ben, Pierre, and Jerry to give the Meadowbrook offer more time and delay the sale of the company. "Perry was cussing mad at me," she said. "He said I was ruining things and that I didn't know what I was doing." Perry had been working hard to close the deal. If the company had taken Dreyer's original offer, a stock swap at $31 a share, Perry would get a pretax capital gain of more than $8 million. But Jennifer held firm. "It seemed to me that the people who loved us were trying to help us," she said, "and we should let them give it their best shot."

Ben started pushing on two fronts. Meadowbrook was his plan A, but Goldstein's skill and flexibility had made Unilever into a possible plan B. "Ben doesn't get enough credit for it, but he is an incredibly shrewd businessman," said Jennifer. "He was disciplined," said Pierre. "He pushed the process. The sale agreements have precise numbers in them. That was Ben."

The Meadowbrook offer couldn't proceed unless Ben had access to current financial data from Ben & Jerry's—but at that time, even though he was vice chair of the board, he couldn't get current numbers from Perry or Fran. "He invited me up to his house and asked me what I thought of Perry," said Tom D'Urso, who was the company's treasurer. "I told Ben I thought Perry was betraying the company, and I'd do anything to help Ben win." Tom started sharing data with Ben and his assistant in after-hours meetings in Ben's downtown office. So even though Meadowbrook didn't have funders, it did have an important advantage. It could base its offer on the same numbers Ben & Jerry's used.

Ben laid out several nonnegotiable conditions at his first meeting with Richard Goldstein at Unilever. Even after a sale, he said, the company must have an independent, self-perpetuating board to act as a watchdog, with legal powers to maintain the social mission and the quality of the product. "This was highly unusual," said Goldstein. "Ordinarily when we bought a company, we bought it all. For a company to retain its own board after they have been wholly acquired, it would have to be because the country's government insisted on it."

Goldstein thought that this one time, Unilever might be willing to make an exception. "I felt that what we were giving him, in the end, didn't matter much to Unilever," he said. "We were getting the brand. We were getting the business. They would have their own board of directors, but we would control what I regard as the key factor in success or failure, which is the selection of the chief executive. The board of Ben & Jerry's didn't have the right to appoint the CEO. Ben needed to be comfortable with the choice, but it would be our choice."

Plus, Goldstein liked Ben and Jerry. "Neither of them ever had a hidden agenda," he said. "They were completely open about what was important to them." Howie Fuguet says he thinks Dick Goldstein was also "awed by our financial performance. He was thinking this is odd, this is crazy, but wow, it makes money too!"

Shaping the Sale Agreements

After Ben and Dick Goldstein had agreed in principle, Gold-stein went to see the chief counsel of Unilever USA, Ronald Soiefer. "He told me I was going to work on this acquisition, and that it was going to be complicated," Soiefer said. "He said the job was to collaborate with them to create a gover-nance structure that would set our bid apart from any others."

It wasn't hard to figure out each side's goals. Unilever mainly wanted to buy the company and operate it in a way that was consistent with their policies, said Soiefer. They also needed to retain the loyalty of Ben & Jerry's custom-ers, win the competition with Dreyer's, and overcome the general suspicion some Ben & Jerry's board members felt toward multinational corporations. A contract that protected the three-part mission might help achieve the last three goals without interfering with the main ones.

Ben & Jerry's wanted to stay independent, but if that was impossible, the company wanted to preserve its historical mission and the integrity of the brand forever. "Perpetuity is what really distinguishes this deal from other deals involving socially responsible businesses," Soiefer said. "The board of Ben & Jerry's is not going away. They will always be pushing to integrate the social mission throughout the company and keep the company's operations transparent. It isn't like Uni-lever can run out the clock."

The legal structure Soiefer suggested was a "close corpo-ration." "It's basically a corporation that has only one stock-holder," said Howie Fuguet, the lawyer for Ben & Jerry's. "And in the case of Ben & Jerry's, the stockholder grants cer-tain powers to the board. One of the board's powers is to appoint new members without the shareholder's approval. This means that the shareholder can never fire the board." These non-Unilever directors control nine of the board's eleven seats.

The guiding principles of the contract are set out in a four-page Shareholders Agreement and parts of a sixty-five-page Agreement and Plan of Merger, along with several attachments. (Together, they are referred to as the sale agreements.) The documents allow the board of directors to protect its independence from Unilever, and they give the board primary responsibility for "preserving and enhancing the objectives of the historical social mission of the company as they may evolve," and for "safeguarding the integrity of the essential elements of the brand." Unilever has primary responsibility for the financial and operational aspects of the business, and it also retains all powers not expressly given to the board.

"The idea was to follow the historical pattern of the three-part mission," said Howie. The agreements captured the tension that had always existed between the product quality, economic, and social parts of Ben & Jerry's and set up a system of checks and balances so the three parts could keep moving forward together. "The important thing, historically, was that no part of the mission should be more important than any other part," he said. "They are supposed to be equal."

The sale agreements also describe the job of the CEO in detail. They require the board of Ben & Jerry's to agree with Unilever on an annual business plan and delegation of authority to the CEO, with Unilever having the final decision on both counts. They also allow Unilever to hire and fire the CEO after "good faith consultation" with the board. But the board has the express power to prevent the CEO from changing product standards, introducing new products, or changing marketing materials or any use of the Ben & Jerry's trademark. Some of the CEO's compensation is pegged to the company's social performance, and this part of the compensation package is decided by the board of Ben & Jerry's. The agreements also require Unilever to fund an independently audited annual report of Ben & Jerry's social performance, and they call upon Unilever to develop its own system of social assessments.

The agreements require Ben & Jerry's to maintain a corporate presence and substantial operations in Vermont for at least five years, and they prohibit layoffs and benefit cuts for two years. They require Unilever to contribute $1.1 million a year to the Ben & Jerry's Foundation, plus adjustments to ensure that its contribution will increase in step with inflation and increased sales. They call for a new product development unit to be headed by Ben Cohen for as long as he remains a member of the board and an employee of Ben & Jerry's. And they require all board members and employees to sign Unilever's Code of Business Conduct and abide by the company's financial, accounting, and legal procedures. This provision puts boundaries on how Ben & Jerry's people do their jobs, and what they can and can't say about their jobs in public.

It took a long time to settle on these points. "It was by far the most unique deal I have ever been involved in," said Goldstein. "When we were getting toward the end of it, Ben used to call me at home at all hours. My wife would answer the phone and he'd say 'Yo, it's Ben.' She'd say, 'Ben, he's traveling. I'm going back to sleep.' And after we signed the deal, Jerry and his wife asked my wife and me to come to their house for dinner. I can't remember ever doing something like that. I was flattered."

On January 25, Unilever sent the board a cash offer of $36 a share, with an offer to sign the sale agreements as a sweetener. But Ben and Terry Mollner were still looking for a funder for their preferred plan to take Ben & Jerry's private. They had found a prospect in Todd Berman, who ran a venture fund called Chartwell Investments. Berman had no interest in the social mission. In fact, he was exactly the kind of guy Ben gave speeches against. In 2005, Berman was even sentenced to five years in prison for embezzling. But in 2000, Berman did have the money.

On January 26, Meadowbrook and Chartwell made their offers. On January 27, the board rejected these offers as well as Unilever's and decided to move forward in negotiations with Dreyer's. This was the option preferred by many of the company's top managers, including Perry. Because of the distribution agreement, a merger with Dreyer's would be easier to accomplish. The Dreyer's offer was also a stock swap, so the taxes on capital gains for individual shareholders would be less than the income tax from a cash deal. But on January 28, Unilever increased its bid to $40 a share. At the same time, Ben and Jerry told Dreyer's that they would not vote their shares in favor of a merger with Dreyer's and that they would also gladly share their low opinion of Dreyer's with any reporter who asked them.

On February 4, Meadowbrook resubmitted an offer for $32 a share, in cash. The offer emphasized the social mission and was backed by Ben's friends Judy Wicks and Anita Roddick, along with twenty-three other luminaries from the Social Venture Network. Judy Wicks called this the "white knight" plan, and after a story ran about it in the *Wall Street Journal*, many other potential investors, including Barbra Streisand's representative and several of the distribution companies that contracted with Ben & Jerry's, contacted Terry. They were each willing to commit a minimum of $10 million to get in on the deal. The Meadowbrook offer started to look more credible.[6]

Once again, the board was deadlocked. Goldstein then tried a different tack. Unilever would be willing to join Meadowbrook, he said, and allow Ben to retain control. He also told Terry, privately, that Unilever could more than match any money Chartwell had offered, and on better terms. Goldstein said that this was his fallback plan. If he couldn't

buy Ben & Jerry's outright, "This was the least worst alternative," he said. "I would consider doing it if it were the only
way to keep the business from going to Dreyer's."

A Dreyer's takeover of Ben & Jerry's would be a disaster
for Unilever because the chances were excellent that Dreyer's would eventually merge the brand with Häagen-Dazs.
This would leave Unilever without a super-premium brand
in the world's biggest ice cream market. So it was critically
important for Goldstein to win the competition for Ben & Jerry's. "But I wasn't sure my bosses would go for the Meadowbrook deal," he said.

The Deal Goes Down

A lot of shareholders weren't going for the Meadowbrook
deal, either. They wanted a decision, and they didn't want
it to be Meadowbrook. The company's senior managers
were especially alarmed at the prospect of Ben returning as
their boss. On March 10, Perry asked seven senior managers,
including Liz and Fran, to report to him on how the board's
protracted deliberations were hurting their decisions in hiring, franchising, employee morale, and other areas. The managers began threatening to sue the board. At the same time,
three groups of shareholders were preparing class-action
lawsuits to block the Meadowbrook deal.

The atmosphere around the office got nasty. "I came into
my office after 5 p.m. one day and found my boss sitting at
my computer, going through my email," said Tom D'Urso.
He says that his boss was looking for evidence that he was
sending numbers to Ben, "and I knew what that meant. But
at that point, I didn't care."

On March 23, Meadowbrook submitted a new proposal
to take the company private. It was a cash offer for $38 a
share backed by Ben's stock (but not Jerry's) and other investors (but not Chartwell). By far the biggest investor was

Unilever, which would own some equity outright and loan Meadowbrook enough money to cover the rest. Meadowbrook would make these loan payments from future revenues. The proposal was essentially a leveraged buyout, with Unilever buying the junk bonds. And if Meadowbrook failed to make the payments consistently, Unilever would eventually take control of the company.

The board approved this deal in principle. But there were still lots of legal and technical issues to resolve, and Dreyer's and Unilever were still interested in buying the company outright. Then, as the lawyers were working on the details, someone called a reporter. The *New York Times* reported on March 29 that the board had chosen the Meadowbrook deal. Four days later, Dreyer's offered a stock swap at $40 a share.

The board knew that because of the Vermont legislature's 1998 "Ben & Jerry's Law," they could consider other things besides just selling the company to the highest bidder. But they also knew that law had never been tested in court, that they would certainly be sued if they accepted a lower bid, and that every lawyer in the room was urging them to focus on their fiduciary responsibility to shareholders.[7] "We paused and went into the other room," Terry said. "And we said to ourselves, if we use this law we'll lose and have to appeal. It could go to the Supreme Court."

Terry says that the Meadowbrook team was ready to go to court. Although they did not know how they would finance the lawsuit, he says, they saw a chance to add an important precedent to corporate law by testing the Vermont statute. But the Meadowbrook offer became unacceptable to most members of the board of Ben & Jerry's if a lawsuit would be attached to it. The suit would add expense and complications to a company that was already in crisis.

Meadowbrook matched the $40 offer, although at that price it was doubtful that the company would produce enough revenue to make the loan payments to Unilever.

Then Dreyer's, tipped off again, indicated that it was prepared to raise its offer to $41 or $42 a share. It was April 6. "I knew we couldn't match that," said Terry. "So we agreed that we had done our best and failed. Somebody would own the company, but we didn't know who. Ben, me, and the rest of our team were in a Unilever boardroom. We all stood up and put our hands on top of each other's hands in the middle of the table. As we raised our hands toward the ceiling, we made an increasingly loud noise until it became a scream —'Wee, ee, ee, ee'—and we threw our offer through the ceiling. We let go of it in true Ben & Jerry's style. We went out in a blaze of glory."

"I'm awfully glad it fell off the table," said Goldstein. "We didn't know how in hell we would write the agreements with Meadowbrook and who would have the responsibility for what." But even though Ben had cleared the way for the company to be sold in an auction with Dreyer's—an auction Goldstein was determined to win—Goldstein still needed to make sure that Ben and Jerry were satisfied with the Unilever deal. So at the end of the negotiation, Goldstein offered a few extras to Ben and his allies. He offered Meadowbrook two seats on the new board of directors of Ben & Jerry's, with Terry Mollner holding one of them. "We weren't going to have a majority on that board anyway, and I needed to cement the deal," he said. He offered to donate $5 million to a venture fund that Ben and Pierre would control, separate from the sale agreements, to launch more social ventures. And he offered a one-time grant of $5 million to the Ben & Jerry's Foundation, with no strings attached.

There was just one more thing. "At the end, I felt like if this deal was going to go down, I was at least going to try to get some money for the employees," said Jeff. "We were supposed to be about linked prosperity, but if you didn't own a lot of stock, you weren't going to get anything." So Goldstein made three concessions to Jeff. He set aside another $5

Ben and Jerry with Richard Goldstein, president of Unilever North America, announcing the company's sale on May 10, 2000.

million to distribute directly to plant employees as bonuses after the sale. He added a clause to the sale agreements that requires Unilever to pay a living wage to all full-time employees of Ben & Jerry's. The wage level would be based not on the official state minimum wage but on estimates of how much it cost to live in minimal comfort and security in Vermont. Jeff and the staff of Ben & Jerry's would produce these estimates. Jeff and one other director were also granted the authority to sue Unilever if it ever stopped paying a living wage, with Unilever picking up the legal bills.

"It was not difficult for us to make donations," said Goldstein. "As I said, Unilever is a generous company. And the living wage thing wasn't a question of increasing their wages, it was about maintaining a policy. I'm sure I called my boss and told him we needed to do this and he said, 'Is that the end of it?'" It was. On April 11, 2000, the board voted to sell the company to Unilever for $43.60 a share, subject to the terms of the sale agreements.

Looking back on it, Jeff says that several things came together to cause the sale. "The distribution problem was real, and it caused a sense of crisis," he said. "Ben was gone, so we didn't know who was going to lead us. Many of the managers wanted to sell. And the board was out of its league. We were dealing with all of these big-business issues, and we didn't have the knowledge or experience to handle them."

Ben was absent when the board voted to sell the company. He came to the meeting on April 11 to hear the final presentations from Dreyer's and Unilever, and he listened to the discussion until the board broke for lunch. Then he left before the votes were actually taken.

Ben, Jerry, and Jeff were exhausted and heartbroken. In a 2008 interview with the *Guardian*, Jerry said, "We did not want to sell the business; it was a very difficult time. But we were a public company, and the Board of Directors' primary responsibility is the interest of the shareholders. So that is what the decision came down to. It was extremely difficult, heart-wrenching. It was a horrible experience for me and I can probably say it was horrible for Ben too.

"It is not as if we sold it feeling great about the situation and ended up regretting it. We didn't feel great about it from the start and throughout. It was nothing about Unilever. We didn't want to get bought by anybody."[8]

Viewed in strictly financial terms, though, the sale was a huge success. The company's stock price had more than tripled in three years, and bidding had gone from $32 a share in November 1999 to more than $43 in April. After only forty months with the company, Perry booked a capital gain of $12.6 million, or $3 million more than Jerry. To many shareholders who had watched their holdings languish for a decade—and especially to shareholders who had bought in 1997, when the stock was a bargain—Perry was a hero.

By the time the sale happened, though, the atmosphere inside the company had become toxic. "Perry gathered the senior managers together on the day of the sale to explain the deal," said Tom D'Urso. "He went through its terms, and said that no employees would lose their jobs for two years. Then he paused, looked directly at me, and said that the only exception to this rule was the Treasurer, who would be terminated immediately. I left at the end of the day. The only thing I had done was give information to the cofounder and vice chair of the board."

The sale was also a big potential gain for socially responsible businesses, although everyone in that community saw it as a big loss at the time. A small socially responsible company had written the essential noneconomic elements of its mission statement into a contract, had insisted that the contract be perpetual, and had persuaded a much larger company to sign that contract before agreeing to sell. No one knew how the relationship was going to turn out, of course, because no one had ever done anything like it. And a cynic would add that none of it mattered.

None of it did matter to Ben and Jerry, who both felt that they had suffered a terrible loss. "It was a heartbreaking, horrible thing for Ben because his business was the vehicle for expressing the love he felt toward the world," said Judy Wicks. "A business becomes beautiful when it is powered by that love and compassion. Ben & Jerry's was built on that love, and also on an authentic, beautiful friendship. And now the beautiful business was gone.

"I remember trying to make Ben feel better. I told him that now he could do other things, and what a good influence the company could have on Unilever. It could even spread caring capitalism globally. But he was inconsolable. He said, 'No matter what good Ben & Jerry's does from now on, the money will all go to Unilever.' There was no longer a social activist in control. The leader had been focused on the common good, and that was gone. It was an enormous loss to society, and to the socially responsible business movement."

Jeff, Pierre, Jennifer, and everyone else who was devoted to the three-part mission went into mourning. They were all deeply shaken and wounded. But they were still in the game.

ELEVEN

A Thousand Cuts

A lot of socially responsible entrepreneurs sold their companies at the beginning of the twenty-first century. In 2000, a few months before Unilever agreed to pay $326 million for Ben & Jerry's, the vegetarian food company Boca Burger sold itself to Kraft, a subsidiary of the tobacco giant Philip Morris. Coca-Cola bought the organic juice company Odwalla in 2001, and it bought Honest Tea seven years later. In 2006, Colgate-Palmolive bought Tom's of Maine, while L'Oreal paid nearly $1 billion for the Body Shop. Et cetera, et cetera.

Corporate social responsibility caught on in the 1980s and 1990s because the biggest and most lucrative consumer market in history rewarded it. As the enormous baby boom generation moved through middle age, the peak years of earning and spending, millions of boomers held on to their youthful desires to change the world. Corporate marketers of the 1990s talked about "cultural creatives" or "the LOHAS (lifestyles of health and sustainability) Market" and started looking for ways to attract this kind of consumer. Some companies bought established brands. Others did good deeds and arranged for lots of publicity. The strategies and tactics pioneered by Ben & Jerry's went mainstream.

What Ben told Jennifer in 1985 really is true: businesses have enormous power that can be harnessed to generate enormous social benefits. L'Oreal has greatly expanded the Body Shop's historic commitment to fair trade, for example.

L'Oreal is also several years into an environmental audit pro-gram that has greatly reduced its environmental footprint.

But just as often, corporate social responsibility is a hol-low promise. The advocates who work with multinational firms are almost always contractors who can be hired and fired at the pleasure of the CEO. The cause-related activi-ties of multinational corporations are usually a branch of the marketing department, to be cut when times get tight. As the century turned, several leaders of the socially responsi-ble business movement warned that their cause was being co-opted.

The sale agreements with Unilever were unusually tough, however, and they had the potential to generate an entirely new kind of corporate enterprise. They mapped out a way for the three-part mission of Ben & Jerry's to keep growing in perpetuity under Unilever's ownership. And Unilever did support the company's social mission activities with a gener-osity no other company was willing to match. But a contract is not a mission statement, and the promises in a contract are only as good as the people who enforce them. For many years, Unilever supported the social mission only because they were required to.

The employees of Ben & Jerry's still wanted the company to pursue linked prosperity, and the board did too. But the two groups were not working together any more, and the new owners did not understand the spirit that made their acquisition so valuable. The result was stalemate, infighting, and drift.

Lost Sailor

"Once in a while you get shown the light / In the strangest of places if you look at it right."

Ben quoted the Grateful Dead song "Scarlet Begonias" to explain why he had agreed to sell. "Under this new arrangement, Ben & Jerry's will be independently operated, our values will continue, and we hope our efforts to make positive change will even expand," he wrote on April 12, 2000. "Unilever has contractually agreed to increasing socially beneficial activities as a percentage of sales, every year. Ben & Jerry's will be doing more good than it does today."

For the next decade, Unilever made its required annual contribution to the Ben & Jerry's Foundation. It also allowed Ben & Jerry's to run several effective social mission campaigns, and it worked aggressively to reduce the company's environmental footprint. But something important was missing. The company's traditions of open communication and transparency were abandoned. Key decisions were no longer being made in Burlington. And the people who ended up supervising Ben & Jerry's had, as Ben once put it, a tragically narrow conception of business.

Things started to go wrong just two weeks after the sale when Richard Goldstein, Unilever's chief negotiator and the man in whom Ben and Jerry had placed their trust, announced that he had taken a job with another company. Goldstein told Ben and Jerry that his departure wouldn't matter because his bosses understood the three-part mission and wanted it to grow.

At first, it seemed that Goldstein might have been right. Antony Burgmans, cochairman of Unilever, flew to New York and put on a T-shirt for his first meeting with Ben. "He came back from that meeting and said, 'Don't touch Ben & Jerry's,'" said Kees van der Graaf. "He said it was a jewel, a diamond, and that we need to cultivate it. Our instructions were to learn from Ben & Jerry's."

Niall Fitzgerald, Unilever's other cochair, also seemed to get it. He briefed the board and employees on Unilever's good works when he visited Vermont in May, and the list was impressive. Unilever was one of the world's largest processors of fish, so they helped start the Marine Stewardship

Council in 1997 out of concern for the long-term sustainability of fisheries. The company's Code of Business Principles, a separate document from the Code of Conduct all employees and board members sign, commits it to "the long-term goal of developing a sustainable business." It also forbids Unilever from buying products made by forced or child labor, giving or taking bribes, and hiring or firing anyone for any reason other than job performance. Fitzgerald described Unilever's first social assessment, which was under way, and there was even talk of Ben participating in it.

Goldstein's departure did matter, though, for several reasons. First, it was a rude awakening to a new way of doing business. Ben, Jerry, and Jeff liked to base their deals on long-term personal relationships, not written contracts. But "all the seats in big business are rented," said Jennifer. "We didn't understand that at first." The team that had put together the deal quickly scattered. The Gordian Group walked away with its fee and an award for Middle Market Deal of the Year. Henry Morgan and Fred Miller left. Perry Odak bought a home on Fisher Island, an ultra-exclusive enclave in Miami. Within a year he was the CEO of Wild Oats, a chain of organic grocery stores (that was sold to Whole Foods in 2006, four months after Odak resigned). And Richard Goldstein was just a distant advisor after September, although he officially remained on the Ben & Jerry's board of directors until the end of 2001.

There was one Unilever person who came to all Ben & Jerry's board meetings and understood the company exceptionally well, because he had cowritten the sale agreements. But Ron Soiefer was an observer. He was there to take the minutes and to answer legal questions. Soiefer did not run Ben & Jerry's, and he also was not responsible for seeing that the terms of the agreements were being followed. That was the board's job.

Promise vs. Practice

The sale agreements required Unilever to choose a CEO to run Ben & Jerry's "after good faith consultation" with the board. Shortly after he signed the agreements, Ben Cohen began interviewing CEO candidates. He considered hiring Walt Freese, the president of Celestial Seasonings Tea, another prominent socially responsible business. But he eventually decided that he wanted to hire Pierre Ferrari, whom he had first met when interviewing candidates in 1997.

When Ben presented his choice, Richard Goldstein told him as politely as possible that the CEO decision was up to Unilever. So Ben flew to London with Pierre and Terry Mollner to make his arguments to the top brass. "They were cordial, but it became clear that the people in charge of Unilever's sustainability initiatives didn't really want to collaborate with us," said Terry. "They hadn't cut the deal, and no one was telling them to take us seriously." Shortly afterward, Ben's recruiter called all the prospects to apologize and say that the search was over.

On November 20, 2000, Unilever announced that Yves Couette, director of their ice cream business in Mexico, would be the next CEO of Ben & Jerry's. Jeff and Jennifer flew to London to meet Yves and show that they were working in good faith. But Ben's reaction was swift and unequivocal. "I'm not interested in hanging around and supporting what I'm sure will be the destruction of the company," he told Reuters on December 1. "Ben & Jerry's will become just another brand like any other soulless, heartless, spiritless brand out there— that's my concern," he told the Associated Press.[1]

Ben had always been ambivalent about working with Unilever. But now he was emphatically out, and Jerry followed him. There was no longer any talk of either of them serving on the board. Ben had other things on his mind,

anyway. A few weeks after he made those comments, at the
age of forty-nine, he checked himself into a Vermont hospital for quadruple heart bypass surgery, followed by several months of rehab. Shortly after the operation, Ben agreed
to take a one-year sabbatical from the board and to keep
silent about Unilever in public during that time. He started
his rehab by taking slow walks with Jerry through the aisles
of the local Home Depot and spent the rest of the winter in
Daytona Beach. On doctor's orders, he also changed his diet.
"There had always been a stocked ice cream freezer case in
his kitchen," said Terry. "That went away."

Liz Bankowski also left the company in 2001, turning the
director of social mission job over to a marketing specialist.
Liz remained on the foundation's board of directors, occupying the seat Naomi Tannen had vacated in 1994, but she no
longer had any relationship to the company. Ben and Jerry
did maintain a relationship with the company, however, and
it's complicated. In 2014, they are still officially employees of
Unilever, and the terms of their employment are described
in long-term contracts. Unilever pays each of them well over
$200,000 a year and asks little in return. Ben and Jerry occa-
sionally appear as spokespersons for Ben & Jerry's products,
particularly those that advance the social mission, but their
contracts do not require them to endorse anything.

Unilever's Code of Business Conduct prohibits employees
from disparaging the company in public. But Ben says lots of
things in public that are critical of Unilever, and he and Jerry
freely lend their star power to edgy political causes, including the fight against genetically modified food and other
issues that make multinational companies nervous. Everyone assumes that their public criticism or praise of Unilever
will probably affect sales of Ben & Jerry's, too. In this way,
Ben and Jerry retain some influence over the company they
founded. "I have no responsibility, and yet I have no authority," Jerry told a lecture audience at Cornell University in

2013. "It's something we can all shoot for."

So if Ben and Jerry were out, who would be the watchdog for the sale agreements? The agreements say that the board of Ben & Jerry's has eleven seats. Nine are controlled by "independent directors," which means people who were on the board before the sale, representatives of Meadowbrook Capital, or the people they assign. The CEO and one other Unilever representative fill out the list. But the people who resigned from the presale board were not replaced. After the dust settled, the board membership totaled six: Jennifer, Jeff, Pierre, and Terry on the Ben & Jerry's side, and the CEO and one other Unilever executive on the other. Dick Goldstein turned the Unilever seat over to Hans Eenhorn, who had recently retired from managing ice cream and other brands. Eenhorn was active in global antihunger and sustainability causes and had a continuing role as a consultant to Unilever, working on revising the company's environmental strategy.

In August 2000, when the sale was final and the board officially re-formed, Jennifer agreed to be the chair. "I didn't think that one through," she said. "Jeff was the natural choice, but he didn't want the job. And so I found myself in charge of this group that had contractual obligations, but did not have the energy or the strategy to meet them.

"At the time, we all thought that the most important thing was to play nice and be professional. Remember, we were coming off an eighteen-month period where our meetings would just blow up. People were almost throwing furniture. And so, my overarching goal was to show them we were not nuts."

The Emerald City

With Ben and Jerry gone, the board lacked larger-than-life leaders to carry the vision forward. They had agreements that their leaders had negotiated, but what they did with those contracts was up to them. Looking back on that time, Jennifer says that she and other board members were naïve. "We tried to be professional, but we also believed that Unilever was ultimately evil," she said. "We imagined that at the center of it there had to be an all-powerful enemy like Palpatine [the Emperor in *Star Wars*], and we couldn't negotiate with someone like that. We didn't trust them, and we kept waiting for the other shoe to drop."

Jeff says that he did trust Unilever, as far as it went. "I felt that they were just another big company," he said. "Their world was very different from ours, and I did trust them to be who they were. They were pursuing profits. That meant I should have been vigilant. But I was tired. I was happy with my reduced role."

Yves made it easy for them, too. He was much friendlier than Perry had been, and he also grew more interested in the social mission as time went by. Yves hired Walt Freese as chief marketing officer so that the company's image would be in the hands of an outsider who was committed to socially responsible business, instead of a Unilever lifer. Walt started meeting with Ben and Jerry regularly, which gave the founders some access to the company.

The board wasn't much of a concern to Yves. It met only four times a year and didn't make many demands, and he had several fires to fight. In 2001, Ben & Jerry's sales were sluggish, dairy prices were rising, the distribution system was transitioning to warehouses, and a disastrous attempt to introduce the product in Japan had to be undone. Also, the sale agreements had prohibited Unilever from making any layoffs at Ben & Jerry's, but only for two years. Everyone knew what would happen in the spring of 2002. Yves was pleasant, intelligent, and a good listener, but he could also be ruthless.

Richard Goldstein had assured Ben that Ben & Jerry's was a separate business and that its CEO would negotiate his annual contract with the head of Unilever North America.

But that didn't turn out as planned, either. Unilever assigned the supervision of Ben & Jerry's to its North American ice cream division in Green Bay, Wisconsin, where all of their American brands, including Breyer's, Good Humor, Klondike, and Popsicle, were managed. Yves was a lot less independent than he had hoped to be.

"Green Bay was a success story," said Kees. "In the late 1980s, Unilever had a $60 million ice cream business in North America that was losing money. Then Eric Walsh came in and started doing acquisitions. He did them very well." Walsh's strategy was to buy a company, cut its costs by laying people off and combining operations, and spend the savings on marketing and promotion. "He turned Green Bay into a $1.6 billion ice cream conglomerate making very nice profits," said Kees. "This man did a miracle for Unilever."

Walsh preferred to work alone, so the top brass didn't second-guess his decisions. But the folks at Green Bay had not negotiated the Ben & Jerry's deal. To them, this was just the next stage in their successful campaign to acquire, integrate, streamline, and expand their ice cream empire. They assumed the Vermonters would get used to the new order, just as others had. One Green Bay manager says that the universal attitude toward what they called "the social mission crap" was "How can we get around this?"

Yves's job title was chief executive officer, but he was neither hired nor supervised by an independent board of directors. He was a Unilever employee whose powers and duties were enumerated in the sale agreements, and who negotiated his job description with a supervisor every year. And it soon became apparent to employees that the man Yves negotiated with, Eric Walsh, either did not understand or did not care that the social mission was at the core of Ben & Jerry's. In 2001, the economies of Europe and the United States were in recession, and Unilever was having trouble meeting its profit goals. Cutting costs was job one.

There was an obstacle to cutting costs at Ben & Jerry's, though. The sale agreements gave the board the right to veto changes in the product formula, consult with the CEO on many aspects of the business, and carry out other powers that protected large parts of the company's budget. Yves overcame this obstacle by putting severe restrictions on communication within the company. Line workers at the plants were no longer invited to headquarters, and employees at one site needed to get a pass to visit any other site. The office complex in South Burlington was twenty-five miles away from St. Albans, twenty miles from Waterbury, eighty-five miles from the novelties plant in Springfield, and one hundred miles from the distribution center in Bellows Falls. As time went on, employees at each site had less and less knowledge of what others were doing.

Yves also put up a wall of silence between the employees, the franchise owners, and the board. Jeff and other board members were no longer invited to the annual meeting of store owners (although Ben and Jerry always went). Board members couldn't just drop by the office to say hello, either. "I was not allowed to go into the plants," said Jeff. "I practically had to get a visa to go visit the scoop shops. I couldn't even talk to the people at headquarters without permission." Employees also knew they couldn't talk to board members without putting their jobs in danger. They began calling Green Bay the "Emerald City," with Walsh the Wicked Witch of the West.

Of course, employees at headquarters had ways of finding out what the line workers were being told to do. The line workers told them privately, after hours, because they were friends. The franchise owners also knew, because their livelihoods depended on the quality of the ice cream, and their customers would tell them as soon as something changed. The founders and the board heard the rumors, but they didn't do anything. "It was like a dysfunctional family," said Debra Heintz. "Everybody suspected that we were cutting corners, but everybody also knew that you did not talk about it. Silence was the normative behavior. You could feel it immediately."

Yves ordered changes in the pints soon after he arrived. These included increasing the overrun (the amount of air in the mix), decreasing the butterfat content, and using smaller, cheaper chunks, all of which decreased the cost of manufacturing. These changes were "a poorly kept secret," says Dave Stever. "Many of us didn't like the idea of touching the recipes, even if we were told they were making the product better. We knew, but at the same time, there was no real way to fight for change. We didn't see a way to push back. We were being told, 'Here's your cost savings target. Go get it.'"

By mid-2001, the employees of Ben & Jerry's were silent and fearful, the chair of the board was intent on not rocking the boat, the founders were almost entirely disengaged, and Jeff was all but convinced the battle had been lost. He kept hanging on, but at times he wasn't sure why.

Enlightened Layoffs

Unilever knew that positioning Ben & Jerry's as a socially progressive company was almost as important as putting tasty chunks in the mix. When asked what made Ben & Jerry's different from Häagen-Dazs, customers in the company's ongoing tracking surveys always mentioned the chunks first—but they also talked about Ben & Jerry's unique business practices, their concern for the environment, and their "sincere desire to make the world a better place." The problem was Unilever's idea of the social mission. It was like the rest of Unilever. It was careful and quiet.

Because Yves did not begin working at Ben & Jerry's until the end of 2000, the employees were left wondering what to do for most of a year. While they waited, they kept advancing the three-part mission in the ways they always had. As 2000 began, Vermont was engaged in a furious debate over whether to legalize civil unions for same-sex couples. Ben & Jerry's had a stake in the debate because the company had offered benefits to the same-sex partners of employees since 1991. So Liz decided to get out in front of the issue. Ben & Jerry's drafted an open letter to the legislature, persuaded forty-six other businesses to sign it, and bought a full-page ad in the *Burlington Free Press* that appeared on March 23, the day the state house voted on the bill.

After the law passed (and the company was sold), employees decided to create a new flavor, made with Vermont maple syrup, to celebrate. Vermont Honeymooner Ice Cream had a rainbow with two entwined wedding rings arching over the top of each pint, along with copy that said, "True commitment tastes universally great."

"Everybody in the company had signed off on it," said Dave Stever. "This was going to be one of those progressive causes we could get out in front of. We were just waiting for the CEO. So as soon as Yves showed up, we showed it to him and told him we all wanted it. He said he didn't. It was too much for him. We were hugely disappointed."

Yves was much more enthusiastic about doing leading-edge work on environmental protection. He led an energetic Ben & Jerry's campaign on global climate change that launched in 2002, five years before Al Gore's movie *An Inconvenient Truth* won its Oscar. The company created a new flavor endorsed by the Dave Matthews Band (One Sweet Whirled), which donated its licensing fee to an environmental consortium. At every stop on the band's spring and summer tour, Ben & Jerry's staffers passed out tips on how to reduce a household's carbon footprint, along with free samples of ice cream. The company also supported basic research on thermoacoustic refrigeration (which does not use ozone-depleting refrigerants), purchased carbon offsets, and expanded its program to reduce the environmental impacts of dairy farming. The Caring Dairy program launched in Europe in 2003, at the same time Unilever began to produce and distribute Ben & Jerry's ice cream there on a larger scale.

All of this environmental work kept Ben & Jerry's in the game as the corporate social responsibility movement went mainstream. In 2002, when CERES and the Association of Certified Chartered Accountants decided to start giving out awards for the best "sustainability reports" in North America, Ben & Jerry's was their first honoree.

It was harder to get Unilever interested in social justice initiatives where measurement is often harder, progress is usually slower, and the potential for controversy is always greater. In the fall of 2000, a media report exposed child slavery in West Africa's chocolate industry. In 2002, the company's social mission director reported that she and Yves had been searching for "an effective and sustainable way to mobilize Ben & Jerry's resources" on this issue, but that "the issue is far more complex than any of us could have imagined." Although the first products using fair-trade-certified cocoa were sold in 1994, Ben & Jerry's did not start transitioning to fairly traded cocoa until 2011.

Unilever was least enthusiastic about the part of the mission statement that promised to "expand opportunities for development and career growth for our employees." They were far more interested in boosting profit margins, and there was one way to do that quickly. "It was not hard to see," said Pierre Ferrari. "The company was overstaffed even before the sale."

As the two-year anniversary approached, employees showed that the sarcastic heart of Ben & Jerry's was still beating. The *Daily Plant*, the unauthorized employee newsletter that had ceased publication in 1993, rose again on April Fools' Day, 2002. It announced that the new "lean and mean" Ben & Jerry's would handle the impending layoffs as a game that mimicked the TV show *Survivor*, with each group meeting weekly to fire one of its own members. The *Daily Plant* also announced that instead of getting free ice cream, all employees were now being offered Unilever rice "and any rodents they can catch in the building."

Talk about gallows humor. A few days after the anniversary passed, Yves announced that the company would be closing the plants at Springfield and Bellows Falls. The board had actually discussed closing those sites in 1999, and plans were in the works when the sale happened. The board and Yves worked together so that each employee who got a pink slip was offered either a job elsewhere or an enhanced severance package. The company also gave the employees a year's advance notice, which was unheard of in corporate circles. It even found buyers for both facilities so that both of them stayed open. It was the first time Ben & Jerry's had ever done serious layoffs, and it did them with care.

The second round of layoffs showed Yves's ruthless side. One morning in October, the finance department and several dozen other people who worked at South Burlington didn't show up for work. One-quarter of the employees at the company's headquarters were suddenly gone. "That section of the office turned into a little ghost town," said Sean Greenwood. "It was like an island that had been swept away. I didn't like walking by there. It felt eerie." Then, in January 2003, Greenwood himself got laid off, along with others in the marketing department. The number of employees declined from 750 at the end of 2001 to 520 at the beginning of 2003.

Sean says he quickly found other work, and he also got a great severance package. "But it was still painful to leave this place," he said. "The social mission was a big part of why we all worked here.

"I actually thought that the people who kept their jobs suffered more than I did. They were miserable. I often found myself trying to make people feel better who had full-time jobs, even though I was looking for work. They were telling me they felt like they could get laid off at any time.

"It was hard to believe that Ben & Jerry's really had a three-part mission statement when you also had that feeling. The mission statement was still on the website and the marketing and public relations people were still selling it, but we were no longer practicing it internally."

Dwelling on the Edge

Courage is a consistent theme in the Ben & Jerry's story. It is the word that Chuck Lacy used to describe the way the company was managed during the years of rapid growth, and it is the quality that the board of directors needed to challenge Unilever. How much are we willing to risk for our beliefs? Why can't we do better?

Pierre and other board members kept urging Yves to be more radical. Pierre even argued that social initiatives he characterized as "edge-dwelling" would increase sales because the product would never appeal to the general population. The few people who were alienated by the company's support for something controversial, such as same-sex marriage, would be more than outweighed by a much larger number of educated, affluent urbanites who would love the company for its courage.

Yves listened and, as time went by, he started to agree with the board that taking risks was important. But he worked for Unilever, so he had to be careful. In 1990, Ben & Jerry's had participated in a full-page newspaper ad to protest America's invasion of Kuwait. In March 2003, the board requested another public statement, and the managers asked Yves for permission to take out a newspaper ad registering Ben & Jerry's official opposition to the war in Iraq. Yves said no, but he did allow employee volunteers to charter two buses to a weekend antiwar rally in Washington.

The buses left Burlington at night, arrived in time for the rally the next morning, then immediately headed home so that nobody would miss work. The employees marched together, carrying signs and wearing rain slickers that identified them as being from Ben & Jerry's. The march fired up the employees. It encouraged them to keep acting on their beliefs, regardless of Unilever's position.

"THREE-PART MISSION STATEMENT, INNOVATIVE MODEL FOR COMPANIES AROUND THE WORLD, DIES AT 16," read the headline for an item in the April 2004 *Daily Plant*. "The mission died after a long, devastating illness, originally contracted in August of 2000, surrounded by employees, former employees, and friends. During the course of its three and one-half year illness, the Mission Statement weathered a series of setbacks to all three of its parts ... more recently, doctors said that the Product Quality part of the Statement had to be amputated. After that, it is believed that the Mission Statement lost its will to live. In lieu of flowers, donations may be made to the Ben & Jerry's Foundation." The board never saw that *Daily Plant* article. If they had, maybe they would have acted.

Ben & Jerry's had plenty of money to spare for new initiatives in 2004. Savings from the layoffs had dropped straight to the bottom line, and the alliance with the Dave Matthews Band and the One Sweet Whirled flavor had been extremely successful. The long-term outlook was brighter, too. In 2002, after a lot of training and supervision by Vermonters, a Unilever factory in the Netherlands started producing Ben & Jerry's Homemade Ice Cream. "It isn't easy to make this product, but the folks in Hellendorn did much better than anyone expected them to," said Helen Jones, who was appointed director of brand development for Europe in 2002.

The United States accounted for just 29 percent of global ice cream sales in 2003, according to Euromonitor. Western

Europe was another 29 percent, and the rest of the world was 42 percent. Helen supervised the introduction of Ben & Jerry's to Sweden, Denmark, and Ireland, with the long-term goal of pushing it through Europe and eventually making it a global brand. She relied on the idea that she had come up with in the United Kingdom, which she calls "seed marketing." "Unilever opens a scoop shop as a flagship in the country, and uses that to bring the Ben & Jerry's experience to life in the market," she says. "As we did in the UK, the shops and kiosks build demand, and this puts us in a stronger position when we start making deals with grocery stores." Helen also used Unilever's global presence to tailor the company's social mission to each new country. "We absolutely need to lead with our values," she says, "but we also have to adapt our messages so they are culturally relevant."

Back in the United States, however, the social mission was stuck in neutral. At its August 2004 meeting, the board debated whether or not a new flavor should be named "Dave Matthews Magic Brownies." Was that "edge dwelling," or was it just being naughty? "I was alternating between getting pissed off and not giving a shit," remembers Jeff. He stayed in that unhappy state for three more years. The board of Ben & Jerry's had an ace in the hole, however. If all of the seats on the Unilever side were rented, the Vermonters weren't going anywhere.

Enter Walt Freese

Yves left Ben & Jerry's at the end of 2004, and Walt Freese, the company's chief marketing officer, replaced him. Ben, Jerry, and the board were pleased with the choice. Walt had been one of Ben's original candidates for CEO back in 2001. Ben and Jerry had been meeting regularly with Walt since then, and they had become friends. After three years of exile, it seemed as if Unilever had seen the light and put a socially responsible business leader in charge. The board would have another chance.

As the number of socially responsible businesses that sold out to multinationals continued to grow, various kinds of deals were being made to keep social missions alive under new ownership. In 2003, for example, Stonyfield Yogurt happily sold itself to Group Danone, the French conglomerate. Socially responsible businesses cheered because the deal allowed Gary Hirshberg to remain as Stonyfield's CEO for as long as he wanted, provided that the company posted sales growth in excess of 10 percent a year. Hirschberg lasted nine years. But the Ben & Jerry's board goes on in perpetuity.

The three-part mission was also seeping into Unilever's collective consciousness during Yves Couette's tenure at Ben & Jerry's, although no one knew it at the time. Yves's next assignment at Unilever was senior vice president with responsibility for the strategic planning of Lipton Tea, which is sold in more than one hundred countries and, in 2012, had annual revenues of about $2.7 billion. "Yves was a smart guy,

Walt Freese, Ben & Jerry's "Chief Euphoria Officer" from 2005 to 2010, participating in the day of community service that has been part of every annual meeting of franchised store owners since 1996.

and he saw what made Ben & Jerry's work," said Pierre Ferrari. "By the time he left, he had begun to integrate the three bottom lines into his thinking." In 2007, two years after Yves left Burlington, Unilever announced that it was partnering with the Rainforest Alliance to evaluate the supply chain for its tea, with the goal of sourcing 100 percent of it from "sustainable and ethical" vendors by 2015.

Hints of a new attitude were emerging at Unilever. But in 2005, as Walt moved into an office that now has the three-part mission statement painted on the wall, Ben & Jerry's board members were becoming increasingly suspicious of the men who led their branch of the giant corporation. Board members say they saw a steady stream of evidence for violations of the sale agreements, but that Walt deflected their concerns. They say he dealt with their inquiries by stalling and stonewalling, while employees fumed and the three-part mission sputtered.

Some employees say that Walt's commitment to the mission was genuine. He rehired several key employees who had been part of the organization during the glory days of the 1990s; he switched more ingredients to "values-led sources," such as eggs from chickens that are not confined in cages; and he continued the company's aggressive campaign to bring attention to climate change. Several managers said that Walt would have welcomed it if the board had adopted a more aggressive attitude toward Unilever. But there wasn't much change.

The lack of forward motion made the employees of Ben & Jerry's doubt that Unilever really cared about social responsibility. "Unilever is committed to communicating using lengthy, vague documents to ensure you have no idea of what our intentions are," according to a "press release" that ran in the April Fools' 2005 edition of the *Daily Plant*. The article went on to announce a new "One Unilever Crystal

Meth Vitality Strategy" to make all the company's ice cream out of Unilever products, with new flavors like "Marsha Marsha Mayonnaise" and "Wishbone Salad Swirl."

Cracks in the Dike

Walt's biggest problem wasn't the social mission of Ben & Jerry's. It was the profit margins in Green Bay. They were too low, and heading lower, because the strategy that had worked so well for Eric Walsh—acquire a company, cut its costs, and spend the savings on expansion—had run its course. With no ice cream companies left to acquire, and overall sales of ice cream not growing, Walsh could only watch his division's costs continue to rise while sales did not. Cost cutting could only go so far. The performance of Breyer's Ice Cream was especially poor, possibly because it no longer tasted as good as its rivals Dreyer's and Edy's did. Green Bay had been cutting costs by making Breyer's with cheaper ingredients, and people weren't buying it as they used to.

"Eric Walsh knew how to make a penny scream," Jennifer said. So as his revenues stalled, he kept tightening down on costs. "He used a classic tactic," Pierre said. It was called difference testing. "It's like slicing a salami. You reduce quality a bit, then compare the original to A, and you see no difference. Then you reduce it more, and you compare B to A, and you see no difference. Slowly but surely, they migrated the quality of Ben & Jerry's pints down over time. So when they said there hadn't been any changes to quality, they were talking about their research, but they were basically lying."

Walt also had to cope with a rapid expansion in the number of franchised scoop shops. By the end of 2005 the company had contracts with 435 shops, almost twice as many as they had in 2000. Ben & Jerry's had gotten caught up in a gold rush. Food industry forecasters had predicted in the late 1990s that middle-aged baby boomers would cope with their busy lives by spending a lot more at quick-serve restaurants, whether or not the restaurants sold fast food, take-out food, or desserts. All kinds of companies competed with each other to secure the best locations for quick-serve operations, and as the rush continued, stores started popping up on sites that had less and less traffic. Ben & Jerry's had always gotten many more franchise applications than it had approved. But now the big focus was on the number of stores opened each year, and there was less of a focus on how successful these stores were.

The company faced two significant business problems. Some of the new stores were struggling, and the advisory committee of franchise owners was not shy about letting Walt know how much these stores needed help. At the same time, Walt was caught in a pincer between his boss in Green Bay, who wanted him to cut costs by cheapening the pint product, and the board of directors, which had the power to veto any changes that would affect the product's integrity.

If he wanted to keep his job, however, Walt had to do as he was told. He was the CEO, but he wasn't an independent executive. Unilever had changed his official job title to General Manager/Chief Euphoria Officer, so Walt took orders directly from Eric Walsh. This was a clear violation of the sale agreements, which enumerate the independent powers of the CEO in detail.

Walt's solution to this dilemma was to keep the board, staff, and Unilever from communicating with each other directly. He kept the walls of silence in place and insisted on being each group's sole point of contact. While he ran the company, employees who knew what was happening in the plants could not meet directly with board members to tell them what they knew. The employees also did not know what the board knew. The board and Unilever were also kept separate from each other—each thought the other was acting irrationally, so neither could be effective.

Walt controlled the information each group received. Board members and employees say that he also characterized the interests and motivations of groups in ways that would deflect criticism, thereby preventing the board and Unilever from engaging each other. This made things easier for Unilever, so Walt could continue supporting his family. "Walt had good intentions and he did his best, but he couldn't get respect from the Unilever people he reported to," said Terry. "He couldn't represent our interests to them effectively. It took us a long time to realize that this was a serious problem."

From the employees' perspective, the most serious problem might have been that Terry and the other board members were not paying attention. They were plainly told by the company's social auditor that Walt's lack of authority was a concern soon after he was hired, and they ignored the warning. The new job description "is a perilous move so far as the social mission is concerned," wrote James Heard in his report on 2004, which was written halfway through 2005. Making key decisions in Green Bay "creates enormous reputational risks if Ben & Jerry's fails to live up to its three-part mission." Heard feared that Ben & Jerry's would become "a Unilever marketing operation using the brand's reputation for social responsibility to promote sales."

The board and the founders liked Walt, though, so they didn't raise a stink about the job change. "I missed the importance of it," said Jeff. "They always said he was the CEO, and I didn't understand that it was a big change. I thought they were just being cute." James Heard was not invited back, either. In fact, the company's social report was not audited again until 2009, in one more violation of the sale agreements.

In the summer of 2005, seven months after he was promoted, Walt told the board that the butterfat content of Ben & Jerry's pints had been reduced by one-half of a percentage point, and that customers who tasted the new formula could not tell the difference. The board told him this was a violation of the sale agreements, and they asked that he tell them in advance next time. But the damage had already been done. The percentage of butterfat in the mix decreased from nearly 16 percent to below 14 percent in some flavors, with a noticeable difference in taste and creaminess. There was also a lot more air in the mix.

The chunks got smaller and cheaper, too. "They took Cherry Garcia, a best-selling flavor, and put new kinds of cherries into it that were smaller and tasted like rubber," said Pierre. "I eat a lot of Cherry Garcia so I could tell, this was definitely not superpremium ice cream. And Jeff, who always pays close attention to customer complaints, saw that the rates were starting to climb. Unilever also tried to meet their sales target one quarter by shipping a huge quantity of our product to warehouse inventory, which was against their own rules. I really blew up over that one." Pierre and Jeff started to become more vocal, and board meetings got increasingly tense.

Store owners started complaining, too. "The management kept telling us that they were following the proper guidelines, but we all believed that the product had changed," said Roger Kaufman of San Francisco, who was on the board of the franchise owners' advisory council. "Eventually we took our concerns to the board."

As time went by, the pressure on Walt kept growing. "He was like the boy who puts his finger in the dike to stop leaks," said one senior manager. "The problem is, he only has ten fingers." But even if the three-part mission wasn't being respected by the people who owned Ben & Jerry's, many employees still believed in it, and it still had the power to change people's minds.

Whenever a Unilever person was introduced to Ben & Jerry's, he or she usually had the same reaction: that only an idiot would have negotiated the sale agreements. Ron Soiefer changed their minds. He understood why the agreements were structured as they were, and he also attended Ben & Jerry's board meetings. He spent hours explaining the company's philosophy to skeptical Unilever executives, and as the years wore on, he brought a lot of people around.

Jane Bowman had worked in human resources for several big companies when Walt hired her in August 2005. "Walt asked me to calculate a livable wage for Vermont, with the help of this guy Jeff Furman," said Jane. "I thought that a livable wage was the craziest idea I had ever heard. Why would you ever pay your employees more than the market rate? That was the practice everywhere else. And when I met Jeff, my first impression was that he's a lunatic. He comes in wearing a T-shirt with jeans and wild hair, and I'm thinking, where am I? Then he started talking, and I figured that he worked for some advocacy group."

The sale agreements gave Jeff the authority to ensure that Unilever paid every Ben & Jerry's employee a living wage, along with the power to sue Unilever at Unilever's expense if the company fell behind. Jeff used that threat to get a rare invitation to South Burlington. "Jane was nice and very smart, but she didn't get what we were doing at first," he said. "The general atmosphere inside that office at that time was pretty grim."

No one was eager to explain the three-part mission to a newcomer back in 2005—it seemed like ancient history. "But the more Jeff talked, the more I started to see the sense in a living wage," Jane said. "Jeff and I argued constantly. We would get into it about things like mileage and the cost of a car and what people really needed to get by." Jeff smiles when he remembers a long argument with Jane about how many pairs of shoes a person needed. "It got so hot that we had to close the door," he said. "We were sitting in her office yelling at each other about shoes."

"I got sold on this principle gradually," said Jane. "But when I presented our findings to people from Unilever, they didn't get it at all. It was difficult to be in the middle. I had been asked to do a job I didn't fully understand, and in the beginning I didn't even support. Then I felt beaten up pretty well for doing it. But it was my job, so I just put my head down and kept going." One Unilever person who did cooperate with Jane was Ron Soiefer, "and he was just a gem of a man," she said. "He was my shepherd. By the time we were done, our numbers and methodology were absolutely bombproof."

The updated living wage was approved in July 2006, and the formula has been updated every year since. In 2013, the company's new hires in Vermont started at $16.13 an hour plus benefits, which was almost double the state's minimum wage and far above the state's average entry-level wage for manufacturing jobs.

"I have become the reluctant livable wage expert, with scars to prove it," Jane said. "It was hard on me, because I always want to be a peacemaker. But Jeff taught me on that, too. He would say, 'Pissing people off is good. I want to piss people off.' He showed me that this kind of a journey is how real social change is made. You don't get people to change by always being nice. And now I am extremely proud of our living wage and the conversations it provokes. I have become an activist for it, in a quiet kind of way. A lot of businesspeople understand and respect the idea once you explain it to them."

In the public's mind, the halo over Ben & Jerry's was still firmly in place. In December 2006, the company finished first in an annual poll of five thousand Americans that ranked 152 brands according to twelve aspects of "corporate citizenship," such as authenticity, generosity toward their communities, being open and honest, and treating employees well. But the public didn't know that the three-part mission was almost out of fuel. Ben & Jerry's was still publishing annual social reports, but these reports did not have independent audits, and an increasing amount of the stuff in them was fluff.

The same month the poll came out, the board approved a Unilever plan to shift 17 percent of Ben & Jerry's pint production to a factory in Henderson, Nevada. The board was told that making ice cream closer to western markets would save fuel and also put a big dent in the company's carbon footprint. But Henderson was not a Ben & Jerry's facility. Its employees would not be covered by the sale agreements, so they were not guaranteed a living wage or given the same benefits as employees in Vermont were. The board wasn't sure that the milk used to make Ben & Jerry's in Nevada would be supplied by family farms or co-ops. And the same problem applied to Europe, where sales were growing quickly. No one was making sure that linked prosperity would extend to people who made Cherry Garcia in Nevada or the Netherlands.

Ben & Jerry's was growing and changing. It was becoming a global brand, and the board needed to decide whether to give up or fight. In 2007, they decided to fight.

TWELVE

Counterattack

Jeff Furman didn't take it easy after Ben & Jerry's was sold. He refocused his activist energies on other organizations. He served on several local and national boards, including the Ithaca School Board, where he ran on a promise to begin a long-term commitment to eliminating race and class as predictors of performance. He tried to bring the concerns of low-income people to business and government. He stayed busy, and he mostly left Ben & Jerry's alone. But in 2007, he found that he couldn't ignore the company any more. "We couldn't get off square one with Unilever," he said. "We talked endlessly about the social mission and read lots of reports, but it was clear that we were losing ground.

"We were getting by on our old reputation, but I was having a hard time believing that we still deserved it. I had been around the longest, and I knew the founders best, and the other board members often looked to me to see how I would react. If I didn't challenge Unilever, they wouldn't either. So I finally decided that it was up to me."

Jeff, Pierre, and their colleagues took a fresh look at the documents that controlled the board's relationship to Unilever. They focused on the big company's legal obligations, and they started taking a tougher line. As their negotiations proceeded, Jeff also prepared a plan B. He persuaded Howie Fuguet, who had retired from Ropes & Gray, to come back and advise the board on a potential lawsuit against Unilever.

Jeff and the board also worked with Ben and Jerry to plan

Howard Fuguet, the company's lawyer from 1984 to 2000, came out of retirement to advise the board of directors as it battled Unilever in 2009 and 2010. His only pay was free-pint coupons.

a guerrilla-style public relations campaign, in the spirit of the campaigns they had waged against Pillsbury in 1984 and Monsanto in the 1990s. "If I was going to stay on the board, I needed to do something," said Jeff. "Grassroots action campaigns were what we knew how to do. But we were also aware that this time was different. We were talking about attacking our own people."

Familiar Faces in New Jobs

Things started breaking in the board's favor around that time, although they did not know it at first. Walt had rehired several employees who had helped build the three-part mission in the 1980s and put them in new, more important roles. Sean Greenwood had started as a scooper and tour guide in the late 1980s, and he had stayed until he was laid off in 2003. He is a musician with stage presence, and his irreverent, fun attitude made him a great spokesman for the company. In 2005, Sean returned to Ben & Jerry's as the director of public relations.

Another key hire was Rob Michalak, who met Jerry while hitchhiking in 1977 and directed public relations from 1989 until 1998. Rob returned in 2006 to direct the social mission. With Walt's encouragement, Rob gathered the department

Ron Soiefer, chief counsel for Unilever North America, cowrote the sale agreements and defended them to skeptical Unilever executives over the next decade. When Soiefer retired, the board thanked him for his "steadfast support & insightful guidance" by designing a commemorative pint of his favorite flavor—chocolate, with chocolate cows and peace signs added in.

heads to talk about the status of different social initiatives, trade ideas, and encourage cooperation. He also went back to improving the measurement of Ben & Jerry's social performance, a job that had been largely neglected since the sale. Rob was picking up where Liz Bankowski had left off.

Walt also brought Debra Heintz back into the center of things. Deb had never left the company, but her old job as materials director had been eliminated in the 2002 layoffs. "I was told that Eric Walsh didn't want to lose me, but that he needed to get me out of the headquarters," Debra said. "The idea was to get people to look to Green Bay for answers. So if I wanted to keep my job, I needed to be invisible."

Debra spent five years managing the company's distribution from Waterbury, but she was capable of doing more. In January 2007, Walt brought her back to South Burlington

to help bring some addi-
tional expertise to the company's retail operations. Debra
and the rest of the retail team
focused on untangling some
of the problems created by the
expansion plan.

The number of Ben & Jer-
ry's stores had nearly doubled
since 2000 and competition
had also increased, but the
industry's predictions had been
wrong—the overall demand
for ice cream shops had barely
budged. Many stores were in
financial trouble when Debra

Sean Greenwood (left) and
Rob Michalak performing at
the company's Global Franchise Meeting in 2010.

took the job, and the franchisees were demoralized. "This was
also a moral issue for me," said Jeff. "We had encouraged the
franchisees to take risks, and I felt that we had to take some of
the responsibility for what happened."

The problems at Ben & Jerry's in 2007 were minor when
compared with the problems other ice cream companies
were having, including other Unilever ice cream brands. By
2007, Green Bay had been putting up anemic sales numbers for several years, and Nestlé was gaining market share.
"Timing is extremely important when you're managing a
brand," said Pierre. "You can realize tremendous savings right
away by cutting the cost of goods and marketing." This is
what happened to Breyer's. Its ingredients got cheaper and
cheaper, and today some Breyer's flavors are labeled "frozen
dairy dessert" because they no longer meet the US government's definition of ice cream. You can also boost revenues,
temporarily, by running promotions and specials that cut the
price of the product. "It's a suicidal strategy in the long run,"

said Pierre. "But it takes time for the image of a brand to erode, and in the short run, you look like a hero."

Eric Walsh's boss finally got it. He decided to close the office in Green Bay, move those jobs to the New Jersey headquarters, and look for a new ice cream chief whose strengths were in marketing and innovation. "You can get away with anything in business as long as you perform," said Pierre. "But when you stop performing, you are quickly killed."

The board heard that Eric Walsh was leaving about the same time they decided to meet without Unilever people in the room. Jennifer invited Jeff, Pierre, and Terry to her home in March 2007. "I didn't want to be the chair any more, for several reasons," she says. "One was that we needed to signal a tougher stance toward Unilever." The group decided that Pierre would take the chairman's seat in January, and that Jeff and Jennifer would start looking for new board members. "And it sounds crazy now," said Jennifer, "but this was also the first time since the acquisition that I thoroughly read the sale agreements. I realized what a powerful tool we had."

Jeff started looking. "I called a bunch of white guys and asked them who would be good for our board, with just one condition: no white guys," he said. The calls led him to Anuradha Mittal, a native of India who had come to Berkeley as a young economist in the mid-1990s. Mittal is founder and director of the Oakland Institute, a progressive think tank focused on agriculture, development, and human rights. "Jeff launched into a long story about how his team had lost the company, and how they felt unable to protect the social mission," she said. "He was almost in mourning, but at the same time, he was quite inspiring.

"I got interested because it was a new kind of role for me. I was given the chance to work inside a corporate system instead of just standing off to the side and throwing rocks at it. I could take ownership of the problem."

Like Jeff, Anuradha spends a great deal of time representing the interests of low-income people–specifically farmers in developing countries, many of whom sell their goods to Unilever. She is a polished speaker and an accomplished writer, with experience leading high-profile advocacy campaigns. "I think the board wanted someone who would not shy away from conflict," she said. "When I met with Jeff's colleagues, they were still acting as if they had been defeated. Changing that attitude was the first thing on my list. I was only going to take the job if it could be a vehicle for change." She joined the board in October 2007.

Meet the New Boss

Eric Walsh's retirement, which happened at the end of March, gave the *Daily Plant* its lead story for April Fools' Day 2008. "Ding Dong the Witch Is Dead!," the anonymous employee wrote. This was "what no one is really saying, but wants to."

Walsh left behind a wounded company. The *Plant* joked about a tunnel dug by Ben & Jerry's employees so that they could escape to new jobs at Seventh Generation, a privately owned business with a strong social mission that is also based in Burlington. And it also took a swipe at Walt and his fondness for Buddhism: "Instead of using cherries in Cherry Garcia, we will ask production workers to think about cherries when they make the product. 'Philosophically, it will still be Cherry Garcia. We think it's Cherry Garcia, therefore it is,' said Walt Freese."

The board didn't see this issue of the *Daily Plant*, either. But by this time it didn't matter, because they finally understood that the company's future depended on them. Every year, Jeff attended a three-day meeting with the grant-making committee of the Ben & Jerry's Foundation, which is made up of company employees. They were eager to tell him what they knew. Ben and Jerry always attended the annual meeting of franchise owners, so they had also gotten earfuls. The board had asked for hard information on product quality and the social mission dozens of times, in many different ways, and they were getting tired of hearing excuses. Maybe Walsh's replacement would have a new attitude.

Pierre stepped up in January 2008, supported by Jeff as behind-the-scenes connector, and Jennifer, Terry, and Anuradha pushing them forward. "I changed the tone," Pierre said. "I was totally confrontational. It was the right time to be like that. Unilever's management was professional, but it was eroding the value of our brand. The clouds of war were on the horizon."

The independent board members were acting in the entrepreneurial tradition of Ben & Jerry's. They were finding their way in a job no one had done before. "None of the board members had top management experience, although Pierre came the closest. So it was a new experience for everybody," said Howard Fuguet. "And to this day, we have not found another company that has a governing document similar to Ben & Jerry's. The authority for their board does not depend on who the people are. It goes on forever. That is a big difference."

In his first meeting as chair, Pierre asked Ron Soiefer to review the sale agreements and outline the board's duties and powers. Ron affirmed that the board has the duty to protect the social mission and the power to veto changes in the product and other operational decisions made by the CEO. He added that the veto is a blunt weapon and should be used sparingly, if at all; its purpose, he said, is to encourage cooperation and consultation. Jeff replied that since Unilever had taken away a lot of the CEO's authority, it had left the board with fewer alternatives than a veto.

The board also objected to the target Unilever had set for the company's profit margin. It was too high, Jeff said, because a business with a three-part mission needed to invest in social programs and product quality. The mission wasn't an optional thing, Jeff said. It was a big part of "the essential integrity of the brand," and the sale agreements gave the board the right to defend it. The employees watched and cheered, silently.

John Le Boutillier, the man who took over from Eric Walsh, was not a political activist. But he wasn't a career executive from Unilever either, and he had been hired to make changes. He was from Kraft Foods, a notoriously tough place to work. And when he started dealing with the board of Ben & Jerry's in the spring of 2008, he actually had less experience with Unilever than the board did. "He came off like a hard-assed business manager, but we quickly found out that he had a heart," Pierre said. "We usually didn't agree, but there was something loveable about him."

Le Boutillier was initially skeptical about the business model of Ben & Jerry's, but he kept listening. "He comes from a corporate background, but we connected," said Anuradha. "We found common values. We both love a challenge. So if the question is how to pay people a living wage, and it's clear that the rules require us to do that, he will jump into the details with you and make it work, instead of dismissing it out of hand." Unlike Eric Walsh, John was also available. He was a regular presence at board meetings, and he was easy to reach.

Good things started to happen. Le Boutillier removed the barrier that had kept board members from working directly with employees, which allowed everyone to look at the same information. Debra Heintz and her team evaluated stores on their overall financial and operational health, and they started offering first aid. They supported owners who decided to close their stores, and they offered growth and investment strategies to owners who wanted to ride out the downturn. Complaints dropped.

In August, the board met in the Netherlands, toured the Unilever factory there that made Ben & Jerry's products, and visited a farm that was following the company's Caring Dairy standards for labor and environmental impact. The board learned that all the farms in the European co-op that supplied milk to Ben & Jerry's were on track to meet those standards, which meant that the European co-op was actually ahead of the St. Albans co-op, the company's supplier in Vermont. The European farmers were enthusiastic about Caring Dairy because they believed it would also give a marketing edge to their own brand, Beemster Cheese.

Rob Michalak's reboot of social metrics started yielding results, too. He and the board worked together for most of a year to develop measurements of Ben & Jerry's social mission performance that would meet the standard Ben had put into the sale agreements. The agreements say that social metrics should "increase at a rate in excess of the rate of sales increases."

"We had been measuring how much extra we spent to buy ingredients with a social benefit, like milk that didn't have artificial growth hormone," said Rob. "This did not do what the agreement said, and it also rewarded spending instead of performance. We needed to quantify the social mission so we could measure performance against sales." Rob's goal was similar in some ways to the work Liz Bankowski had been doing in the late 1990s, but there was a difference. Now his task was to measure progress on eleven specific "social mission priorities" listed in the sale agreements, including:

- improvements in packaging, leading to a compostable pint container;
- complying with CERES environmental principles, leading to "sustainability" for the entire business;
- continuous improvement in sustainable agriculture;

- continuing the relationship with the St. Albans dairy cooperative;
- opposing the use of recombinant bovine growth hormone (rBGH);
- making products that are free of genetically modified organisms (GMOs);
- continuing the PartnerShop program;
- purchasing ingredients from "values-led" suppliers (those whose core practices advance social mission goals);
- partnering with nonprofit organizations focused on environmental protection and social justice;
- supporting the Ben & Jerry's Foundation; and,
- continuous social auditing and assessment.

"Our task was to design measurements that spoke specifically to the agreement," said Rob. "The process took a while, because it had to be approved by the board, Unilever, and the management. We also had to decide how much weight to give to each point."

John and Suzy Le Boutillier with their daughter, Eleanor, in July 2008.

Rob also decided to bring in a third-party social auditor to replace James Heard, who had left after 2004. "I ran into a CPA, Brendan LeBlanc, who told me he would be interested in working with us," Rob said. "We decided to use him to help us design the methodology, so our reporting of social metrics could reach a level of assurance that would satisfy an accountant." Rob said that in 2008, he could not find another business or organization that could give him advice on how to design social measurements to this standard. The company was again pushing the edge of socially responsible business practices, which was just where the board wanted it to be.

The Other Shoe

Despite the progress, the board remained suspicious. "These were all long-term things," said Jeff. "In the first few months, a lot of it just seemed like talk. We were still waiting for results." Seven years of miscommunication and frustration had not helped the board build a relationship of trust with Unilever, either. Jeff and his colleagues were still waiting for the other shoe to drop. So in the fall of 2008, Jeff started moving on plan B. He contacted Howie Fuguet, who agreed to give the board legal advice without pay. Howie began looking at the sale agreements to identify the areas where Unilever was in violation.

"It was clear that Unilever had seriously breached the agreements," said Howie. "They were running roughshod over the provisions relative to the powers of the CEO. They had admitted to changing the product quality, and the CEO had not told the board. The overseas operations were not in compliance. And there was more. It wasn't hard to see."

Jeff called on two other old friends, too. He asked Ben and Jerry to work with the board on effective ways to organize the public behind the board's objections. Ben especially was happy to get involved. He started talking about organizing a boycott of Unilever products. "It was a rerun of our history," said Jeff. But this time, Ben wasn't running the show. The board was.

By the middle of November 2008, John Le Boutillier had been working with Ben & Jerry's for more than eight months. He also had responsibility for several other ice cream brands, some of which were much bigger than Ben & Jerry's, but the Burlington company got more of his time than any of the others. Although Ben & Jerry's was not an easy company to manage, John understood that it was strategically important to Unilever, and he felt the relationship was going well. And so, respecting the terms of the agreement, he threw out an idea to see whether or not it was something the board would consider.

At the November board meeting, Walt and John proposed that the company stop producing pints at Waterbury and expand the site's capacity as a tourist attraction. The cost of producing a pint was far higher using the old equipment, so moving all of the production to St. Albans would save millions of dollars a year, which could be used to fund more social mission initiatives. Expanding Waterbury would also improve the visitor experience and turn the site into a monument to Ben, Jerry, and the company's vision of social justice. From John's point of view, this was an operational decision that would save money while enhancing the integrity of the brand. It was a clear win-win.

After the presentation, Pierre stopped the meeting so that he could meet privately with Jeff, Jennifer, Terry, and Anuradha. They came back with a long list of questions for John and Walt, and they insisted that John meet with Ben and Jerry to get their reactions. The board did not see the proposal as a win-win. They saw it as proof of malicious intent. This was the signal they had been waiting for. The other shoe had dropped.

"Waterbury is hallowed ground to us," said Jeff. "So I objected to the proposal on such a fundamental level that I still have a hard time putting it into words. I thought they were going to eliminate jobs and then talk about how great we were. It came from a marketing and cost-cutting mindset, and it was more than offensive to me. It was absurd."

Jeff also insisted that the board visit Waterbury the next day, and "that was a turning point for me," said Anuradha. "I saw people my own age who had worked there for twenty years, and it had been their only job. They were so happy to meet us. And Unilever was considering shutting down the plant because it wasn't efficient. When I met those workers, I realized the weight I carried. It wasn't about the ice cream. It was about providing dignified lives for people who were the backbone of the company."

Le Boutillier says it was clear that the idea was dead on arrival, and he didn't pursue it further. But it was too late. To the board, the proposal was proof that Unilever still had the wrong approach toward Ben & Jerry's. They decided to defend Waterbury by going on the attack. Jeff drafted a letter for the independent directors to sign and send to Walt, John, and four of their bosses at Unilever on December 14. The letter asked for "a serious and complete review of where we are, where we have fallen off the track, where we want to head, and how we can all get there."

"Our board stands united behind the three-part mission and the Leading with Progressive Values statement," the letter continued. "We see business as a powerful force for social change ... we are all aware of the complexity of redefining business from the Milton Friedman perspective to the Ben & Jerry's perspective. We know that it is not simply a matter of trade-offs, it is not simply a matter of a program here or there, it is not philanthropy, and it is not building a brand. It is a philosophy of how we run our business day to day, keeping a social justice and environmental perspective on the table as we make all of our decisions for a profitable business."

The letter went on with a long list of "unresolved issues." It began with changes to the product that the board had never approved and asked for an accounting of those changes. It continued with a request to appoint a chief executive officer for Ben & Jerry's who had the broad discretion over the business outlined in the sale agreements, including the authority to choose suppliers based on their social practices rather than cost. It also asked that Unilever reduce the targeted profit margin for 2009 by four percentage points.

The letter also made specific requests to add employees who would be dedicated to the social mission, reinstitute the independent social auditor, and more. Although the letter never threatened Unilever directly, the tone was serious and the implication was clear. "To maintain our reputation, we must continually challenge the business status quo," Jeff wrote. "We want the world to say, 'There goes Ben & Jerry's again, aren't they ever satisfied?' The answer is 'No, not yet.'" The letter ended with a request to meet with "Unilever representatives who are empowered to make the decisions necessary to help us all move forward."

Le Boutillier says that the letter made it harder to move forward. It was not necessary for the board to have a contentious relationship with Unilever because both sides wanted the same thing. "Unilever bought the company because of its three-part mission," he said. "We loved the social justice component and the focus on product quality. There was just a massive misunderstanding brought about by personality differences, geography, and years of miscommunication."

The proposal and the letter led to months of tense meetings with lots of lawyers and threats, implicit and otherwise. But looking back on it, Le Boutillier says that the blowup needed to happen. "There was all this resentment," he said. "It needed to come out, and it wasn't getting done by staying nice. The result was a very nasty stretch, but we were like two lovers having a bad fight. The minute we turned the corner, it was like a curtain had been lifted. It was incredible."

Ways of Working

In another way, the timing of the letter was fortunate for the board. As they sent it, Paul Polman was becoming the new CEO of Unilever, and like Le Boutillier, Polman had been hired to deliver change.

In 2005, Unilever had abandoned the old cochair system for a more traditional business structure that had clearer lines of authority, with a CEO and a nonexecutive board chair. In January 2009, for the first time in the company's 120-year history, it brought in a leader from outside the company instead of promoting from within. Polman took the helm as a severe global recession was complicating everyone's business plans, and he arrived ready to shake things up.

Polman had previously been a leader at two big multinationals: first at Procter & Gamble, where he turned around their European business, and then at Nestlé, where he had been the CFO. With Unilever, it was finally his turn to hold the top job. "It's great to start at a time of uncertainty," Polman told a British newspaper on February 9. "When there is a lot of wind, even the turkeys can fly, but with no wind, it's only the eagles. I'd hate to be a turkey."[1]

On Polman's first day at Unilever he froze employee salaries, cut the travel budget, and shocked analysts by saying that the volatile economy had rendered the company's financial projections worthless. Three months later, at an international conference on climate change, Polman called on businesses and governments to work together to end global deforestation, especially in the tropics. He committed Unilever to managing its impact on climate change throughout its supply chain, including the farms it bought from and the consumers it sold to. His comments got a lot of attention because Unilever is one of the world's largest customers for palm oil and other products of tropical agriculture.

Polman brought Unilever a bolder style of leadership that was more focused on corporate social responsibility. "This was smart," said Pierre, "and it was also taking a page from Ben & Jerry's. When consumers know that Unilever is out in front on sustainability, it distinguishes their products from the competition. That had been our strategy for twenty years."

As soon as they heard the news about Polman, Ben Cohen and Jerry Greenfield tried to meet with him, casually going over the heads of John Le Boutillier and his boss, Michael Polk, president of Unilever Americas. Going over your boss's head is a big corporate no-no. They didn't get the meeting with Polman until March, and at a five-hour meeting Ben and Jerry held with Walt, John, and Polk in Vermont in January, the vibe in the room was as chilly as the air outside. But the January meeting also got results. The board quickly got word that if product quality had slipped, it would be fixed.

Things were looking up. But returning to the original standards of product quality, and verifying that those standards had been met, would be a complicated task. What were the original specifications? How should the company restore them, and should they tell customers the standards had been changed back? Should the people who test product quality be ordinary customers or sophisticated taste testers? And what about the board's other demands, such as restoring the power of the CEO? John says that at the meeting with Ben and Jerry, he agreed to negotiate a "ways of working" document to resolve these and other issues. The board spent the rest of their January meeting talking with him about it.

On March 9, Ben and Jerry flew to London to have dinner with Paul Polman and Michael Polk. They covered most of the topics in the board's December 14 letter. The top guys reassured them that Waterbury would remain unchanged, and the pints would be returned to their original, pre-Unilever specifications. But Ben and Jerry were not happy with Polk's summary of the meeting. Unilever was still insisting on a profit margin that was too high, they said, and the three-part mission was still being crippled by attempts to integrate Ben & Jerry's into Unilever's hierarchical "matrix" management structure, instead of allowing the CEO to draft an annual plan and operate according to its terms. They responded to Polk with a threat: "Should Unilever refuse to abide by the terms of the sale agreements, Ben and Jerry are not going to be quiet about it."

The ways of working document, or WOW (no kidding), was going to be a kind of manual—not a legal document, but an annually updated memorandum that described the complicated relationship between the board and Unilever in writing. "When you think about it, being the CEO of Ben & Jerry's is a very hard job," said Jeff. "You report to the company's board of directors, and you also report to Unilever executives, and you can be certain that your bosses will often disagree with each other. At the same time, you need to run the company. So how do you do that? The CEO will be a lot more likely to succeed if we all agree on where the boundaries are."

Walt was struggling to placate the board and Unilever while also running the company, and the pressure was becoming unbearable. "Walt was adamant that he should be the board's sole contact, so we didn't talk to the board except in highly controlled ways," said Sean Greenwood. "I think Walt did this because he thought it was his best chance to protect Ben & Jerry's. But ultimately that tactic undid him, because after a while, no one trusted him."

Howie Fuguet started putting in a lot of hours sending drafts of the WOW back and forth with Unilever's lawyers. His only pay was pint coupons, along with the satisfaction of making some of the country's highest-paid lawyers squirm.

"At first we just traded papers," Howie says. "But with each subsequent draft, they got friendlier, until they were more or less on our side. They saw that Unilever was going to lose on a lot of these questions, and they risked a lot of bad publicity if they didn't satisfy us. I think that Ron Soiefer and the other Unilever lawyers eventually had to bring the Unilever executives along and make them see that."

"Remember, social initiatives take a long time to yield benefits, while cost-cutting has an immediate benefit," said Pierre. "This is the key to the WOW. We need to come up with a way to manage these components. What is going to be the return on various kinds of investments, financial and social? How can we calculate the margins? How do we link the social mission to profitability? Let's figure it out!"

Turning the Corner

As the drafts of the WOW became more detailed, Rob Michalak and his team started working on the company's first audited Social and Environmental Assessment Report (SEAR) since 2004. The auditor Rob had hired reported to the board in June 2009 that he had found twenty-four deficiencies in the way the company measured social mission activities. For example, the company had purchased carbon offsets so that it could claim that activities that put carbon dioxide into the atmosphere, such as driving trucks, would be balanced by tree-planting and other actions taken by the vendor who sold the offsets. Yet Ben & Jerry's had never followed up with the vendor to make sure it had actually done what it promised to do. And that was one of the simpler fixes.

Measuring social performance was going to be extremely complicated. Lots of new territory needed to be mapped out, and statistical measurements would have to be created from scratch. An even bigger problem was that half of the auditor's recommendations were up to Walt to fix, and the board doubted that Walt had the authority to fix them.

Meanwhile, the board and the founders kept working on plan B in case the WOW fell through. Howie wrote a press release outlining their legal complaint, and Ben thought up ways to present the board's objections to the public in old-school Ben & Jerry's style. There was talk of a new ice cream flavor called "Unilever Squash" (because the company was squashing Ben & Jerry's) and a road trip with the founders in a motorcycle and sidecar, evoking the cross-country journey they had once taken to scoop ice cream in a van named the Cowmobile. But Howie hoped they wouldn't ever use these ideas. "We were using a fairly common tactic," he said. "You threaten to keep your opponent at the negotiating table, and to show them you're serious. But it is very expensive to actually go to court, and you never know where it's going to end up."

"I was looking at the drafts of the ways of working agreement, and I was looking at the PR campaign, and I was uncomfortable with both choices," said Jeff. "The negotiation wasn't moving fast enough, but our alternative was to attack Unilever, which meant that our employees would get hurt."

Jeff was also increasingly uncertain about letting Walt in on the board's plans. In April, Walt had telephoned him to relay the news that the changes in butterfat, chunks, and other aspects of product quality over the last eight years had been much more extensive than he had previously reported to the board. "He said he hadn't known about the changes," said Jeff. "And that left me thinking that one of two things were true. Either he really didn't know, or he did know and hadn't told us. Either one made him look bad."

The board put the PR plan on hold and continued to negotiate. After a meeting in July, John Le Boutillier wrote to

Pierre and Jeff that there are "lots of tough topics that promise to continue into the future, but we are much closer than
ever before and are in agreement on philosophy and direction. Now we just need to work through the how." John
went on to summarize a long list of agreements and open
items concerning product quality, new hires, social metrics,
the CEO reporting relationship, and so on.

Jeff, Ben, Jerry, and Pierre also met with Walt to work on
a three-year plan for the company. "It was a forward-look-
ing meeting," said Jeff. "We were trying to help him balance a
lot of competing goals, and we were working well together."
But the sales numbers, at the depth of a severe global recession, were far below expectations. At the August 2009 board
meeting in London, Walt presented the financial data along
with his three-year plan, and no one was happy with either
one. The profit margin was the crux of the matter. It had
declined since 2008, which made John unhappy. And Walt
projected that it should remain at a fairly high level over the
next three years. This made the board unhappy, because
they wanted more investment in the social mission. "It was
the same old stuff," said Jeff.

Around this time, Jeff took Walt aside for a private conversation. "I warned him about keeping the board from communicating with employees and Unilever directly," he said.
"I told him that you can only walk that line for so long, and
that people were finding ways to communicate. I also told
him that when those walls came down, it would happen
quickly."

The London meeting was the first for Kees van der Graaf,
who had retired from the board of Unilever and was preparing to take the place of Hans Eenhorn on the board of Ben
& Jerry's. "I remember two things from that meeting," said
Kees. "First, Hans took me aside and said, 'Be careful what
you say, because the board is about to go to court with Unilever.' And the second thing was, no one seemed to like Walt.

I think social mission people tend to be too nice. No one was satisfied with him, but no one was willing to tell him the truth, either."

Still, signs were accumulating that the new relationship was bringing life to the social mission. Unilever agreed to extend the living wage policy beyond Ben & Jerry's employees in Vermont so that people who made and sold Ben & Jerry's in Vermont, Nevada, the Netherlands, and everywhere else would be paid according to the same system. And in 2009, the company started using paper for its pint containers that came from sustainably managed woodlots, as certified by the Forest Stewardship Council (FSC). They had stopped using chlorine-free paper in 2007, after it became clear that a new kind of paper production using much smaller amounts of chlorine would become the industry standard. Yet the sale agreements required Unilever to make progress toward a "compostable pint," and this was progress.

In September 2009, Vermont made it legal for same-sex couples to marry. Ben & Jerry's had been a supporter of gay rights since the early 1990s, but Unilever had vetoed an employee proposal to celebrate the state's civil union law for same-sex couples by releasing a special flavor in 2000. This time was different. The company temporarily renamed its Chubby Hubby flavor "Hubby Hubby," donated ice cream to the wedding receptions of Vermont's first same-sex spouses, and publicized the efforts of the national advocacy organization Freedom to Marry.

In the fall of 2009, John Le Boutillier and the board negotiated a five-year plan aimed at "re-radicalizing" the company. The plan called for all the ingredients used by Ben & Jerry's to be free of genetically modified organisms (GMOs) by the end of 2012. By the end of 2013, all ingredients would also come from farms and processors who were paid fairly and met minimum environmental and social standards. New youth training initiatives would be put in place, too. Few

Where, after all, do universal rights begin?

In small places, close to home – so close and so small that they cannot be seen on any maps of the world. Yet they are the world of individual persons; the neighborhood he lives in; the school or college he attends; the factory, farm, or office where he works. Such are the places where every man, woman and child seeks equal justice, equal opportunity, equal dignity without discrimination. Unless these rights have meaning there, they have little meaning anywhere. Without concerned citizen action to uphold them close to home, we shall look in vain for progress in the larger world.

Eleanor Roosevelt / 1958

We urge members of the Vermont Legislature to Support the Civil Union Bill (H.847)

Autumn Harp · Adult & Family Therapy, PC · A.T. Land Use Consulting · Ben & Jerry's · Bradford G. Elliot · Danforth Pewterers Ltd. · Debby Bergh Consulting · Dynamic Business Solutions · Eastern Systems Group · Farm & Wilderness Camps · ForesTrade, Inc. · Gardener's Supply Co. · Hubbardton Forge · Hemmings Motor News · Keller & Fuller, Inc. · Light-Works · Mamopalire of VT, Inc. · Magic Hat Brewing Co. · Marketing Partners, Inc. · Main Street Landing Co. · Merritt & Merritt · Montgomery & Merrill, CPA's · Norrell Services · Page Designs, Inc. · R.H. Scott Associates, LLC · Seventh Generation · Sleeping Lion Associates, Inc. · SoHo Modular Design · Social Architect Associates · The Negotiation Center · Tall Paul's Tall Mall · TK Consulting

companies of Vermont Businesses for Social Responsibility. VBSR

Ben & Jerry's has supported the rights of same-sex couples since it began providing health benefits to gay and lesbian partners in the early 1990s. In March 2000, it lobbied for Vermont's pioneering law allowing same-sex civil unions. In 2001, Unilever's new CEO vetoed an employee proposal to celebrate that law's passage by releasing a flavor called Vermont Honeymoon. Eight years later, Unilever allowed the company to release Hubby Hubby to celebrate the Vermont legislature's decision to legalize gay marriage.

companies of this size had made a similar commitment to the fair trade and values-led sourcing movements before, and the pledge to eliminate GMOs was even more audacious. This was just where the board of Ben & Jerry's wanted the company to be.

"The plan is just a document," John said. "What is significant is how we got to a plan. For the first time, we escaped from the old pattern of Unilever defending the economic mission while the board defended the social mission. As we were negotiating, there were even role reversals." There were times when John would question whether or not a proposal was radical enough, and also times when a board member would push for additional economic growth. Jeff was surprised and pleased at the way John threw himself into things.

"This was when the old acrimony and distrust between the board and Unilever finally dissolved," said John. "It happened very quickly. It was the first time senior Unilever people and the board united in the desire for a business with a healthy three-part mission. There was no more us and them. There was only us." Le Boutillier put limits on the company's profit targets, which Paul Polman approved, and this helped give Ben & Jerry's the cash it would need to reach their social mission goals.

Jeff says that while the re-radicalization plan did improve the relationship between the board and Unilever a great deal, the tension between the two sides did not go away completely, and he adds that it probably never will. Every year there are social mission targets and profit targets, and if the company doesn't hit either of them, both sides should come back to the table. The difference, he says, is that both sides started negotiating in good faith.

Another fundamental change came when the Social and Environmental Assessment Report for 2008 was released in September 2009, with large sections certified by the CPA. The report was grounded in new metrics that would make it possible to measure the productivity of social mission spending and fund the social mission according to sales. The new metrics divide the social mission into categories, such as "environment," "scoop shops," and "values-led sourcing," and give each category a certain number of points. A perfect score is 200, although the company will never reach that because it keeps changing its goals. The distribution of points allows the company to distribute spending on the social mission according to its priorities, and also to ensure that social spending grows faster than sales.

In mid-November 2009, Jeff flew to Burlington for two meetings. On November 17, he went to Ben's house with Jerry and the independent directors to talk about the public relations campaign against Unilever. "We were all struggling with it," Jeff said, "and eventually Jerry said he couldn't participate in it because he didn't want to hurt the employees. I was relieved to hear him say that because I wasn't comfortable with the plan either. By that time, I had a lot of skin in

The plant in St. Albans took more than three years to build. When it opened, it was capable of producing 50 percent more ice cream than Ben & Jerry's actually sold.

this game." Ben was taken aback, but he said he wouldn't do any public appearances without Jerry.

The next day, at the board meeting, a lot of good things happened. The company's research and development director announced that seventeen flavors had been restored to the original specifications and would ship in the first quarter of 2010. The board decided not to announce the formula changes to the public; instead, they would emphasize Cherry Garcia in promotions designed to lure lapsed customers back. The board also heard that the company would commit to having all of its ingredients come from fairly traded sources, and also to be free of genetically modified ingredients (GMOs) by the end of 2013. Sugar would be especially hard to find, but the company was going to do it.

On the second day of the board meeting, Rob led a long discussion of the social metrics and the 2008 audit, and he outlined plans to improve reporting for the audit of 2009. The board asked Rob and the auditor to come back and present their findings to the board first, every year. They also set quality assurance procedures for the restoration of more flavors to "gold standard" specifications, and they ended the meeting with a celebratory tour of the St. Albans plant.

"When I got back to Ithaca I felt a huge sense of relief, like we had dodged a bullet," said Jeff. "We had walked right up to the edge of a cliff. At the last minute, we decided not to jump. And that's when we turned the corner."

Early in 2010, Rob got the green light from Unilever to start integrating the "quality of results" model into the annual evaluation of the company's social performance. Every gallon of milk, scoop of sugar, special employee benefit, and advertisement would be evaluated and ranked for its contribution to the social mission, to ensure that the company's social performance increases faster than sales. It was an almost unimaginably complex goal for a company with large manufacturing plants that mixed more than a hundred ingredients. No one had ever done anything like it before. But Ben & Jerry's was going to try.

One person would not be coming along, however. By the beginning of 2010, Walt had played all of his cards. The board and Unilever made a joint decision that the company needed a new CEO.

John had someone else in mind for the job, someone he knew well. Jostein Solheim was a veteran Unilever executive who had spent the last few years developing ice cream brands. He had a broad resume and a lot of creativity. He was capable of performing at a higher level, and John knew that he would love to run Ben & Jerry's. So John made the call.

THIRTEEN

Pursuing Linked Prosperity

Three years after John made the call, on the morning of January 19, 2013, in the ballroom of a Las Vegas resort, about three hundred people gathered for the annual meeting of the independent businesspeople who own Ben & Jerry's stores. The crowd buzzed about the afternoon they had just spent together at the Shade Tree, a shelter for victims of domestic violence. Store owners and employees, many wearing well-designed T-shirts made for the meeting, had painted, hauled trash, fixed things, and handed out free ice cream to smiling women and delighted children. They had also contributed $3,000 to the shelter, a donation the company had triple-matched. The annual meeting had included a project like this every year since 1996.

The program that morning was a lot like the company: it was smart, friendly, and fun. Banners on the stage were decorated with doodles of ice cream cones and peace signs, interspersed with enthusiastic phrases like "Great Idea!" printed in a font that looked like lower-case handwriting. People wiped away tears as they watched a slide show of themselves hugging their new Shade Tree friends, as the song "Home" by Phil Phillips, the 2012 winner of *American Idol*, boomed over the loudspeakers. Then, after a lot of thanking, Ben Cohen and Jerry Greenfield took the stage.

Just to the Side

Ben also thanked everyone for the day of activism. "But there are two kinds of activism," he said, as Jerry looked on.

"There's direct action, which is what we did yesterday—helping people who need help. And then there's advocacy, which is about changing the system that creates the conditions that require direct action in the first place. The only reason the Shade Tree needed us is that our government is not funding organizations like it at the level that is required. They are finding other things to do with our money."

Political donations from corporations and the ultrawealthy have seriously warped the priorities of governments, said Ben, which is why, in 2012, Ben & Jerry's launched a campaign called "Get the Dough out of Politics." The campaign is aimed at passing a constitutional amendment to overturn the Supreme Court's *Citizens United* decision and make it clear that corporations do not have constitutional rights. But people have criticized the "Dough" campaign for sending mixed messages. During the 2012 election cycle, Unilever also contributed $467,100 to a lobbying group aimed at defeating a California referendum that would require the labeling of products that contain genetically modified organisms (GMOs). Unilever did this despite Ben & Jerry's long-standing position in favor of labeling. The referendum was defeated, and a torrent of corporate money ($46 million against, $9 million for) probably had something to do with it.

"Ben & Jerry's has a heritage of being an edgy, cutting-edge company," said Ben. "It is supposed to do things that haven't been done before. But the reality is that Ben & Jerry's is owned by a major corporation that is not particularly edgy." A nervous chuckle crept into Ben's delivery as he prepared to make his pitch. "You, as franchisees, are in the middle," he said. "You're free—heh, heh, heh—to pretty much do whatever the heck you want. You're independent operators ... and when the cat's away, the mice will play."

The audience leaned forward as Ben described his new organization, Stamp Stampede, which sells rubber stamps designed to print messages on US currency, such as, "Not to be used for bribing politicians," or "Money is not speech." "This is not exactly a Unilever-sanctioned activity, but it does what the company says it wants to do, which is get the money out of politics," said Ben. "It is a form of monetary jujitsu. We're using money to get money out of politics. Once this spreads, we can make hundreds of millions of impressions."

Setting up a stamp station in a Ben & Jerry's store, he said, is a way for owners to "act in that edgy, never-been-done-before kind of way that is the company's heritage." He and Jerry would be selling the rubber stamps at the company's trade show that afternoon. He invited everyone in the audience to stop by for a hug, a photo, and a stamp.

Ben is a great salesman. He made it seem like buying a stamp was a cool, subversive act and dared the audience to do it. "You can join the stamp stampede and be like Ben, or you can not join and be like Unilever," he said, and the audience gasped. But during his comments, Ben had asked the CEO of Ben & Jerry's to hold up one of the stamps and the CEO was happy to do it, because, after all, he had a stamp station in his office. And by mid-January, the company's site, GetTheDoughOut.org, had already persuaded thirty thousand people to join the movement to overturn *Citizens United*.

So there was Ben, smiling as he told the people who run the business he cofounded that, despite their best efforts, they could still do a lot better. The global franchisee meeting was a long seminar on how to use the three-part mission to win in the competitive world of ice cream stores. Ben briefly hijacked the proceedings to describe his crazy stamp idea, which actually seemed brilliant once he had made his case. Then he invited everyone to join him, just as he had been doing for thirty-five years. He and Jerry were standing just off to the side of the company. They had almost come full circle.

That was as close as I got to Ben and Jerry. They declined my request for an interview, saying they didn't want to relive the past. I didn't blame them. If I had faced as many

The independent board of directors of Ben & Jerry's in May 2013.
From left: Helen Jones, Kees van der Graaf, (kneeling) Terry Mollner
and Pierre Ferrari, (standing) Jeff Furman, Jostein Solheim, Jennifer
Henderson, Anuradha Mittal, and Daryn Dodson.

annoying questions about uncomfortable topics as they
have, I probably wouldn't talk to me either. Besides, I got the
story. Although their names are on almost every page of this
book, the story is not really about them or their history. It's
about linked prosperity.

"You know, when you stand on the shoulders of giants,
you have a great view," said Jostein Solheim, the CEO of Ben
& Jerry's, who took the stage after Ben was through. "I have
worked for about twelve companies, and I have never had
such a great view." Then he thanked everybody, too.

Jostein didn't mention Stamp Stampede except to say
that a Unilever person had recently visited his office and had
stamped his money on the way out, "possibly for evidence."

He talked about linked prosperity, which he said was "the business model of Ben & Jerry's. We don't see ourselves as an ice cream company. If we did, we'd be no different than Häagen-Dazs. We see ourselves as a partner to communities." Linking the company's prosperity to employees means not just paying a livable wage, but guaranteeing a dignified life. Linking it to farmers, processors, and suppliers means "eliminating poverty from our supply chain," he said. Linking prosperity to customers means measuring the social mission and making sure it grows faster than sales.

"We need to keep optimizing for linked prosperity," he said. "This is a very powerful model, but it isn't easy. There will never be an end point, because our ambition is to change the world. We need to keep making choices that are painful. We are on a journey."

A Moment for Capitalism

I left the meeting wondering about two things. The first is the eerie ways a company's culture can mimic the personality of its founders. First the cofounder of Ben & Jerry's told the crowd that although they were doing great things, they still weren't getting it right. Then the CEO said the same thing, and he added that they never would.

I thought of Liz Bankowski, back in the early 1990s, pushing social values throughout the company and saying, "None of us felt like we were getting it right." Or Ben Cohen, in 2000, signing a unique agreement that injected the three-part mission into one of the world's largest corporations and saying, "It was just about the worst day of my life." Again and again, groundbreaking accomplishments were portrayed as insufficient. They were small victories within larger failures. What would it take to satisfy these people?

I also wondered how Ben & Jerry's had pulled off its turn-around. Back in March 2010, when Jostein took over as CEO, the board of directors was still trying to decide whether or not to sue Unilever for breach of contract. Now everybody, including Ben and Jerry, seemed to be working together. There were disagreements, but the center was holding and the company seemed like a reasonably happy family. What had happened?

One of the reasons for all that good feeling is Jostein, who is, by all accounts, an exceptionally talented chief executive. He describes himself as "a dabbler with a lot of curiosity." He is Norwegian, so he arrived already hardened to Vermont winters. His resume includes fourteen years in Unilever's ice cream division, the last three doing brand development. He is also enthusiastically wacky. He started his job as a scooper on Free Cone Day and likes to dress appropriately for company functions: at the Las Vegas meeting, for example, he came to one party in a Holstein-patterned suit jacket.

"Jostein is an ice cream man," said Dave Stever, "but even better, he's a Ben & Jerry's man. He has the right intuition, the stuff that you have to have in your gut. You can be the best spreadsheet person in the world, but if you don't get this company, you don't get it. He gets it."

Debra Heintz in 2008.

I could also think of two other reasons for the turnaround. One is the sale agreements the board negotiated with Unilever in 2000. For most of a decade, the company was whipsawed between a boss who didn't respect the Agreements and board members and employees who did. John Le Boutillier, backed up by his bosses, Kevin Havelock and Paul Polman, changed the tone at Ben & Jerry's from

Ben & Jerry's opened a store in Tokyo in 2012. In 2014, the company's ice cream is sold in nearly three dozen countries.

suspicion to mutual respect. The profit advocates and the social mission advocates came back to the table, started playing by the rules of the sale agreements, and finally began a mature working relationship. When that happened, the company got its heart back.

"I came in with the financial freedom to invest in product quality and put the social mission into high gear," said Jostein. "If I hadn't had that freedom, I would not have taken the job. I could give the managers millions of dollars to make the transition to fairly traded ingredients. It wasn't just talk."

Of course, it's easier to fund the social mission when you're making truckloads of money. And the other big reason for the turnaround is that under Jostein, Ben & Jerry's has been making steady progress toward becoming a global brand. The product is on sale in almost three dozen countries in the spring of 2013, with double-digit revenue growth in Europe, a spectacularly successful 2011 launch in Australia, and a flagship store in Tokyo that opened in 2012. That launch alone could drive growth for years. Sales of Häagen-Dazs in Japan are estimated to be over $400 million a year.

If things go as planned, the United States will account for less than half of Ben & Jerry's revenues by 2020. So the company is changing again, and a new set of challenges has emerged. "It's an exciting time," said Jostein. "The stars are aligned. Ben, Jerry, and Jeff are approaching things with a lot more maturity, Unilever is taking its corporate social responsibility seriously, and I think business in general is at a tipping point. The belief that all a company must do is get maximum short-term profits for shareholders has come to a dead end. The mainstream is now discovering that. It's an important moment for capitalism."

Reaching for Transparency

Unilever's new attitude also changed the role of the board. At the end of 2010, when Pierre became the CEO of Heifer International, he resigned as chair and Jeff took the gavel. "I changed the approach," said Jeff. "I use a lot more encouragement. There's a lot more positive energy in the company now, so it's easier to go around patting people on the back."

Power works by division, but influence works by multiplication. Unilever has most of the power at Ben & Jerry's. The board has just enough to ensure that the product quality and social parts of the three-part mission are taken seriously. But the board has a lot of influence. And if power shared is power lessened, the opposite is true of influence. Jeff's board moves the three-part mission forward by sharing what they know and encouraging others to see what they see.

At the end of 2010, after countless drafts, Jeff and Jostein set aside the "ways of working" document because their agenda was too full. Instead of arguing over ways of working, the board and Unilever were piling on the work. One of the first things Jeff did was add Helen Jones to the board of directors. Helen had left the company in 2009 because she was unable to continue working with Walt. It was another bad breakup, but she still loved Ben & Jerry's. "I was absolutely delighted to get the call," she said.

Around that time, the company started taking actions that would have been unimaginable a few years earlier. In October 2011, Jeff wrote and the board passed a resolution expressing their "deepest admiration" for the Occupy Wall Street movement that had taken over a park in Lower Manhattan, and for its supporters across the country.

"The inequity that exists between classes in our country is simply immoral," the resolution read. "We know that the media will either ignore you or frame the issue as to who may be getting pepper sprayed rather than addressing the despair and hardships borne by so many, or accurately conveying what this movement is about. All this goes on while corporate profits continue to soar and millionaires whine about paying a bit more in taxes ... As a board and as a company we have actively been involved with these issues for years, but your efforts have put them out front in a way we have not been able to do ... we are honored to join you."

The press release grabbed the media's attention, and the company put its support for Occupy back in the spotlight when Ben, Jerry, Jeff, and Jostein talked about it at the National Press Club in December. A lot of the media coverage either attacked or ridiculed Ben & Jerry's. But during the last quarter of 2011, the company's sales in the United States also grew faster than they had in years. While it isn't possible to say that one thing caused the other, Jostein believes it.

Back in 2003, Pierre tried to persuade the CEO of Ben & Jerry's that taking controversial positions on social issues would increase sales. A decade later, the CEO of Ben & Jerry's said the same thing to the crowd in Las Vegas. "The most dangerous thing for Ben & Jerry's is to lean back and not speak up," said Jostein. "The more people get pissed off at us, the more ice cream we sell. This is counterintuitive, and it is hard for any big corporation to understand. But it is true beyond a doubt."

I can't think of another big company, let alone a wholly owned subsidiary of one of the world's largest corporations, that would post a love letter to radical street protestors. It's also surprising that the company's CEO believes that doing "edgy" things also increases sales. And the most incredible thing is that they're sincere. Ben & Jerry's invited Occupy activists, plus people from Jobs with Justice and other activist groups, to participate in the company's annual retreat, talk to the board and top managers, and look for ways to collaborate.

Ben & Jerry's can do these things because most of the company's loyal customers agree with their politics, and also because of another unusual corporate policy: transparency. They do have secrets, of course. Like any food company, Ben & Jerry's keeps most of its product development, financial reports, and marketing plans under wraps. But ask about social and environmental performance, and the company will share information until you beg them to stop. As a result, even people who disagree with Ben & Jerry's positions on the issues usually think of them as trustworthy and committed to making great ice cream.

Transparency lets Ben & Jerry's set audacious goals without fear of failure. Its big goal for 2013 was to procure all of its ingredients from sources that are certified as fairly traded and free of GMOs. "This is a massively complex project," Rob Michalak said in March. "If you measure by volume, we are close to the goal. But we use over 100 ingredients when you count up all the chunks and swirls, and some of them are problematic. We have weekly operational meetings where we go through deep, thick spreadsheets that are full of tiny numbers."

It is essential that the company use corn syrup, for example, because without it, the swirls won't come out right. The company has an urgent need for the caramel stripes that run through Stephen Colbert's Americone Dream, and all their other swirls, to taste nice and smooth. But nearly all of the corn grown in the United States comes from genetically modified seeds, which means that finding a supplier of GMO-free corn syrup wasn't easy. In the spring of 2013, they finally found one.

So the company is pushing hard to make its goals, but if they don't make them, they will simply explain why and keep pushing. "At the same time, we need to keep raising the bar," said Rob. "We struggled for years to find fairly traded sources of cane sugar. Now that we have done it, we can't improve that further, so we need to go back to the sale agreements and set new goals. It's the same for dairy products." A few years ago, he said, Ben & Jerry's was satisfied if its dairy came from family farms that did not use bovine growth hormone. Now it pays farmers to enroll in the Caring Dairy program and continuously improve their practices against multiple sustainability indicators, such as the use of energy, nutrients, and pesticides; emissions of greenhouse gases; and measures of animal husbandry, biodiversity, labor practices, and farm economics.

Transparency also allows Ben & Jerry's to make trade-offs as they approach a social goal. For example, some farms in the St. Albans co-op do not meet Caring Dairy standards. This means that some of the milk stored in the co-op's tanks comes from these noncompliant farms. So Ben & Jerry's documents that the production of farms enrolled in its Caring Dairy program is sufficient to cover the company's needs, even if some of its milk does not come from those farms.

In March 2013, ninety-one farms in Vermont and the Northeast participated in the program, along with most of the farms in the Dutch co-op. This is already more than enough to cover Ben & Jerry's global needs, and the company is constantly signing up more farms. Without transparency, their "batch sourcing" policy would be an opportunity for a muck-raking journalist. With it, Ben & Jerry's is free to encourage conversations about how to reduce the substantial environmental impacts of dairy production while protecting the livelihoods of family farmers.

Pushing those conversations is the real point of the exercise. Ben & Jerry's does not take an official position on whether genetically modified organisms (GMOs) are good or bad, for example, although most of its employees probably oppose them. The company's position is that products containing GMOs should be labeled as such, so that people can learn about the issue and make up their own minds.

The "just label it" strategy is also how Ben & Jerry's fought bovine growth hormone (rBGH). But this time, the stakes are much higher because GMOs are a much bigger, more complicated debate. Most plant scientists say that making genetic modifications to staple crops like corn, rice, and wheat can improve crop yields while decreasing reliance on pesticides and irrigation. As the world's population grows from 7.1

Ben & Jerry's pays a premium to Rudy Hooch Antik, a farmer in the Netherlands, for participating in the company's Caring Dairy program, which aims to minimize the environmental and social impacts of dairy farming.

billion in 2013 to 9 billion in 2043, with a probable decrease in arable land and worsening water shortages, it's hard to argue with improved crop yields. But the environmental and health impacts of GMOs are still largely unknown, and activists say that improving crop yields isn't as effective as improving the efficiency of food systems. They also have a big problem with patenting the world's food supply. The debate is far from over.

Corporations like Unilever oppose GMO labeling because it increases their production costs. Labeling is a go-slow approach, and it reflects the view that big science and big businesses should not be the only ones who get a vote. "All the big food companies are against labeling, including Unilever," said Jostein. "We're having a huge fight with them. But we are committed to the consumer's right to know, and we are not going to go away."

"Social changes depend on transparency," said Jeff. "The movements against the Vietnam War and for civil rights took off when pictures showed people what war and injustice look like. Once people understand what is actually happening, the grassroots movements can start. The best way for us to encourage systemic change is to engage with the public about these issues and let them make up their own minds."

Corporate Radicals

One day in 1985, as the company was organizing its first national stock offering, three bankers from New York City flew up to Burlington to pitch their services. "They showed up wearing yellow T-shirts over their dress shirts," Jeff said, "and they had printed 'We Love Ben & Jerry's' on them in big letters. They looked ridiculous. I turned to Ben and said, 'Hey, how about that, they want to be like us.'"

The "titan in a T-shirt" gag came up several times over the next thirty years, notably when Unilever cochair Niall

Ferguson flew across the Atlantic to meet Ben. But as the years wore on, it also got harder to separate the profiteers from the cool guys. The second generation of socially responsible entrepreneurs does not see a double bottom line as revolutionary. They are more concerned with perfecting the form Ben & Jerry's helped to invent.

Many entrepreneurs are choosing a new business structure called a "benefit corporation," or "B Corp." This type of corporation is required to create a general benefit for society while also providing returns to its shareholders. Its directors must consider how their actions affect their employees, community, and the environment as well as the bottom line, and they must publish audited reports of their social and environmental performance.

B Corps come in two flavors. Some go through a review and certification process by a not-for-profit organization called B Lab.[1] Ben & Jerry's received this certification in 2012. But at press time, nineteen states had passed legislation that establish benefit corporations as a separate category. In California, New York, Illinois, New Jersey—and Vermont—businesses that are chartered as benefit corporations receive different levels of legal protection. If this option had been available and accepted in 2000, Ben & Jerry's probably would have avoided the bidding war and legal threats that led to its sale.

The big boys are stepping up, too. In November 2010, Paul Polman announced a set of audacious social goals for Unilever. By the end of the decade, he said, the company would cut the environmental footprint of its products by half, help one billion people improve their health and well-being by giving them more convenient ways to wash their hands, make safe drinking water available to five hundred million people, work with Oxfam and other not-for-profit groups to add five hundred thousand small farmers and entrepreneurs to its global supply chain, and source 100 percent of its agricultural materials sustainably. The event announcing the

Sustainable Living Plan cited Ben & Jerry's 100 percent fair trade campaign as evidence that Unilever was serious.

"Helping a billion people is a big target, I know that, and that's why we work with a lot of different organizations," said Polman in a speech in October 2012. "I want to show that big doesn't necessarily mean bad, and that it's not only small that is beautiful. I want to show that even big companies can be a force for change in this world. Take Ben & Jerry's. They have championed social and environmental causes since their beginning, and look at the impact that they have increasingly in the mainstream culture."[2]

"We are helped by having an organization like Ben & Jerry's," said Kevin Havelock, who is president of Unilever's refreshment division and Jostein's boss. "We are learning from an organization that has always put stretch objectives into areas such as Fair Trade and finding sustainable sources."[3]

Ben & Jerry's is now sharing information and contacts with Unilever's sustainability staff, says Jostein, and both sides are seeing benefits. "They are helping us do a lot of the mundane work that comes along with switching to fair trade sugar," he said. "And we are helping them work on the definition of a sustainable agricultural product." Unilever's resources are also critical to the international expansion. "We always lead with our values," said Helen Jones, "but we need to be careful to express those values in ways that are respectful to local cultures. The local Unilever people help us in all kinds of ways. We didn't have the resources we needed to expand internationally when we were independent, and now we do."

Another new challenge for Ben & Jerry's is figuring out how to lead with its values in countries that deny their residents rights that Americans view as nonnegotiable. The company is not yet in China, for example, although ice cream is popular there and other Unilever brands are sold. "I think the question is how to have the most influence over human rights," said Kees van der Graaf. "Do you get it by pointing your finger at the bad things, or by working from within? I think we should work from within and not be afraid to go early into suspicious countries. We will have a bigger impact if we help them establish new ways of working."

"Our relationship to Unilever is a balance of integration and separation," said Jostein. "I like to say that we have a four-part vision. We aspire to be a social justice company that happens to sell ice cream, so our mission is to change the world. We want to be a global player and prove that this is a better way to do business. We want to be the world's best ice cream company, and never let the consumer down. And fourth, we want to steer Unilever. We want to do this in a nice, subtle way, not by finger-pointing. So any time we can integrate with them, we do it. And when we can't integrate we will keep ourselves separate, as gracefully as possible.

"At times we might upset people in Unilever by doing and saying things that are contrary to their short-term interest. This is because it is difficult to do the right thing sometimes, although still you know it's right. I think they want us to lead them in that way, and that is why the three-part mission is fundamental to how we stay on course. If your sole mission is shareholder wealth, the negative side effects of your business may cancel out the good you do."

The big short-term interest, of course, is Unilever's quarterly income statement. "I wonder what will happen the next time Unilever has trouble meeting its financial targets," said Pierre. "Will they keep investing in the social mission as they are now? Linked prosperity is all well and good, but how are we going to manage for linked hardship?"

Jeff says he has several good arguments stored up for the next downturn. "Money has a different meaning depending on where you put it," he said. In other words, a few million dollars for the social mission is a tiny sum to a corporation that booked profits of $7 billion in 2012, but an extra $500 is a huge thing to an African cocoa farmer. "It should be clear to everyone by now that our brand equity is in the three-part mission," he says. "Unilever learned the hard way that when you cut costs, you run the danger of destroying brand equity. That is one reason why it is in their interest to give an extra $500 to the farmer."

The longer this message seeps into Unilever, the better are the long-term prospects for linked prosperity. At the 2012 retreat, the managers, board members, and line workers at Ben & Jerry's spent a day and a half pondering the meaning of linked prosperity and how they could deepen the company's commitment to it. It's a work in progress. It was also one of the first meetings attended by Daryn Dodson, who was thirty-two when he joined the board of directors in December. Dodson worked for the Center for Community Self-Help, a large lender that specializes in underserved borrowers. Now he is a venture consultant for Calvert Special Equities, a job he describes as "investing in small companies that might turn into the next Ben & Jerry's. The test is values, social impact, and financial return, same as the three-part mission."

"I saw an extraordinary thing a few years ago," said Pierre. "It was at a big Unilever meeting between the company's buyers and people from Fair Trade International. These buyers are very tough negotiators. They're all about price, and if they can knock two cents off a hundredweight, they're heroes.

"I saw a buyer talking about how the company was applying fair trade to their contracts in Africa, and what it meant to the farmers there. And in the middle of his comments, this extremely tough man started to cry. He had spent his working life beating up people to pay them as little as possible, all the time knowing it wasn't right. But he probably loves his wife and children, and every Sunday his church tells him he should help the poor. That's who he really is. It must have been quite painful for him to put that decent person in the closet whenever he went to work. Now he doesn't have to do that anymore. What an incredible relief!"

The Arc of Justice

Jeff winces whenever he hears Jostein say that Ben & Jerry's aspires to be a social justice company. He has spent his life struggling to find justice for marginalized and oppressed people, so forming a partnership with a corporation that has more money than many countries do doesn't come easily to him. Ben Cohen and Jerry Greenfield probably won't ever be entirely comfortable around Unilever, for two reasons. One is that the loss of their company was so personal and painful. The other is that they have chosen a different path.

"I admire Unilever's efforts to become sustainable," said Judy Wicks, a close friend of Ben's since the early 1990s. "The problems our planet faces are dire. Time is of the essence, and we can't afford to waste it by opposing people who are moving in the right direction, especially when they can do things on a large scale, as Unilever is doing. But Ben is right. Ownership matters. So we are imagining a different world, and our values will never be totally aligned with Unilever's.

"We're pushing for a sustainable economy and environmental survival through decentralization," said Judy, who cofounded the Businesses Alliance for Living Local Economies (BALLE) in 2001 with start-up support from Ben and several others. "As long as large corporations have as much power as they have, there will always be huge economic and social injustices," she said. "The kind of world we want puts economic power back into the hands of communities. Ben's work to get the money out of politics is vital to this power shift."

BALLE's conference in 2013 had more than five hundred attendees who ran the political gamut from socialists to hard-right conservatives. "Self-reliance is a deeply American value that cuts across political lines," Judy said. "I used to see Ben & Jerry's and the Body Shop as little oases of good in a big, bad world. But now I understand that they're just chain stores owned by multinationals. And chain stores are like invasive species to local economic ecosystems. We need to encourage locally made ice cream and soap. Our vision is to keep money and power within our communities."

Being dissatisfied is part of a radical activist's job description. "I am a Hindu, so I believe that I am here as a fighter," said Anuradha Mittal. "The important questions are, who are we fighting, and what are we fighting for." Jeff also believes this. "Sometimes Ben & Jerry's will succeed, sometimes we will fail, and sometimes we will struggle," he said when it was his turn to speak at the franchise owner's meeting in Las Vegas. "But we will always try, and we will always take risks." Ben & Jerry's is still trying to make linked prosperity work, and Jeff can see that something new is emerging. As long as he sees that, he will keep trying.

"We may also alienate people," Jeff said. "But the great movements in our country, like women's rights, civil rights, gay rights, and immigrant rights, have always alienated people. This means that we have to hold ourselves to a higher standard. We need to make sure that our actions match our words, that we honor our commitments, and that we remain completely transparent with each other and everyone we touch. Ben and Jerry have given us their names and their DNA as activists, and we must never deny that."

It was Sunday morning, January 20, the day before the national holiday for Dr. Martin Luther King, Jr. Jeff repeated the line that Dr. King had borrowed from Theodore Parker, an abolitionist minister in the 1850s, and that President

Obama had recently borrowed again. "Dr. King said that the arc of the moral universe is long, but it bends toward justice," said Jeff. "Barack Obama added that it does not bend by itself. It needs each of us to help.

"I have been an activist all my life. Howard Zinn said that to be hopeful in bad times is not just foolishly romantic, and I agree. When you look closely at human history you see more than injustice and struggle. There is also compassion, sacrifice, courage, and kindness. Every time we act, even in a small way, we influence the future. Just to act, to defy the cynics, is in itself a moral victory."

Dr. King was twenty-six years old and new to Montgomery when the bus boycott began and the civil rights movement caught fire. "This makes me think back to 1977, when I helped two men who were also twenty-six and new to the community, and who were also trying to do something that had not been done before," said Jeff. "Ben and Jerry had no idea that all of these amazing things would happen. They just had the right spirit. They wanted to change the world, to make things better. Look at what happened."

Epilogue by Jeff Furman

I have spent about half my life connected to Ben & Jerry's —first and always as a friend to Ben, Jerry, and many others there. During that time I have held various jobs, including consultant, in-house counsel, head of international development, head of franchising, coordinator for a Russian joint venture and other special projects, and trustee of the foundation. I have been on the board of directors since 1982, and since 2010 I have been its chair.

Ben & Jerry's started selling ice cream a decade before Henry Morgan wrote its three-part mission statement. We started the business without any kind of strategic plan, and little business experience. In the early days, we were always trying to combine a social mission with our economic goals, but we did this informally. We had a great opportunity to be creative, which worked well for me, because I had been fired by a bunch of other places.

This book was my idea. It stemmed from the many conversations I had with people who either did not know that Ben & Jerry's had been sold, or did not know that a special board existed to guard the social mission. I regularly had long conversations about this with friends, and eventually Brad and I decided it might be a good idea to write it down. At first we were going to be coauthors, but as the work unfolded, it became clear that this story is not just mine to tell.

The talks I had with Brad were not easy for me. They brought back a lot of the old, hard emotions of personal and collective loss and failure we all went through as we gave up control of the company and struggled for years afterward. So

Ice Cream Social

I understand completely why Ben and Jerry decided not to be interviewed. I still find parts of this story painful to recall, and my name isn't on every pint. But looking back, I also see a lot that makes me proud.

I'm proud when people say that Ben & Jerry's is a pioneer of socially responsible business, and when we do things to encourage a new generation of social entrepreneurs. I fought to make sure that we pay everyone in the company at least a living wage, and I am proud to say that soon all of our ingredients will be fairly traded and non-GMO. We promote sustainable agriculture, publish a transparent social audit, and board member Jennifer Henderson is working with our CEO to implement a linked prosperity framework for our employees, supply-chain partners, and franchisees.

I'm proud that we have supported the rights of same-sex couples for more than two decades. First we provided health insurance for all domestic partners, and more recently we have taken public stands all over the world for marriage equality. We were also one of the first companies to publically support the Occupy Wall Street movement, endorsing its challenges to the top one percent. Brad's book lists many more areas where Ben & Jerry's was unafraid to be the first—sometimes succeeding, sometimes struggling, but always trying.

It's a wonderful record, but it comes with a counterweight. At the same time that Ben & Jerry's was growing in size and ambition, we watched in dismay as the gap between rich and poor got much, much wider. Multinational corporations keep crowding out local businesses on Main Street. The news about the climate crisis is almost all bad. Small farmers and indigenous people are still being forced off their land. The list of injustices seems endless. And as our foreword writer, Annie Leonard, points out in her Story of Stuff project, most big businesses aren't doing much to help. They are still externalizing human and environmental costs, seeking short-term profits, and destroying local traditions and

Norma King, the receptionist at Ben & Jerry's from 1984 until her death in June 2013. Her obituary describes her as "the face and voice of the company ... with a reputation as big as the co-founders', and much more boisterous."

institutions that get in the way. There are days when the accomplishments of Ben & Jerry's seem to me like a scene from *Godzilla*, the one where people throw trash cans at the approaching monster.

When the company was publicly held, Ben and I were the point people for the social mission. Ben, Jerry, and I supported each other, but we never could have been as successful as we were without the many employees who pushed and implemented this vision. Looking back, I see heroes and heroines all over the place. And now some have passed on —beloved employees like Norma King, Diane Cadieux, and Lee Holden.

Recalling the last three decades has also made me revisit the many times when those of us who believed in the three-part mission either weren't paying attention or weren't fighting hard enough. I see more clearly now the importance of vigilance. An advocate must be ever-present to make a three-part mission work. Someone has to go to every meeting, put progressive values on the table, ask about the social impact of our actions, demand that we do better, and ask what else we could be doing. And if you want to stay edgy and keep taking risks for social justice, you have to be as stubborn as a dog with a bone.

As the years went by, I became that dog. It was the role I needed to play and I enjoyed it, but there was a downside. As I focused more of my energy on the social mission, I let important things slide. There were plenty of signs that our company was being prepared for a sale, but I assumed that a sale could never go through. I woke up too late. My focus was too narrow. Looking back, it is clear to me that the enduring division on the board was a big reason why we missed opportunities and ignored obvious warning signs. We kept arguing about the purpose of the company until the company slipped from our hands.

I missed an important chance for Ben & Jerry's when we abandoned the seven-to-one salary ratio in 1994. To me, the ratio meant that we were walking our talk. It was proof that we meant it when we said that everyone in the company was linked, that every contribution mattered, and that the disparities of income in our economic system were immoral. I still feel that way today. But in hindsight, I made a mistake in the way I dealt with it.

The salary ratio may not have been workable any more, but I should have kept fighting harder for the principle of limiting top management salaries and benefits. We could have had a fair, linked compensation system instead of the more traditional business model we ended up following. We suddenly opened the floodgates and started awarding tens of thousands of stock options to our senior employees. I wish I had found a way to prevent that, because we created a compensation system where managers were personally rewarded for putting the economic mission first.

I have had the privilege of being able to bring my heart and my passions to much of my work. This is a rare gift. It can also get you into trouble. A few years ago, I went to a meeting at Unilever's offices. The price of food and fuel had spiked, and I was pushing for a midyear adjustment to our living wage to meet these rising costs. I had my dog-with-a-bone attitude, and I wasn't letting go. Tension in the room was high. When someone suggested that we break for lunch, I heard myself tell the group that we shouldn't stop now because we should all experience what it felt like to be hungry. So everyone just sat there in silence, not knowing what to do. I didn't know either. As the minutes ticked by, I realized that I was also hungry. What the hell had I gotten us into? I don't remember what happened next, but Unilever did agree to the adjustment. I also heard that some people started calling me "Left of Lenin." Well, what's in a name?

I can see how I got that tag. Our three-part mission statement says that product quality, social impact, and economic performance are equally important, but the social mission has always been first among equals for me. Selling Cherry Garcia is a big part of my life, and being in the Free Ice Cream For Life Club is a lot of fun, but I would be okay without them, and I have never been excited by the idea of "economic growth" as a way of curing every problem. I am not convinced that the trade-offs that come with endless growth are worth it, because the wealth of multinational corporations inevitably creates huge imbalances in power. Like Judy Wicks and many others, I am more interested in supporting small businesses and other organizations that are interwoven into their communities and are locally controlled. So I guess I'm not Left of Lenin after all. What a relief!

Of course, I am also keenly aware that the ambivalence that I and some other board members might feel about growth and globalization does not have much of an effect on the overall direction of Ben & Jerry's. I accept that Unilever will always push for international expansion. The board can only insist that whenever Ben & Jerry's enters new communities (we no longer call them new "markets"), our ice cream will be accompanied by real social mission analysis and meaningful activity. We know that living up to our three-part mission statement will be a struggle as long as we continue to expand across our globe.

One of the reasons I stuck with Ben & Jerry's is that I believe what Ben told Jennifer back in 1988, at the organizing meeting of One Percent for Peace. He said, "Businesses are the most powerful institutions on the planet." If we can show that it is possible for a business to embrace social justice while also making a reasonable profit, we might make the moral arc that Dr. King refers to bend toward justice a little faster.

Another reason I was able to stay at Ben & Jerry's for as long as I have is that I never moved to Vermont. This was due in part to family concerns, but it is also because I am deeply rooted in my hometown of Ithaca. I came here in 1961 to attend Cornell University as a chemical engineering student. I flunked, transferred to electrical engineering, flunked again, transferred to unclassified, and finally gave up in 1963. I did end up with a degree in accounting and eventually a law degree, both of them from New York University, but I never would have passed the bar without a lot of help from my friend Robin Gross, and I never really practiced law or accounting.

I moved back to Ithaca in 1977, and my family has lived here happily ever since. The distance from Vermont allowed me to have a different perspective. The work I've done in Ithaca has informed and inspired the work I've done in Vermont, and vice versa. For example, I developed an equity report card for our local school district that was modeled after Ben & Jerry's social audit. The report card is designed to measure our progress toward eliminating race and class as predictors of student success, and our grades are reported to the public.

I could not imagine becoming chair of the board of Ben & Jerry's when Unilever took over in 2000, because I was not sure how and if I could engage with a giant multinational company. But when the opportunity came again in 2010, I was ready to try. During those ten years, I learned a bit about the complex steps Unilever requires to move projects along, and I got a better sense of how the board could be most effective. Ben recently told me, with a smile, that I became chair mostly because I outlasted everybody else. That is probably true.

My goals as chair of the board are simple. I want to make sure all the elements of our sale agreements are being carried out, and I want to secure, as best I can, the legacy of Ben & Jerry's by ensuring that its social mission lives on. I hope that this book can help further both of these goals.

Figuring out how to make the sale agreements work is not easy, and education is one of the board's never-ending jobs. This is because Unilever reorganizes their operating systems and moves staff around so often. Ben & Jerry's board members do not have term limits, and many Ben & Jerry's employees have been with the company long enough to have mastered the three-part mission, but we are always meeting Unilever folks who have never seen the sale agreements and don't understand our culture. So the arguments between people who put profit first and those who are committed to balancing profit, product quality, and social impact have not stopped. The difference now is that we are playing by a new set of rules.

The sale agreements determine our roles and responsibilities, and one of our roles is to be challenging. For example, I applaud when I see businesses sending money to disaster relief in Haiti and New Orleans. But Ben & Jerry's comes from a different perspective. We want to challenge the status quo and address the reasons why poverty, racism, and pain were endemic in Haiti and New Orleans long before the earthquakes and hurricanes hit. At our best, we push for systemic change within the traditional rules of capitalism.

I am a grassroots activist who just celebrated my seventieth birthday, which makes me old enough to have witnessed social change. I understand that one can never fully understand the impact of one's efforts. And I have reaped huge benefits from being around people who combine their deep commitment to social justice with a sense of joy and humility.

In the last few years, people have begun asking me when I am going to retire. Why should I ever do that? I have been fortunate to do work I love with wonderful people. I also have absolutely no hobbies, so I guess I am stuck. And anyway, the work is far from finished, so I'm keeping on.

I remember a day in the early 1990s, when the company was going through a bad stretch of growing pains and we were all working very long hours. Ben and I were sitting together, reflecting on the situation, when we got one of those sudden flashes of insight. We realized that there was no light at the end of the tunnel. This was our path. "There will always be a new challenge," he said. "A new problem will always be lurking around the corner." This new awareness was depressing, liberating, and laugh-out-loud funny, all at the same time.

More than two decades later, however, I occasionally see the light. I see it in our newest board members, who have brought us strong, proven commitments to social justice. Helen Jones nurtured the three-part mission in Europe beautifully, and she combines a passion for social change with the business expertise we need. Anuradha Mittal and Daryn Dodson have the thing Chuck Lacy said we always needed

—courage—and their vigilance should push the social mission forward for decades to come. When I learned more about Anuradha and her international work for justice, I was honored to join the board of the Oakland Institute, where she is the executive director.

I see the light when I meet young social entrepreneurs who are experimenting with new ways to combine social and economic values. They are just getting started now, and they are way ahead of where Ben, Jerry, Chico, and I were when we began. Almost fifty years ago, I helped build a house in the country with a group of hippies who had no electrical tools and very few skills. We lived in it for a few years, and I think it still stands. We were trying to make a statement about living simply. The statements young social entrepreneurs are making now are much more promising. The growing, vibrant movements to promote local economies, local and organic food, clean and green energy, sustainable life styles, local government, and engaged citizens are the most hopeful things I know.

I see the light when I hand someone a coupon for free ice cream and their eyes light up because it isn't just ice cream, it's Ben & Jerry's. I see it when we hire someone who is passionate about the company, when I meet with employees on the foundation's grant-making committees, or whenever our company stands with others who are working for peace and justice. For all of these things, I remain thankful and hopeful.

It is also a huge relief to see younger people stepping up, because as I get older, I'm more and more afraid of embarrassing myself in public. Twice a month I meet with a group of Ithaca's community troublemakers. Most of us are old enough to enjoy the benefits of Medicare. Our meetings have no agenda and no minutes, and we laugh a lot. At one recent meeting, one of us told a story about a woman whose name she couldn't remember, but it began with a *P*. During the next hour, as we discussed one community need or another, someone occasionally shouted a name that began with *P*. By the end of the meeting, we had probably accumulated fifty women's names, but with no success. Eventually she did remember the name, and she sent it to the group by email. It was Deidre.

Last but not least, I am thankful for the pure joy that I have experienced at Ben & Jerry's. It does, after all, make great ice cream. And while I may be biased, I cannot think of another product that brings as much joy, good feeling, and smiles whenever one experiences it. A couple of times a year, my son and I hang out at our local supermarket's freezer case, giving away coupons good for a free pint of Ben & Jerry's. What could be better than that?

Reflection by Anuradha Mittal

As I read this book, my journey through the labyrinth of Ben & Jerry's came alive. It's a drama that unfolds what is, or might be, possible.

The five years I have served on the board are not very long, given all that has happened. When I started, we were devising a legal strategy against one of the world's largest multinationals. Now we are working closely with a team of brilliant and committed staff. There are so many wonderful people at Ben & Jerry's—the director for human resources, the social mission director, the Norwegian CEO dude handpicked by Unilever—and we are all pulling together to execute a mission dictated by compassion, ethics, and a desire to exceed all that we are capable of. This is quite a turnabout for any entity, especially one that is owned by a multinational corporation.

The good news is that our work will never be done. We are restless, setting the bar higher, seeking new ways to determine comparative advantage, to be the case study that sets a new standard for business ethics. The answers are not always obvious, but we do know that we can always do better. In the process, we heal ourselves and all that surrounds us.

Questioning the deeper implications of linked prosperity is our next frontier. When our business does well, how should our workers, our farmers, and the earth also do well? Our fates are tied to theirs, so what is our larger goal and responsibility? And most important, how can we be more unreasonable? These are the questions that nag us.

I am honored and proud to work with amazing colleagues who, in some other settings, might be called cantankerous for all that they aspire and ask for. Their love for what they do every day is captured in this modern translation of Hafiz,[1] the Persian poet, who wrote the original verse almost eight hundred years ago:

Even

After

All this time

The sun never says to the earth,

"You owe

Me."

Look

What happens

With a love like that,

It lights the

Whole

Sky.

Notes

CHAPTER ONE

1. Calvin Trillin, "Competitors," *New Yorker*, July 8, 1985.
2. Molly Ivins, "Is Texas America?," *Nation*, November 17, 2003, 26.

CHAPTER TWO

1. Ben Cohen, interview on *Biography*, CNBC, 2006; transcript at http://livedash.ark.com, searching on "Ben Cohen Biography" (accessed August 11, 2013).
2. Janice Simpson, "Ice Cream: They All Scream for It," *Time*, August 10, 1981.
3. *Biography*, CNBC, 2006.
4. Ibid.
5. Fred "Chico" Lager, *Ben & Jerry's: The Inside Scoop: How Two Real Guys Built a Business with a Social Conscience and a Sense of Humor* (New York: Crown Trade Paperbacks, 1994), 150.

CHAPTER THREE

1. Paul Hawken, *Growing a Business* (New York: Harper Collins, 1987).
2. Anita Roddick, *Body and Soul* (New York: Crown Publishers, 1991), 8.
3. Ibid.
4. Ben Cohen and Jerry Greenfield (with Meredith Maran), *Ben & Jerry's Double-Dip: How To Run a Values-Led Business and Make Money, Too* (New York: Simon and Schuster, 1997).
5. Ibid.

CHAPTER FOUR

1. Lager, *Ben & Jerry's: The Inside Scoop.*
2. See www.bradedmondson.com for more on Ben & Jerry's adventures in Russia.

CHAPTER FIVE

1. Cohen and Greenfield, *Ben & Jerry's Double-Dip,* 144.
2. Ibid.

3. Joe Queenan, *My Goodness* (New York: Hyperion, 2000), 11.
4. Claudia Dreyfuss, "Passing the Scoop: Ben and Jerry," *New York Times*, December 18, 1994.
5. Jon Entine, "The Stranger-Than-Truth Story of The Body Shop," in *Killed: Great Journalism Too Hot To Print* (New York: Nation Books, 2004), 179–212.
6. Jeff Glasser, "Ben & Jerry's Embarrassed in Scoop Over Nuts," *Boston Globe*, July 28, 1995.
7. Paul Hawken, *The Ecology of Commerce* (New York: Harper Collins, 1993).

CHAPTER SIX

1. "Passing the Scoop," *New York Times*, December 18, 1994.
2. Simon Zadek, *Tomorrow's History: Selected Writings of Simon Zadek, 1993–2003* (Sheffield, UK: Greenleaf Publishing, 2004), 163.
3. Ibid., 15.
4. Phred Dvorak, "How Long Courtship Made a Takeover Less Scary," *Wall Street Journal*, July 23, 2007.

CHAPTER SEVEN

1. Lynn Stout, *The Shareholder Value Myth: How Putting Shareholders First Harms Investors, Corporations, and the Public* (San Francisco: Berrett-Koehler, 2012), 29.

CHAPTER EIGHT

1. Perry Odak, lecture at Cornell University, Dyson School of Applied Economics and Management, August 19, 2000, transcript at http://eclips.cornell.edu
2. Constance Hays, "Getting Serious at Ben & Jerry's," *New York Times*, May 22, 1998.

CHAPTER NINE

1. Perry Odak, lecture at Cornell, August 19, 2000.
2. VT.STAT.ANN. tit 11A, § 8.30 (2009).
3. *Biography*, CNBC, 2006.

CHAPTER TEN

1. Kathryn Tully, "My Liquidity Moment: Ben Cohen of Ben & Jerry's," *Financial Times*, June 23, 2010.
2. *Biography*, CNBC, 2006.
3. Jules Marchal, *Lord Leverhulme's Ghosts: Colonial Exploitation in the Congo* (London: Verso, 1998).

4. Unilever Corporation, "Annual Review 2000 and Summary Financial Statements," at http://www.unilever.com/investorrelations/annual_reports/archives (accessed June 26, 2013).
5. http://savebenjerry.com (accessed June 26, 2013).
6. John Hechinger and Joseph Pereira, "White Knight Swirl: Sympathizers Scramble to Rid Ben & Jerry's of 2 Unwanted Suitors," *Wall Street Journal*, February 28, 2000, 1.
7. Jim Steiker and Michael Golden, "Hot Fudge Partners: Insiders Tell How Social Investors Tried to (but Couldn't) Buy Ben & Jerry's," *Business Ethics*, May/June 2000, 7.
8. Jerry Greenfield, "Question Time with Hannah Pool," *Guardian,* July 30, 2008.

CHAPTER ELEVEN

1. Reuters, "Angry with Unilever, Co-Founder Threatens to Quit Ben & Jerry's," *Reading Eagle*, December 1, 2000;
Associated Press, "Company's Direction Worries Ex-Owner," *Vindicator*, December 1, 2000.

CHAPTER TWELVE

1. Rupert Steiner, "Polman Outrages Market as He Tears Up Unilever Targets," *Daily Mail,* February 6, 2009.

CHAPTER THIRTEEN

1. http://www.bcorporation.net
2. Paul Polman at One Young World Conference, 2012; video at http://www.youtube.com/watch?v=ROZeOwuga40 (accessed June 26, 2013).
3. Quoted in Glenn Rifkin, "How Culture Trumps Size," *Briefings on Talent and Leadership*, Korn/Ferry Institute.

REFLECTION BY ANARADHA MITTAL

1. Hafiz (author), Daniel Ladinsky (translator), *The Gift: Poems by Hafiz the Great Sufi Master* (New York: Penguin Compass, 1999), 34.

Sources and Further Reading

I am grateful to the many members of the Ben & Jerry's community who told me their stories, including several who spoke off the record. They include:

Daryn Dodson, Pierre Ferrari, Jeff Furman, Jennifer Henderson, Helen Jones, Anuradha Mittal, Terry Mollner, Kees Van der Graaf, members of the board of directors in 2013; and Liz Bankowski, Charles M. (Chuck) Lacy, Fred Miller, Ronald Soiefer, and Howard Fuguet, former members and advisors to the board of directors. I also interviewed:

BEN & JERRY'S EMPLOYEES IN 2013:

Jostein Solheim, chief executive officer

Andrea Asch, manager of natural resources

Andy Barker, director of social mission

Melissa Bland, assistant to the CEO

Jane Bowman, people mission manager

Michael Graning, finance director

Sean Greenwood, public relations director

Debra Heintz, director of retail operations

Sandy Julius, franchise relations manager

Rob Michalak, director of public relations 1989–97; global director of social mission, 2005–present

Carol Hedenberg O'Neill, franchise site selection manager, senior contract administrator

Lisa Pendolino, managing director, Ben & Jerry's Foundation

Dave Stever, chief marketing officer

Lisa Wernhoff, designer, archivist, "keeper of stuff"

Hanneke Willenborg, global brand development director until July 1, 2012

OTHER INTERVIEWS:

Dave Bruno Sr., franchise owner, Albany, New York, area

Robert Dunn, President, Synergos Institute; former executive director, Businesses for Social Responsibility

Richard Goldstein, president, Unilever USA until 2000

Robert Holland, chief executive officer, Ben & Jerry's, 1995–96

Roger S. Kaufman, franchise owner, San Francisco Bay area

John Le Boutillier, former head, US Ice Cream Leadership Team, 2007–12; president, Unilever Canada, 2012–present

Judy Wicks, founder, White Dog Café, Philadelphia; cofounder, Business Alliance for Living Local Economies

Special thanks to Jostein Solheim and Lisa Wernhoff for making the archives of Ben & Jerry's available to me. This book relies on the company's annual reports (1985–99), minutes of board of directors' meetings, and many other internal documents. The company's newsletters, the *Daily Plant* (1988–93) and *Rolling Cone* (1993–2002), were invaluable for setting dates and giving a flavor of what it felt like in the trenches.

Several documents from the Federal Securities and Exchange Commission (SEC) were helpful, including the company's 10-K reports and many filings related to the sale. One of the most helpful is *Solicitation/Recommendation Statement Under Section 14 (d) (4) of the Securities Exchange Act of 1934: Ben & Jerry's Homemade, Inc.* (Washington, DC: GPO, 2000), which describes the deal and gives a chronology of events leading up to the sale.

The Shareholder's Agreement, Agreement and Plan of Merger, and other documents that govern the relationship between Ben & Jerry's and Unilever are filed in the offices of the SEC and Vermont's Secretary of State. You can download these and many other documents at my website, www.bradedmondson.com, along with a study guide for book groups, links to useful sites, recommendations for further reading, and other resources concerning corporate social responsibility.

Photo Credits

CHAPTER 2
Page 19: Provided by the *Central New York Business Journal.*
Page 25: Photo by David Brewster, *Minneapolis–St. Paul Star Tribune.*

CHAPTER 3:
Page 44: Photos © by Jon Crispin (button) and Arnold Carbone.

CHAPTER 4
Page 64: Provided by Liz Bankowski.

CHAPTER 10
Page 177: Photo by Kathy Willens, Associated Press.

CHAPTER 13
Page 236: Photo by Mike Graning.

ABOUT THE AUTHOR
Page 279: Photo by Jon Crispin.

Index

100 Best Companies to Work for in America (Moskowitz), 82

ACT NOW, 71–72
American Express, 111
An Inconvenient Truth, 192
animal rights, 39, 67, 243
anti-takeover, 144, 152–153
anti-war, 57, 132
  Cold War, 87
  Iraq, 62, 195
  military budget, 42, 131
  One Percent for Peace, 42–46, 50–51, 67, 71, 84, 110, 258
  Vietnam, 38, 245
apartheid, 38, 41, 162
Ark, The, 73
Asch, Andrea, 103–104, 148
Association of Certified Chartered Accountants, 193
audit. *See under* social reporting
Aveda, 159
Aztec Harvests, 133–134

B Corporations, 246
Bank of America, 58–59
Bankowski, Liz
  acquisition of Ben & Jerry's and, 143–144, 174
  board, 53–54, 154
  bovine growth hormone campaign and, 79, 127–129
  CEO search, 91–92, 96, 119
  Foundation and, 186
  Kunin, Madeleine and, 51, 53
  Partnerships and, 149
  retirement, 186
  same-sex marriage and, 192
  social mission and, 55–58, 71, 75, 80, 101, 129, 132, 147, 154, 215
  social reporting and, 60–62, 104–105, 209
  stock options and, 99, 121
  values statement and, 130–131

Barash, Dave, 47
Ben & Jerry's
  anti-takeover, 144, 152–153
  board of directors
    communication and, 190, 201–202, 207–208, 212–214, 219–220
    diversity, 65, 98–99, 110, 211
    management and, 45–47, 65, 68
    Odak, Perry and, 127, 140, 144–146
    salary ratio and, 92, 94, 256–257
    social mission and, 43, 48, 71, 105, 130, 147, 124–125, 240–241 (*see also* social mission)
    stock options and, 121–122, 144
    term limits, 259
    Unilever acquisition and, 142–144, 152–158, 163–167, 173–178; agreements, 4, 169–172, 185–190, 203–204, 213–218, 222–223, 227; conflict, 194–195, 199, 207–208, 212–214, 219–226, 229, 238
  communication within, 190, 201, 204, 226, 240
  distribution 28–29, 100, 112–113, 138–142 passim, 145, 153–160 passim, 173
  diversity, 12, 57, 60–61, 98, 141, 251; of board, 65, 98–99, 110, 211
  environmental policies, 79, 103–104, 130–131, 147–148 (*see also* environment)
  foundation (*see* Ben & Jerry's Foundation)
  franchises (*see* franchises)
  as global brand, 142, 179, 193, 196–197, 206, 239, 246, 248, 260
  Häagen-Dazs and (*see* Häagen-Dazs)
  layoffs, 194–195
  marketing
    ACT NOW and, 71
    Bankowski, Liz and, 57, 186
    cause-related, 111, 129, 182
    Cohen, Ben and, 21–22, 46, 85

Ben & Jerry's
  marketing, *continued*
    cost of, 210, 219
    direct, 24
    Freese, Walt and, 188, 197
    Häagen Dazs and, 107
    layoffs and, 194
    political aspects, 37–38, 44–45
    social mission and, 61, 74–75, 127, 202
    Unilever sale agreements, 171
    in United Kingdom, 100
    Welsh, Jerry and, 111
  plants (*see* St. Albans; Waterbury)
  public relations
    Greenwood, Sean and, 93, 120, 152, 208
    integration of, 150
    Michalak, Rob and, 38, 120, 208
    salary ratio and, 92
    Unilever and, 161, 195, 208, 230
  quality control, 101–102, 200, 203, 210, 222–223, 231–232
  safety, 103
  salaries, 28–29, 63–64, 91–95, 98–99, 256–257 (*see also* living wage)
  sales growth, 21, 36, 90, 93, 102–103, 107, 114, 241–242
  social mission: committee, 105, 130, 147; cost of, 124–125, 132 (*see also* social mission)
  social reporting (*see* social reporting)
  stock: offering, 22–30 passim, 93; options, 93, 99, 121–124, 144, 147, 155, 256; value, 86, 89, 165
  suppliers
    criticism about, 81, 83
    diversity of, 57
    Greyston, 49–50
    linked prosperity and, 4, 10, 50, 118, 146, 152, 237
    social mission and, 58–59, 61, 104, 124, 216, 220
    St. Albans Cooperative, 61, 69, 149, 215–216
  transparency, 240–245 (*see also* Ben & Jerry's, communication)

Unilever
  acquisition, 142–144, 152–158, 163–167, 173–178
  agreements, 4, 169–172, 185–190, 203–204, 213–218, 227
  conflict, 194–195, 199, 207–208, 219–226, 229, 238
  public relations and, 161, 195, 208, 230
Ben & Jerry's Double Dip, (Cohen and Greenfield), 74
Ben & Jerry's Foundation, 25–26, 29, 31, 44, 76, 105, 110, 150, 172, 176, 183, 212
Ben & Jerry's Homemade Inc., 159
Ben & Jerry's: The Inside Scoop (Lager), 30
Berkshire Hathaway, 166
Berman, Todd, 172–173
Boca Burger, 181
Body Shop, 39, 62, 71, 83, 141, 159, 166, 181, 251
bovine growth hormone (rBGH), 78–79, 127–129, 148, 244
Bowman, Bruce, 101, 121
Bowman, Jane, 204–205
Branson, Richard, 83
Breyer's, 90, 113, 189, 200
Bruno, Dave, 73
Burgmans, Antony, 160, 183
Business Ethics, 38–39, 83
Business Leaders for Sensible Priorities, 120, 141
Businesses Alliance for Living Local Economies (BALLE), 250–251
Businesses for Social Responsibility, 67, 71

Calvert Social Investment Fund, 38, 71, 166–167, 249
Campaign to End Childhood Hunger, 73
Caring Dairy, 193, 215
Cascadian Farm, 159
Celestial Seasonings, 185
Center for Community Change, 110
Center for Community Self-Help, 249
Center for Science in the Public Interest, 81

CERES, 79, 148, 193
Chandler, Merritt, 27, 41–46 passim, 53, 91, 96, 110
Chappell, Tom and Kate, 39
Chartwell Investments, 173–174
Cherry Garcia, 36–37
Children's Defense Fund, 72, 129
Chouinard, Yvon, 39
Christmas in April, 73
Citizens United, 234–235
Clavelle, Peter, 167
climate change, 192, 199, 221, 224
Clinton, Bill, 132, 141
Coalition of Environmentally Responsible Economies (CERES), 79, 148, 193
Coca-Cola, 181
coffee, 62, 133–134
Cohen, Ben
  anti-takeover, 144, 153–154
  background, 7, 16–17
  Ben & Jerry's Double Dip, 74
  Ben & Jerry's Foundation and, 26
  board and, 8, 99–100, 121, 144–146, 154, 186
  CEO search, 91–92, 96–97, 114, 116
  Citizen's United, 234–235
  Community Products Inc., 83–84
  founding, 8–9, 15–24, 27–28
  Freese, Walt and, 188, 197, 226
  Goldstein, Jerry and, 157, 159, 169, 172, 183–184
  Greenfield, Jerry and, 7, 17, 30–31, 53, 100, 151, 165–166, 186
  Greyston Foundation and, 49–50
  Harvard prize, 79–81
  Holland, Bob and, 109
  Lager, Charles "Chico" and, 117
  management style, 31–32, 46, 85, 100, 120, 151–154
  Odak, Perry and, 117, 119, 122–127, 144–145, 169
  peace movement and, 42–43, 45, 75
  Polk, Michael and, 222–223
  Polman, Paul and, 222
  salary ratio and, 29, 51, 94, 99
  Stamp Stampede and, 234–235
  stock and, 22–23, 25, 30, 86, 124, 165, 174

Unilever and, 4, 10, 124, 139, 156–159, 163–179 passim; after acquisition, 182–188, 217–218, 222–226, 230–233
  values statement and, 131–132
  Wicks, Judy and, 67, 140–141
Colgate–Palmolive, 181
Common Ground, 77, 136–137
Community Products, Inc., 84
Control Data Corporation, 60
Couette, Yves, 185, 188–195 passim, 198
Council on Economic Priorities, 59
Cronk, William, 113

D'Urso, Tom, 73, 146, 169, 174, 179
Dave Matthews Band, 191, 196
Dean, Howard, 168
Declaration of Sentiments, 11–12
Diageo, 139
Disney, 106
Dodson, Daryn, 249
Dreamery, 153–154, 156
Dreyer's
  acquisition by Nestlé, 90, 113
  competition with Ben & Jerry's, 113, 141–142, 153–154, 164
  distribution of Ben & Jerry's, 28, 112–113, 139, 141–142, 156
  proposed merger with Ben & Jerry's, 143–144, 159, 162–178 passim
Dunin, Robert, 71

Ecology of Commerce, The (Hawken), 94
Edelman, Marion Wright, 72
Eenhorn, Hans, 187, 226
Entine, Jon, 83–84
environment
  bovine growth hormone (rBGH), 78–79, 127–129, 148, 244
  climate change, 192, 199, 221, 224, 254
  Coalition of Environmentally Responsible Economies (CERES), 79, 148, 193
  genetically modified organisms (GMOs), 186, 227, 229, 231, 234, 242–245
  James Bay hydroelectricity, 55

environment, *continued*
  other corporate policies, 39, 54, 62,
    83, 182
  progressive values statement and,
    130–131
  regulations, 59
  reporting, 62, 105–106, 224, 229–230,
    242–246
  Unilever policies, 161, 183, 187, 192–
    193, 215–216, 246–247
  See also Ben & Jerry's: environmen-
    tal policies

Fair trade, 133, 193, 231, 242–243, 249
Fair Trade International, 249
Ferrari, Pierre
  background, 116
  board, 115, 187, 211, 213, 240
  CEO candidate, 116, 185
  Cohen, Ben and, 151, 168
  Couette, Yves and, 195, 198–199
  Dreyer's and, 143, 159
  fair trade and, 249
  Le Boutillier, John and, 214
  Odak, Perry and, 116, 122, 124–125,
    140, 164
  product quality and, 203, 210–211
  stock, 121
  Unilever: acquisition and, 154, 158,
    163–165, 168, 176, 185, 193;
    agreements, 207, 213, 218–226
    passim, 248
  Walsh, Eric and, 200
Fitzgerald, Niall, 160, 183
Flying Friesian, 143
Food from the Hood, 136
Forest Stewardship Council, 227
franchises, 8–9, 20–21
  activism by, 61–62, 72–73, 136–137,
    147, 235, 254
  advisory board, 203
  Ben & Jerry's Foundation and, 83
  conflicts with, 190, 210, 213, 234
  growth of, 87, 200–201
  Russian, 67, 136
  social metrics and, 104, 147
Free Cone Days, 16, 21, 77
Free Ice Cream for Life, 97, 137

Freese, Walt, 185, 188, 197, 199–204,
    208, 212
Friedman, Milton, 118, 219
Fuguet, Howard "Howie"
  founding, 24
  stock offering, 25
  distribution agreements, 139
  Odak, Perry and, 119
  Unilever: acquisition and, 142, 144,
    153, 163–164, 169, 170; agree-
    ments and, 171, 207, 217, 223–225
Furman, Jeff
  background, xi–xiii, 7, 16, 258–259
  Ben & Jerry's Foundation and, 26, 31,
    76, 100
  board and, 11, 26, 46, 121, 137, 140,
    187, 208, 240, 259
  founding and, 1–2, 6–9
  linked prosperity and, 9–10
  management and, 91, 96, 98, 109–
    110, 116–117, 140–142
  Oakland Institute, 261
  Occupy Wall Street and, 241, 254
  One Percent for Peace and, 42–45, 51
  PartnerShops and, 8–9, 67, 77, 135,
    137
  salaries and, 28–29, 51, 94, 177,
    204–205
  staffing, 32, 34, 41
  stock offering and, 19, 22, 25, 245
  suppliers and, 50, 57, 212
  Unilever and, 184–191 passim, 197,
    207–220 passim, 225–226, 229–
    231, 248–250, 259
  Unilever negotiations, 154–260 pas-
    sim, 164–165, 168, 176–178

Gaines, Brian, 73
Garcia, Jerry, 36–37
gay rights, 227–228
genetically modified organisms
    (GMOs), 186, 227, 229, 231, 234,
    242–245
Goldstein, Richard
  CEO selection, 185
  Cohen and Greenfield and, 157, 159,
    184
  Eenhorn, Hans and, 187
  leaves Unilever, 183–184

Odak, Perry and, 139
social mission and, 156, 162
Unilever acquisition: agreements and, 160, 169–176 passim, 188
Good Humor, 189
Gordian Group, 142, 162, 164, 184
Gore, Al, 192
Grand Metropolitan, 107, 113, 139
Grateful Dead, 36–37, 40–41, 182
Greenfield, Jerry
background, 16, 20
Ben & Jerry's Double Dip, 74
Ben & Jerry's Foundation and, 26, 31, 76
board and, 52–53, 92, 99–100, 121, 145, 151, 154–155, 185
bovine growth hormone campaign and, 128
Cohen, Ben and, 7, 17, 30–31, 53, 100, 151, 165–166, 186
founding, 1–2, 7–8, 15–21
Freese, Walt and, 188, 197, 226
Goldstein, Jerry and, 157, 159, 169, 172, 183–184
peace movement and, 42–43, 45
Pillsbury and, 24
Polk, Michael and, 222–223
Polman, Paul and, 222
stock and, 19, 29, 124, 165, 174, 178
Unilever: acquisition and, 10, 139, 144–146, 156–159, 165, 168, 178–179; agreements and, 186, 230–233
Greenpeace, 148
Greenspan, Alan, 118
Greenwood, Sean, 49, 62, 111, 120, 152, 194, 208, 223
Greyston Bakery, 108, 134–135
Greyston Foundation, 49–50
Group Danone, 198
Growing a Business (Hawken), 39
Guinness, 139

Häagen-Dazs
acquisitions and, 113, 138–139, 153, 163, 174
competition and, 85, 89–90, 107–108, 154, 156, 191
distribution and, 23, 28, 112–113
global market and, 100, 142, 240

Haggerty, Rosanne, 76, 137
Hanson, Kirk, 61
Harvard Kennedy School of Government, 79–80
Havelock, Kevin, 238, 247
Hawken, Paul, 39, 42, 94
Heard, James, 62, 105, 150–151, 202, 217
Heintz, Debra, 102, 133–134, 146, 191, 209, 214
Henderson, Jennifer
board, 2, 110, 187–188, 211
One Percent for Peace, 42
sale of Ben & Jerry's, 143–145, 151–154, 160–168 passim, 211
Highland Community, 7, 26
Hirschberg, Gary, 198
Holland, Robert
as CEO, 98–101
Cohen, Ben and, 109
cost controls and, 102–103, 107
distribution and, 111–112, 144–145
La Soul and, 109
resignation, 113–115
style, 110–111, 120
Honest Tea, 166, 181
Horizon Organics, 159
Housing Vermont, 74
Huerta, Dolores, 89
human rights, 38, 41, 54, 106, 162, 211, 247–248

Ice Cream Partners LLC, 153, 156
Imus, Don, 127
Institutional Shareholder Services, 62
International Dairy Foundation, 78
Ivans, Molly, 12

James Bay, 55
Jobs with Justice, 242
Jones, Helen
marketing and, 100–101, 142–143, 196–197
social mission and, 143, 150, 197, 247, 260
Juma Ventures, 136

Kant, Hal, 36–37
Kaufman, Roger, 73, 203

Kelly, Marjorie, 38
King, Martin Luther, Jr., 12, 251–252
Klondike, 189
Kraft Foods, 113, 160, 181, 214
Kunin, Madeleine, 51, 53

L'Oreal, 181–182
La Soul Bakery, 107–108, 134
Lacy, Charles M. "Chuck"
   board and, 53, 55, 91–92
   bovine growth hormone campaign,
      78, 128
   employee safety and, 103
   founding role, 34, 36, 41–43
   growth and, 63, 85–86, 93, 195
   Lager, Chico and, 43, 49
   plants and, 82, 85–86
   Rathke, Fran and, 52
   salary ratio and, 64, 92
   turnaround, 91
   United Kingdom and, 100–101
Lager, Fred "Chico"
   Ben & Jerry's Foundation and, 26
   Ben & Jerry's: The Inside Scoop, 30
   board and, 20, 41–42, 46, 49
   CEO, 49
   founding role, 20–21
   general manager, 20, 32
   Lacy, Chuck and, 34, 43, 49
   One Percent for Peace and, 43
   Pillsbury and, 24
   plants and, 27, 91, 101–103, 135
   salary ratio and, 29, 51, 92
   social mission and, 117
   stock offering, 22–23, 25
   transition and, 96
Lawson House YMCA, 136
Le Boutillier, John, 214, 218–222, 225–
   229, 238–239
LeBlanc, Brendan, 217
Lee, Spike, 89
Lever Brothers. *See* Unilever
Liberty Mutual, 103
linked prosperity
   as business model, 237
   stock options and, 147, 176
   Unilever and, 248–249
   vision of, xii–xiii, 4–5, 9–10, 47, 94–95

   See also living wage; Ben & Jerry's:
      salaries
Lipton Tea, 198
living wage, 10, 177, 204–205, 237. *See
   also* linked prosperity; Ben & Jerry's:
      salaries
LoPorto, Garrett, 168
Lunbeck, Martha, 149

Mailman, Josh, 38
Marine Stewardship Council, 183–184
Marlin, Alice Tepper, 59–60
Marlin, John Tepper, 59–60
Meadowbrook Capital, 167–169, 173–
   176, 187
Michalak, Rob, 38, 81, 82, 120–121,
   208–209, 215, 224
Miller, Fred, 65, 110, 184
Mirvis, Paul, 42, 47
mission. *See* social mission
Mittal, Anuradha, 211–212, 214, 219,
   251, 260–261, 263–264
Mollner, Terry
   acquisition of Ben & Jerry's, 166–167,
      172–176, 185
   board and, 187, 202, 211, 213, 218
Mondragon Corporation, 28–29
Monsanto Corporation, 78, 80, 129,
   154, 208
Morgan, Henry, 41, 42, 43, 46, 47, 65,
   154, 184
Moskowitz, Milton, 82

National Farmworkers, 89
Nestlé, 90, 113, 138, 153, 158, 160,
   163, 221
New Economics Foundation, 104–105
Nike, 106
Nobel Prize, 132
Norris, William, 60

O'Neill, Carol, 120, 136–137
Oakland Institute, 211
Obama, Barack, 251–252
Occupy Wall Street, 241–242
Odak, Perry
   acquisition of Ben & Jerry's, 138–140,
      143, 154, 162–164, 168, 173–174

bovine growth hormone campaign
    and, 128
Cohen, Ben, and, 117, 119, 122–127,
    144–145, 169
conflicts, 117, 122–127 passim, 139–
    140, 143–147, 162–164, 179
international markets and, 142
philosophy of, 118–119, 145
social mission and, 118, 124–127,
    129, 132
stock and, 116, 121–124, 144, 178
turnaround, 115, 117, 119–120
Wild Oats, 184
Winchester, 114
Odwalla, 159, 181
One Percent for Peace, 42–46, 50–51,
    67, 71, 84, 110
One World One Heart, 74, 122, 151
Oprah, 97
Organic Valley, 128

Parker, Theodore, 251
PartnerShops, 8, 67, 77, 135–137, 143,
    149. See also franchises
Patagonia, 39, 54
Patti, Andrew, 116, 143–144
Peace Pops, 43, 45, 132–133
Philip Morris, 181
Phish, 123
Pillsbury, 23, 24, 107, 139, 154, 208
Polaroid, 41
Polk, Michael, 222
Polman, Paul, 221–222, , 229, 238, 246
Popsicle, 189
Proctor & Gamble, 221

Queenan, Joe, 81

Rainforest Alliance, 199
Rainforest Crunch, 84–85
Rathke, Fran, 52, 53, 92, 99, 101, 121,
    169, 174
rBGH (bovine growth hormone),
    78–79, 127–129, 148, 244
Reagan, Ronald, 46
Religious Society of Friends, 40
Rhino Records, 71
Roddick, Anita, 39–40, 83, 140–141,
    173

Roncadin, 165
Ropes & Gray, 23, 207
Russia, 42, 45–46, 50–51, 67–68, 87,
    136

Sanders, Bernie, 167
School Breakfast Program, 73
Scooperdome. See St. Alban's
Seale, Bobby, 89
Seeger, Pete, 89
Seventh Generation, 71, 212
shareholder primacy, 117
Shareholder Value Myth The (Stout), 118
Shopping for a Better World, 60
Silby, D. Wayne, 38
Smith & Hawken, 71
social mission, 10, 12, 50, 53–58
    passim, 70–71, 75, 111
    committee, 105, 130, 147
    cost of, 124–125, 132
    financial health and, 117–118, 126,
        249, 257
    global operations and, 150, 235
    public support of, 93, 205
    statement of, 47–48, 51, 65, 129–132,
        139, 196, 219
    Unilever and, 159, 171, 182–183,
        196–199, 202–203, 213, 220, 223,
        229
social reporting
    audit, 58, 59–62, 104–106, 150–151,
        202
    awards and criticism, 82–83, 94, 193,
        205–206
    B Corps, 246
    metrics, 103–106, 215–217, 224, 229–
        230, 231
Social Venture Network, 39, 54, 94,
    140–141, 166, 173
Soiefer, Ronald, 170, 184, 203–205,
    213, 224
Solheim, Jostein, 232, 236–243, 245,
    247–248
South Africa, 38, 41, 162
South Shore Bank, 41, 42, 74
St. Albans plant,
    construction of, 68–70, 82, 85–87
    production capacity at, 86, 123, 142,
        218

St. Albans plant, *continued*
  jobs at, 69, 106
St. Albans Cooperative
  bovine growth hormone and, 78
  sales to Ben & Jerry's, 61, 69, 149,
    215–216
  standards at, 243
Stamp Stampede, 234–236
Stever, Dave, 146, 166, 191, 192, 238
Stonyfield Farms, 54, 128, 166, 198
Stout, Lynn, 118
Streisand, Barbara, 173
sugar, 231, 242–243, 247

Tannen, Naomi, 26, 31, 76, 185
Time magazine, 17
Times Square Hotel, 76–77
Tom's of Maine, 181. *See also* Chappell,
  Tom and Kate
Trillin, Calvin, 7

Unilever
  brands, 90, 113, 138–139, 189, 210
  environmental policy, 161, 183, 187,
    192–193, 246–247
  history of, 160–162
  Ben & Jerry's: acquisition, 142–144,
    152–158, 163–167, 173–178;
    agreements, 4, 169–172, 185–190,
    203–204, 213–218, 222–223, 227;
    conflict, 194–195, 199, 207–208,
    219–226, 229, 238
U.S. Department of Agriculture, 89
U.S. Food and Drug Administration, 78
U.S. Securities and Exchange Commis-
  sion, 23
U.S. Social Forum, 11–12
Utne Reader, 54, 71

Values statement. *See* social mission,
  statement of
van der Graaf, Kees, 138–139, 162, 183,
  189, 226–227, 247
Vancura, Dave, 135
Vitrano, Rosalie, 121

Walsh, Eric, 189, 190, 200–201, 209,
  211–212
Waterbury plant
  construction, 26, 34, 218
  efficiency, 69, 91, 104
  financing, 22
  layoffs, 219, 222
  production, 28, 34
  seconds, 102
Wavy Gravy, 89
ways of working document (WOW),
  221–225, 240
Welsh, Jerry, 111
Wernhoff, Lisa, 31, 49, 111
Westheimer, Ruth, 62
White Dog Café, 65–67, 140, 167
Whole Foods, 128, 184
Wicks, Judy, 65, 67, 140, 167, 173, 179,
  250–251
Wild Oats, 184
Winfrey, Oprah, 97
women. *See* Ben & Jerry's, diversity
Woodward, Charlotte, 12
Working Assets, 54, 71
Worldwatch Institute, 148
WOW, 221–225, 240

Xapuri, 83–84

Zadek, Simon, 104, 106

About the Author

B rad Edmondson is a writer and consultant who helps people and organizations understand and benefit from social change. He is fascinated by how change happens, and why. A few years ago, while writing about New York's six-million-acre Adirondack Park, Brad learned that the wilderness preserve at the core of it was once privately owned. The land reverted to state ownership after loggers cut down all the trees and walked away. Now the park is the crown jewel of the Empire State, thanks to one far-sighted law, a vigilant public, and one hundred growing seasons.

Brad was raised in rural south Florida, on a farm that was established in 1923 and is still operated by his family. He attended Deep Springs, a college with an unusual curriculum that trains students for lives of service. By the time Brad got a history degree from Cornell in 1981, he knew he wanted to be a writer and storyteller. Instead of going to graduate school, he took editorial jobs at the *Ithaca Times* (1981–85), a weekly newspaper that covered peace and social justice issues, and *American Demographics* magazine (1985–98), a monthly Dow Jones magazine that explained the impact of population change and consumer trends on businesses, organizations, and society. During Brad's tenure as editor in chief of *American Demographics*, the magazine was nominated three times for the National Magazine Award for General Excellence.

Brad's articles have appeared in *AARP The Magazine, American Scholar, Utne Reader,* and *Atlantic Monthly*. His recent corporate clients have included Head Start, Honda, the National Bicycle Dealers Association, and the Private Label Manufacturing Association. But he keeps returning to the power of long-term, multigenerational commitments. While serving on the board of the Finger Lakes Land Trust (1994–2007), Brad helped create a fifty-year plan for a regional network of protected land in a scenic region of Upstate New York. He also helped manage an endowment while chairing the investment committee of Deep Springs College (2000–2010). These visionary organizations taught Brad the power of good stewardship and managing for perpetual return. Brad also noticed that people who are devoted to the greater good usually lead fun and exciting lives, have lots of interesting friends, and have more inspiring funerals.

Brad has two grown children, Will and Emma. He lives in Ithaca, New York with his wife, Tania Werbizky, who works in the field of historic preservation. They daydream about cross-country skiing or bicycle touring, depending on whether or not there's snow. Current trail conditions are posted at Brad's website, www.bradedmondson.com.

Berrett–Koehler
Publishers

Berrett-Koehler is an independent publisher dedicated to an ambitious mission: *Creating a World That Works for All.*

We believe that to truly create a better world, action is needed at all levels—individual, organizational, and societal. At the individual level, our publications help people align their lives with their values and with their aspirations for a better world. At the organizational level, our publications promote progressive leadership and management practices, socially responsible approaches to business, and humane and effective organizations. At the societal level, our publications advance social and economic justice, shared prosperity, sustainability, and new solutions to national and global issues.

A major theme of our publications is "Opening Up New Space." Berrett-Koehler titles challenge conventional thinking, introduce new ideas, and foster positive change. Their common quest is changing the underlying beliefs, mindsets, institutions, and structures that keep generating the same cycles of problems, no matter who our leaders are or what improvement programs we adopt.

We strive to practice what we preach—to operate our publishing company in line with the ideas in our books. At the core of our approach is stewardship, which we define as a deep sense of responsibility to administer the company for the benefit of all of our "stakeholder" groups: authors, customers, employees, investors, service providers, and the communities and environment around us.

We are grateful to the thousands of readers, authors, and other friends of the company who consider themselves to be part of the "BK Community." We hope that you, too, will join us in our mission.

A BK Business Book

This book is part of our BK Business series. BK Business titles pioneer new and progressive leadership and management practices in all types of public, private, and nonprofit organizations. They promote socially responsible approaches to business, innovative organizational change methods, and more humane and effective organizations.

Berrett–Koehler
Publishers

A community dedicated to creating
a world that works for all

Dear Reader,

Thank you for picking up this book and joining our worldwide community of Berrett-Koehler readers. We share ideas that bring positive change into people's lives, organizations, and society.

To welcome you, we'd like to offer you a free e-book. You can pick from among twelve of our bestselling books by entering the promotional code **BKP92E** here: http://www.bkconnection.com/welcome.

When you claim your free e-book, we'll also send you a copy of our e-newsletter, the *BK Communiqué*. Although you're free to unsubscribe, there are many benefits to sticking around. In every issue of our newsletter you'll find

- A free e-book
- Tips from famous authors
- Discounts on spotlight titles
- Hilarious insider publishing news
- A chance to win a prize for answering a riddle

Best of all, our readers tell us, "Your newsletter is the only one I actually read." So claim your gift today, and please stay in touch!

Sincerely,

Charlotte Ashlock
Steward of the BK Website

Questions? Comments? Contact me at bkcommunity@bkpub.com.

MIX
From responsible sources
FSC® C113845
FSC www.fsc.org

Certified
(B)
Corporation
bcorporation.net

3790023